COLD RECALL

-REFLECTIONS OF A POLAR EXPLORER

Edited by Geir O. Kløver

D0126216

The Fram Museum
Oslo – Norway
2009

The Amundsen lantern slides. Photo NB

TABLE OF CONTENTS

INTRODUCTION — PAGE 6

TO THE NORTH MAGNETIC POLE AND THROUGH THE NORTHWEST PASSAGE — PAGE 8
    - READ AT THE ROYAL GEOGRAPHICAL SOCIETY, 11 FEBRUARY , 1907

THE NORWEGIAN SOUTH POLAR EXPEDITION — PAGE 65
    - READ AT THE ROYAL GEOGRAPHICAL SOCIETY,15 NOVEMBER, 1912

APPENDICES

TO THE MAGNETIC NORTH POLE, THE NORWEGIAN "GJØA" EXPEDITION UNDER THE COMMAND OF ROALD AMUNDSEN — PAGE 164
    - READ AT THE GEOGRAPHICAL SOCIETY OF THE PACIFIC IN SAN FRANCISCO, CALIFORNIA, ON 28TH FEBRUARY, 1905 BY THE HON. HENRY LUND, CONSUL OF SWEDEN AND NORWAY

LETTERS FROM THE ROYAL GEOGRAPHICAL SOCIETY 1906-07 REGARDING THE NORTHWEST PASSAGE LECTURES — PAGE 172

ROALD AMUNDSEN'S THE PROPOSED NORTH POLAR EXPEDITION — PAGE 183
    - READ AT THE ROYAL GEOGRAPHICAL SOCIETY , 1909

ROALD AMUNDSEN'S ACCOUNT ON EXPANDING THE SCOPE OF THE NORTH POLAR EXPEDITION TO INCLUDE THE COMPETITION FOR THE SOUTH POLE — PAGE 194

LETTER FROM ROALD AMUNDSEN TO FRIDTJOF NANSEN DATED AUGUST 22, 1910 EXPLAINING THE CHANGE OF PLANS FOR THE NORTH POLAR EXPEDITION — PAGE 198

FACSIMILE OF THE LOGBOOK OF THE FRAM RECORDING THE ONBOARD ANNOUNCEMENT ABOUT THE NEW PLAN FOR THE NORTH POLAR EXPEDITION — PAGE 202

LETTERS FROM THE ROYAL GEOGRAPHICAL SOCIETY 1912, REGARDING THE SOUTH POLE LECTURES IN GREAT BRITAIN — PAGE 204

LETTERS FROM THE LECTURE AGENCY. LTD 1911 – 12, REGARDING THE SOUTH POLE LECTURES IN GREAT BRITAIN — PAGE 209

LETTERS FROM THE LEE KEDDICK LECTURE AGENCY 1911 – 13, REGARDING THE SOUTH POLE LECTURES IN THE USA — PAGE 225

SOUVENIR BOOK FROM THE SOUTH POLE LECTURES IN THE USA — PAGE 234

NEWSPAPER ARTICLES ABOUT ROALD AMUNDSEN'S SOUTH POLE LECTURES — PAGE 241

INTRODUCTION

When preparing for *Cold Recall - Reflections of a Polar Explorer* at the Fram Museum, our main objective was to show visitors images from the lantern slides that Amundsen used in public lectures about his expeditions through the Northwest Passage and to the South Pole. The texts in the exhibition are primarily abridged versions of Amundsen's own manuscripts from these lectures.

When planning the accompanying book to the exhibition, we had the opportunity to expand the exhibition and share some of the many interesting sources we encountered in our research. First of all, this book includes the complete manuscripts from the lectures, as they were held in Great Britain and the USA. We have also included background information on many of the episodes that Roald Amundsen describes, all too briefly, in his lectures. Further background information is given about some of the contents of many of the lantern slides printed in the book, but not specifically mentioned in the manuscripts.

The book includes a large appendix covering many of the letters, articles, brochures and pamphlets related to Amundsen's lecture tours. These are rare brochures, published in connection with the actual lectures, along with letters from the Royal Geographical Society in London, the Lecture Agency in London and the Lee Keddick Lecture Agency in New York. The letters illustrate the time-consuming and thorough preparation of the lecture tours that, in the USA alone, included more than 150 lectures. It is especially interesting to follow the discussion about the fate of Robert F. Scott who, at the time, had not been heard from. Had he reached the South Pole? What would the interest in England be for Amundsen's lectures when Scott was heard from, even though Amundsen undoubtedly had been the first to the pole? The uncertainty regarding Robert F. Scott also explains the different promotion of the lecture tours in England and the USA. In England, the lecture tour was called: "How we reached the South Pole", while Roald Amundsen in America was marketed as: "Discoverer of the South Pole and Winner in the International Race for the Southern Extremity of the Earth".

As many will know, the Norwegian Antarctic Expedition was originally planned and promoted as an expedition to the Arctic. We have used this opportunity to include in the appendix, Roald Amundsen's original lecture on the proposed North Pole expedition to the Royal Geographical Society in 1909. We have also included and translated Roald Amundsen's account on why he changed the destination of the expedition, along with his very personal letter to Fridtjof Nansen on why he kept his new destination a secret.

Roald Amundsen's own collection of lantern slides printed in this book, have a history of their own. They were all used by Amundsen for his lecture tours, and are mostly made from the same negatives he used to illustrate his books. The lantern slides used for his lectures, however, were coloured by hand to increase the entertainment value for the audience. Even though most of the photographs exist in Amundsen's books and in public archives like the National Library of Norway, these slides are the greatest collection of lantern slides in existence actually used by Roald Amundsen. They present a unique glimpse into how Roald Amundsen presented his expeditions, face to face with an international audience, and also the first pictorial account of his successful unlocking of the Northwest Passage and the expedition to the South Pole.

Other explorers very often brought professional artists and photographers on their expeditions. This was not the case for any of Amundsen's expeditions. He and the regular crew members took all the photos themselves. While Godfred Hansen took most of the photos during the Gjøa expedition, Olav Bjaaland is credited with most of the photos from the sledge journey to the South Pole. Many of Roald Amundsen's own photographs proved to be damaged when they were developed in Hobart, making Bjaaland's pocket camera the only source of photos from this historic journey.

In letters regarding the Northwest Passage lecture in 1907, the Royal Geographical Society in London asked Amundsen to reduce his number of lantern slides from 150 to 80 or 90. This collection included only 24 slides from the Gjøa expedition, making it far from complete. A number of other photos and some lantern slides exist in different public archives, but the majority of these are not hand-coloured. Some of these are included in this book.

The lantern slides from the South Pole, as they are presented in this book, must be very close to how the expedition was presented to Amundsen's audience. As the slides were not numbered, we have used the manuscript of the lecture and Roald Amundsen's published account "The South Pole" to guide the order in which they are now printed.

The majority of the slides from the South Pole expedition were developed by J.W. Beattie in Hobart, Tasmania and coloured by TW Cameron. They were the first made from the expedition negatives. Roald Amundsen stayed in Hobart for only 13 days, thus showing the importance of developing the films and making the lantern slides for the imminent lecture tours and the image-hungry newspapers worldwide.

The lecture tours were an important source of revenue for Amundsen and needed immediate attention on his return to guarantee as many bookings as possible while the story was fresh.

This collection of lantern slides was thought lost, before they were discovered in the attic of a member of the Amundsen family in 1986. The interest in the collection resulted in Roland Huntford's book "The Amundsen Photographs", published in 1987. "The Amundsen Photographs" contained 150 of the 250 lantern slides in the collection, including 44 photographs from the Maud expedition not included in this book. These will be the focus of another exhibition at the Fram Museum together with lantern slides from Roald Amundsen's *N24/N25* and *Norge* expeditions from the museum's own collection.

In 2006, the owners of the *Amundsen lantern slides* offered the collection for sale at an auction house in London. The collection was bought by a private Norwegian collector. Immediately after the auction in London, the buyer contacted the Fram Museum to inform staff about the future whereabouts of the collection. This contact led to an agreement whereby all publishing rights to the collection would be donated to the Fram Museum, while the original photos would be restored and kept at the National Library of Norway.

Due to this cooperation between a private collector, a polar history museum and a national library with its restoration and long-term storage expertise, this collection of unique lantern slides can be made available to the general public whilst being kept in the best storage facilities available.

Through the generosity of the collector, we have avoided that such important material ended in a private vault with no access for the public, for technical research or for historians.

This exhibition and the associated book would not have been possible without the cooperation of the National Library of Norway and their friendly and knowledgeable staff: Kristin Bakken, Anne Melgård, Arthur Tennoe, Guro Tangvald, Wlodek Witek and Tom Erik Ruud. They have restored and digitized the *Amundsen lantern slides* and provided many of the additional illustrations in the exhibition and the appendix of the book.

The Norwegian Geographical Society has donated its historical archive to the Fram Museum. This has given us, amongst many other topics, detailed accounts from the preparation of the South Pole Expedition and information on the restoration of the Fram.

My colleagues Anne Rief and Charlotte Westereng Syversen have provided valuable contributions to the exhibition and book, while Edwin Pasco and Josefino Caraig made sure that the exhibition was mounted in time.

Our designer Marcus Thomassen of Psycho Penguin Productions agreed to work night and day to get the expanded version of the book and the exhibition ready for the printer's deadline.

- Geir O. Kløver
Director of the Fram Museum

A photo from the Amundsen lantern slides collection.

An additional photo added to give further illustrations to Roald Amundsen's text.

Editor's note:

"At 8 a.m. my watch was finished and I turned in. When I had been asleep some time, I became conscious of a rushing to and fro on deck. Clearly there was something the matter, and I felt a bit annoyed that they should go on like that for the matter of a bear or a seal.

Editor's comments or additional texts added to give more details on topics mentioned in Amundsen's text or to describe some of the motives in the lantern slides in further depth.

The Gjøa undergoing her reconstruction before the expedition to the Northwest Passage.

AMUNDSEN LANTERN SLIDE 001: FM/JFO

To the North Magnetic Pole and through the Northwest Passage

Read at the Royal Geographical Society, February 11, 1907

Roald Amundsen(1872-1928). Photo: Fram Museum (FM)

To Sir John Franklin must be given the honour of having discovered the North-West Passage, and to Admiral Sir Robert McClure that of being the first to pass through it, partly in his vessel the Investigator and partly on foot. On the foundations laid by the splendid work done and the rich fund experience gained by English navigators in these regions, I succeeded - in the track of Sir James Ross, Dr. John Rae, Admiral Sir Leopold M'Clintock, Sir Allen Young, and many others – in making my way in the Gjøa to the region around the Earth's north magnetic pole, and, furthermore, in sailing through the North-West Passage in its entirety. If I have thus been the first to sail through the North-West Passage, it is with pleasure that I share the honour with those brave English seamen – the seamen who here, as in most of the other parts of the world, have taken the lead and shown us the way.

The scheme of the Gjøa Expedition I had welcome opportunity of laying before the Norwegian Geographical Society on November 25, 1901. It was briefly as follows: With a small vessel and a few companions, to penetrate into the regions around the Earth's north magnetic pole, and by a series of accurate observations, extending over a period of two years, to relocate the pole observed by Sir James Ross in 1831, and also to make investigations in its immediate vicinity. This was the chief object of the expedition.

The condition of the ice still farther west allowing of it, it was furthermore my intention to attempt to sail through the North-West Passage in its entire extent, this being a problem which for centuries had defied the most persistent efforts. I chose a small vessel, with the view to be better able to pass through the sounds of these regions, which are narrow, shallow and generally packed with ice. In preferring a small number of members to a larger one, it was – apart from want of space – because, in the event of such a misfortune occurring to us as the loss of our vessel, it would be easier to find means of subsistence for a small than for a greater number of men.

John Franklin (1786-1847). Photo: FM

Robert McClure (1807-1873). Photo: FM

It was the Norwegian minister to England, Dr. Fridtjof Nansen, who, by his great experience and his many good counsels, made the Gjøa Expedition what it was, in all respects well planned and excellently equipped. In order not to tire my hearers, I will give in as few words as possible the earlier history of the expedition.

Fridtjof Nansen (1861-1930). Photo: FM

Drawing from James Clark Ross' account of locating the North Magnetic Pole. Photo FM

My undertaking, as soon as it became known, awakened great interest in very wide circles, and several wealthy men came forward and supported the enterprise with donations. It would take too long to name all the persons who gave the expedition pecuniary support, but I must in respectful gratitude mention the names of their Majesties King Haakon and King Oscar II.

The vessel of the Gjøa Expedition was built in Hardanger in 1872 and was my only contemporary on the trip. She had originally been used in the herring fisheries along the Norwegian coast; later she was sold to Tromsø, whence she sailed for many years in the Arctic sealing trade. She had weathered many a storm, through not always scathless. After my purchase of her, I had a small petroleum motor, of 39 indicated horse-power, put into her, to help us along in calm weather. The ice-sheathing, which before only reached a couple of planks under the water-line, I had lengthened right down to the keel; stout cross-beams were put into the hold and connected with massive joints to the deck and keelson, and the old hempen rigging was replaced by wire rigging.

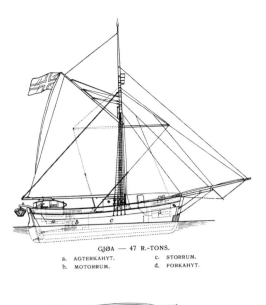

GJØA — 47 R.-TONS.

a. AGTERKAHYT.   c. STORRUM.
b. MOTORRUM.   d. FORKAHYT.

GJØAS DÆK.

The Gjøa at Frognerkilen before departure, 1903.
Photo: National Library of Norway (NB)

Photo: FM

AMUNDSEN LANTERN SLIDE 005: FM/JFO

AMUNDSEN LANTERN SLIDE 004: FM/JFO

Photo: NB

AMUNDSEN LANTERN SLIDE 003: FM/JFO

AMUNDSEN LANTERN SLIDE 002: FM/JFO

Photo: NB

I had chosen my companions by degrees. First in order I must mention the man who sacrificed his life in the service of the expedition, Gustav Juel Wiik. He was born in 1878, at Horten, and thus lived to be somewhat over twenty-seven years of age. From six weeks' study shortly before the departure of the expedition, at the Magnetic Observatory at Potsdam, where he particularly studied the use of self-registering magnetic instruments, he returned with the most excellent testimonials for industry and thoroughness. I had a good opportunity of seeing, during our three years of work together, that these testimonials were not exaggerated, and the magnetic data we brought back with us I owe, in the first instance, to this young man's painstaking and accurate labour. In addition to his position as assistant in the meteorological observations, he was also second engineer.

The second in command of the expedition was Lieut. Godfred Hansen, of the Danish navy, born in Copenhagen in 1875. His light-hearted disposition was of absolute benefit to us, and during the three years – more than three years – that he and I spent together in the little cabin of the Gjøa, 6 x 9 feet, I became more and more attached to him. It was prophesied before our departure from Norway, that within a year we should not be able to bear the sight of one another; this prophecy, however, we thoroughly gave the lie to, and I almost think we could have managed three years more. He was the navigator of the expedition, the astronomer, geologist, surgeon, photographer, electrician, and an expert in dealing with our explosives. He also played star-parts as meteorologist and magnetician.

Sergeant Peder Ristvedt was born in Sandsvær in 1873. Besides being first engineer, he was also our meteorologist, smith, clockmaker, copper and tinsmith, gunsmith, etc. I knew Ristvedt before I engaged him, as he had taken part as assistant in my first expedition in the Gjøa in 1901. I was thus aware of what I was doing when I secured the service of this capable man and pleasant companion.

Anton Lund was the first mate of the expedition. He had sailed from his earliest youth on our Norwegian sloops to the Arctic ocean, and was consequently an unusually experienced man in all matters connected with the condition of the ice and navigation through it.

Helmer Hansen was born in the Vesteraal islands in 1870. He had previously been a peasant, fisherman, and Arctic navigator. His position was that of second mate, and he was careful and conscientious in all that he did.

Last of all, then, comes the cook, Adolf Henrik Lindstrøm, born at Hammerfest in 1865. He took part in Sverdrup's expedition in the Fram, and had thus extensive experience as an Arctic cook. I will confine myself to informing you that, besides providing us for three years with excellently prepared food, served to the minute, he voluntarily filled the vacant posts of botanist and zoologist. His kitchen work ended, he was pretty sure to be seen abroad on arctic summer evenings with his botanical collecting-box, his shotgun, and his butterfly-net, and woe to the flower, bird, or insect which came his way! After this description of my comrades, I feel sure that none of my hearers will be surprised that we succeeded in accomplishing what we did.

At twelve o'clock on the night between June 16 and 17, 1903, we cast off, and the Gjøa was towed down the Christiania fjord. It poured with rain, and was as dark as in a sack. Some of my friends tried to console me by saying that the weather was much the same when Nansen started in 1893, and that it was a good omen. However, I had never been a believer in omens, and I therefore felt myself, in spite of these auspicious torrents, very uncomfortable in my soaking clothes. At six in the morning we entered the harbour at Horten, where we took our explosives aboard. At eleven in the forenoon the last tie which bound us to home was broken, for the tow-rope snapped, and left the Gjøa to her own fate. We were then just outside Færder lighthouse. After the tug had given us the proper farewell civilities, it stood up the fjord again, and the Gjøa, by her own exertions, worked her way slowly forwards against a southerly breeze. The voyage across the Atlantic has been made countless times, and does not offer any particular interest. A great number of people had, indeed, designed this ocean as the Gjøa's last resting-place; but, in spite of many prophecies and many warnings, our good little Gjøa quietly and calmly worked her way onwards, giving not a moment's thought to all wiseacres. How glorious it was to have exchanged the narrow hot streets for the open sea - and not only we human beings enjoyed the change, but our dogs likewise. We had, I should explain, six dogs with us which had taken part in Sverdrup's expedition, and they seemed to enjoy the voyage exceedingly, running about and getting into as much mischief as was to be attained. Their spirits were particularly high on rough days, as then they had an agreeable change in their monotonous diet (consisting of a stockfish and a quart of water), in the shape of the delicious viands sacrificed to them by my seasick companions.

On July 9 we sighted the first ice, in the vicinity of Cape Farewell, the southern extremity of Greenland, and on the 11th the land round the cape itself appeared in sight. The wind, which had not been particularly favourable to us up to this, did not improve now, and our voyage up the whole of the west coast of Greenland was thus one single struggle against the ever-prevailing north wind. We had to console ourselves with the proverb that "it is an ill wind which blown nobody any good." Though the contrary wind from the north hindered our progress, it at any rate set the ice in motion southwards, and made a way for us.

The voyage, which had hitherto been somewhat monotonous, became more lively on the appearance of the ice. Icebergs of varying shape glided past us and took captive our attention. Now and then we made an excursion into the drift-ice, and shot some of the beautiful large bladder-nose seal that were lying about on the higher parts of the ice. Both men and dogs were longing for fresh meat, and this seal-flesh provided us with an agreeable change in our menu.

On July 24 we sighted Disco Island, and the day afterwards anchored at Godhavn, whither the Royal Danish Greenland Trading Company had been kind enough to bring some of our equipment in their ships. Here we spent five days, enjoying the great hospitality of the inspector and the governor of the colony. After having taken a series of magnetic and astronomical observations, and shipped all our things, we left the place on July 31.

Godhavn on Disko Island. Photo: NB

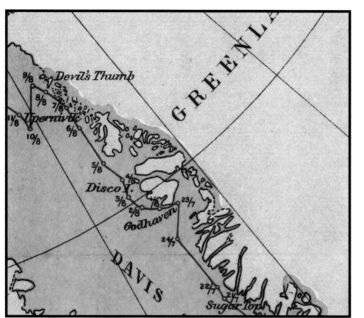
The Disko Island area. Photo: FM

On August 8 we reached Holm Island, which marks the beginning of the redoubtable Melville Bay. The ice was packed close, but, however, proved to be broken. We kept cruising backwards and forwards alongside the edge, watching for an opportunity to enter it, and at last, on the evening of the 10th, it so far slackened that we were able to slip in. In thick fog, we wound our way about through fairly practicable ice, a few icebergs now and then breaking up the dense masses of the fog with the strength of their flashes, calling to us their own warning. On August 13, at half-past two in the morning, we saw the last of this fog, the *Gjøa* quietly and calmly gliding out of the thick masses, which had surrounded us as in a nightmare for several days, into a new world, lighted up by the loveliest sunshine, and with a marvellous beautiful view. In the east we saw the head of Melville Bay filled with impenetrable icefields; in the north lay the fine mountain scenery around Cape York, beckoning

Inuit from Greenland aboard the Gjøa. Photo: NB

and calling to us in the sunshine – the feeling was overwhelming; before us, shining in the blue and white, lay the huge masses of drift-ice. There was not much open water to be seen from the masthead, but then we did not want very much. On August 15 we reached Dalrymple Rock, where two Scotch captains, Milne and Adams, had left a largish depot for us. Here we fell in with the Danish Literary Greenland Expedition, and spent a few lively and pleasant hours with the members of it. On August 17 we continued our voyage, and bore across Baffin Bay, in sight of the Carey Islands. It was lucky for us that we met with calm weather here, for with our deeply laden vessel a storm might have had serious consequences. Besides our sky-scraping deck cargo, there were on the top of it all our eighteen dogs, the greater number of which had been shipped at Godhavn.

By way of making the time go quicker, they had divided themselves into two about equally strong sides, and from time to time made inroads on each other's territory. This game, needless to say, was hardly to the liking of the man who happened to have the watch, and many a round oath found its way out into the world. On August 20 we stood into Lancaster Sound; a few icebergs, which had collected round Cape Horsburgh, and some slack ice stretched straight across the sound. We kept in under the northern shore. The land made an exceedingly barren impression; there was no vegetation to be seen, and the mountains were high and table topped. It was, however, not often that we were able to see land, the fog for the most part being thick and heavy.

The members of the Danish Literary Greenland Expedition, Harald Moltke, Knud Rasmussen, Jørgen Brønlund and Ludvig Mylius-Erichsen, aboard the Gjøa at Dalrymple Rock on August 15, 1903.

AMUNDSEN LANTERN SLIDE 007: FM/JFO

On August 22 we reached Beechey Island, where I had arranged to stop and take a series of magnetic observations, which were to decide our future course. Before the departure of the expedition, several persons more interested than learned in terrestrial magnetism had written to me, pretending by a subtle method, which, however, they did not disclose, to have discovered that the magnetic pole had moved, with a speed of I don't know how many miles in the year, in a north-westerly direction, and was now on Prince Patrick's Land. They might as well have said in the moon for all they knew.

Beechey Island gives a barren and dismal impression; and particularly sad are the ruins of the house erected by the British Government for the succour of the Franklin Expedition. Five graves did not make it more cheerful. The memorial stone to Sir John Franklin was the only thing which in the least brightened all this sadness – a handsome marble tablet, put up to his memory by his faithful wife.

The ruins of the Franklin depot at Beechey Island left a sad impression on Amundsen. Photo: NB

The John Franklin memorial at Beechey Island.

The Beechey Island area Photo: FM

AMUNDSEN LANTERN SLIDE 008: FM/JFO

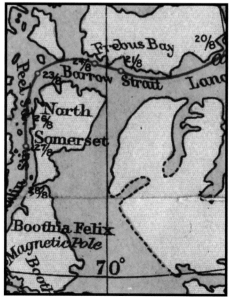

The magnetic observations indicated the pole as being in a southerly direction, and Prince Patrick Land was this time left in peace. We left Beechey Island on the 24th, and shaped the course for Peel Sound, entering those waters in dense fog. The ice was the whole time fairly practicable, and we met only loose streams which presented no hindrance. At Prescott Island the compass, which for some time had been somewhat sluggish, entirely refused to act, and we could as well have used a stick to steer by. Navigation, as we now practiced it, was at first a somewhat unfamiliar proceeding, and when one watch released the other, the fog lay close and compact, as it always did, strange remarks might have been heard. "What are you steering?" would ask the relieving watch, in a cross and sleepy tone. "Supposed to be steering south, but ain't sure we're not going north;" and as he handed the tiller to the other, one would hear, "Steady-so." So there one would be at two o'clock in the morning, just up from a comfortable warm berth, the fog pouring down over everything, and absolutely nothing to be seen in any direction, and one was to steer steady! This was certainly great fun; but custom is a remarkable thing. Within a short time we became quite at home even with this sort of navigation, and we made way. On August 28 we passed the spot where Sir Allen Young was stopped in his vessel the Pandora by impenetrable ice. Later in the forenoon the western entrance to Bellot Strait, where Sir Leopold M'Clintock in vain tried to get through, was passed. Now began our voyage along the west coast of Bootia Felix – a voyage that more than once looked dark for us. We were not hindered by ice to any great extent; the land lead was, as a rule, so wide that we could get along without difficulty; but that which was

worse for us were the shoal water, the constant fog, and the pitch-dark nights. On August 31 we struck ground for the first time. The weather, however, was fine, and we got off without injury. In the evening we anchored off a low island to wait for daybreak, for I no longer dared to go on now that the nights were so dark, and in such foul waters. How peaceful everything was that evening! It was an unusually dark night and absolutely calm, and what greatly increased our already romantic position was the fact that we – I confess it openly and without shame – had no idea where we were! The land had been mapped in winter, and many of the small islands which we came across were not marked at all, the snow covering them at the time having rendered them invisible. All was so peaceful, quiet, and calm. We had all retired, and left the watch to one of the engineers whose turn it happened to be. I had just got out my log to enter the events of the day, when I was suddenly interrupted by the cry of fire. I knew what this meant on board a small vessel carrying 7000 gallons of petroleum, great quantities of gunpowder and explosives, and whose hull was, besides, saturated with tar. We were all up on deck in less time than it takes to tell it. The first thing that met our eyes was an enormous pillar of fire rising up through the engine room skylight. Things didn't look peaceful any longer. We all ran like mad for vessel and life! The engineer on watch had not left his post; he was holding out bravely down below in the suffocating smoke, trying to the best of his abilities to subdue the fire, which had arisen in some cotton permeated with petroleum. This was Wiik. We succeeded by united exertions in becoming master of the fire, and got off without much damage.

An artist's impression of the fire on the Gjøa. Photo: FM

The evening of this same day we beat up under an islet and anchored there. We took this to be one of the small islands lying north of Malty Island. It was blowing hard and night coming on. At four the next morning we weighed, and continued our course. It was a fine morning, partially clear, and with a westerly breeze. I was at the tiller, and my two comrades were hoisting the sails. Suddenly there was a shock, and we struck three times. All expedients to get off were in vain, and there we were for thirty hours. A strong breeze blew up from the north, and came to our assistance, and under crowded sail we succeeded in forcing the Gjøa across a 200-yard-long bank, and out into comparatively deep water.

We only lost our false keel; but from that day to this it has been a matter of wonder to me that human handiwork could have withstood the treatment which the Gjøa underwent on that occasion. During this enforced delay we got a determination for position, and thus knew where we were. About midday we cast anchor of Cape Christian Frederik, on Bootia Felix, so as to get things a little in order after grounding. The wind was then slack and off shore. At eleven in the evening, it suddenly went over to the south-east, and blew hard. There was no question, in the darkness and the shoal and foul sea outside, of getting under way. There was only one thing to be done, and that was to pay out our cables to the bitter end and await results. The wind soon increased

to a gale, the seas were high and short, shaking our chain cables violently. The land did not look as well now as when we came in and anchored into it leeward. All hands were on deck, and getting ready for the stranding which seemed inevitable. Each man had had his work allotted to him, and at the moment when the cables gave would be in readiness at his post.

The petroleum motor was going at full speed, and the vessel was kept well up to the wind and sea, by which means I hoped to ease a little the violent strain on the cables. We had anchored at midday on the 3rd, and it was not till four o'clock on the 8th that the wind dropped sufficiently for us to get out again. Then another drifting night in pitch darkness among shoals and rocks, and then at last release. It is impossible to describe the well-being, the feeling of calm and safety, which came over us after these ten days of ceaseless fighting, when we dropped anchor on September 9, at half-past three in the afternoon, at the head of Petersen Bay, in King William Land. There, approached by a narrow inlet, lay the harbour which was to be our place of sojourn for two years – "Gjøahavn," or Gjøa Harbour. A fresh land breeze prevented us from standing in, and it was not till the evening of the 12th that it fell sufficiently for us to beat up against it and drop anchor. Now we could breathe. We had done a good bit of work.

The Gjøa aground. Photo: NB

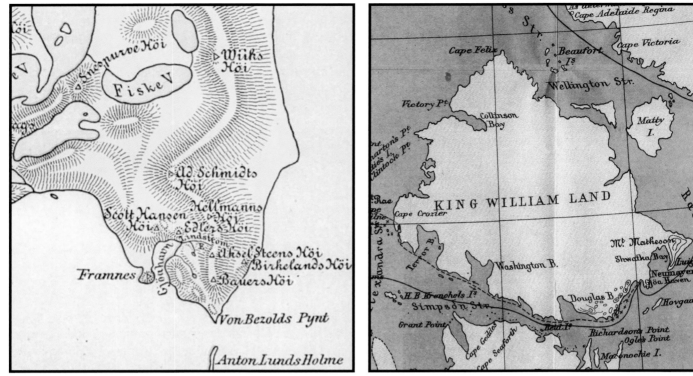

Detailed map of Gjøa Haven. Photo FM

Map of King William Land. Photo FM

"Gjøahavn" was all that the heart could desire, small and landlocked. Low sandy land, covered with moss, rose gently upwards from all sides, until it reached a height of 150 feet, and thus formed a sheltered little basin where we could lie safe and snug. The day after our arrival here I rowed ashore with my instruments to ascertain the state of the magnetism in this area, and, strange as it may sound, we had found the very spot which, accordingly to my scheme, was the most suitable for a magnetic station – about 100 nautical miles from the magnetic polar area. There was no longer any doubt; this would be our home for the next two years. The time after this was very busy. The vessel was hauled close up to the shore, which fell abruptly away, a conveying rope rigged to the masthead, and all our provisions passed ashore by means of it. Everything was put in order, and the house which we built covered over with a sail.

The Gjøa at anchor in Gjøa Haven. Photo: NB

*The Gjøa
discharging by
aerial ropeway.
Photo: NB*

Unloading the Gjøa at Gjøa Haven.

AMUNDSEN LANTERN SLIDE 020: FM/JFO

Gustav Juel Wiik, Godfred Hansen and Helmer Hansen building the magnetic variation house. Photo: NB

The magnetic variation house.

AMUNDSEN LANTERN SLIDE 247: FM/JFO

Uranienborg, the observatory for absolute magnetic observations. Photo: NB

Uranienborg in winter.

Building the store house. Photo: NB

Then came the observatories, and of them a mushroom growth sprang up. First the magnetic variation house, then a dwelling-house for the meteorologist and magnetician, the two latter being built of empty provision cases filled with sand. After that came the house for the absolute magnetic observations: the walls were built of blocks of snow, and the roof made out of thin transparent sailcloth. Finally, we built the astronomical observatory, which was known as "Uranienborg," this also being of snow, with a sailcloth roof. Besides all this building, we had done another good stroke of work in the shape of killing a hundred reindeer, and we had thus abundant provisions for ourselves and our dogs throughout the winter. The ice formed on October 1 and 2. The vessel was then covered with a winter awning, and everything got ready to receive the approaching winter.

On October 29 the first Eskimo made their appearance. Expectation on this point had always run high, and we had talked daily about meeting with them. Sir John Ross, in his description of his voyage gives the word "Teima" as the usual salutation between white man and Eskimo; and we had therefore carefully laid this word to heart in order at once to check any warlike desires, should they be apparent. This first meeting was exceedingly ridiculous, and is one of our liveliest reminiscences.

With two companions, armed to the teeth – namely, Anton Lund and Helmer Hansen – I started off to meet the Eskimo, walking first myself, with two comrades following me at about three paces' distance. They had shouldered their guns, and had such a fierce expression on their faces that it alone would have been enough to put a warlike detachment to flight, to say nothing of the five unfortunate Eskimo who were approaching us. The step and set-up of my detachment were unexceptionable. Arrived at about a hundred paces from us, the Eskimo stopped, and we, not wishing to show less strategic ability, did likewise. Now, I thought, is the moment to set this matter at rest, and shouted "Teima" at the top of my voice. It did not seem to affect them in the least, and after a short parley among themselves, they recommenced their march on us. They were five in number, had formed in a sort of fighting line, and now advanced towards us smiling and humming. Two of them had their bows firmly secured to their backs, and the three others were apparently unarmed.

Netsilik Inuit carrying spears several meters long. Photo: NB

We on our side, of course, reassumed our advance, repeatedly shouting, "Teima, teima," and the Eskimo answered, but with quite another word, namely, "Manik-tu-mi." We now approached one another quickly, and finally ended by meeting. It was a remarkable encounter. The Eskimo stroked and patted us both in front and behind, all shouting "Manik-tu-mi" as hard as they could. We, true to our original plan of campaign, copied our adversaries, and shouted and howled, patted and slapped, to the best of our ability.

They were fine men, these Eskimo, tall and strongly built, and in their appearance reminded me more of Indians than of Eskimo, having their redskin type of complexion; they were, moreover, slim, and, as I said before, tall. The ordinary broad and fleshy Eskimo nose was exchanged for one better in shape, somewhat hooked; their hair was cut short, with the exception of a small crest of long hair which stretched from one temple round the nape of the neck to the other temple. We now proceeded, laughing the whole time, to the vessel. These Eskimo called themselves "Ogluli Eskimo," and looked upon the North American coast from Back River westwards to Adelaide Peninsula as their hunting fields. We made many good friends among this race, but it was not till later, when we met with the "Nechjilli Eskimo," that we made inseparable allies.

Magito, a woman frequently mentioned in Amundsen's book from the expedition. Photo: NB

Netsilik women and children on a fishing expedition. "Netsilik" means "the seal people". They hunted seal and reindeer, and fished for salmon, trout and cod. Photo: NB

On November 2 the permanent station began its work. I will try, in as few words as possible, to explain terrestrial magnetism and the use of our magnetic instruments.

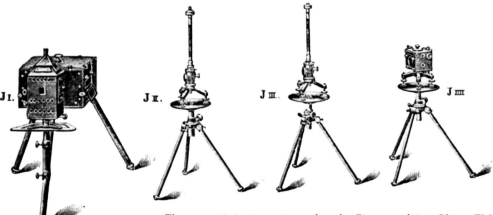

The magnetic instruments used on the Gjøa expedition. Photo: FM

Instrument for astronomical research.

AMUNDSEN LANTERN SLIDE 010: FM/JFO

Terrestrial magnetic power is, with regard to direction and force, different on every point of the surface of the Earth, nor is it always the same in one and the same place. It is subject to regular daily and yearly changes, and, similarly, there often occur irregular more or less violent disturbances. Finally, small displacements show themselves from year to year, which continue in the same manner for a long series of years. All this has been discovered through observations undertaken during the course of time at various parts of the surface of the globe, partly during travels, and partly by permanent stations. A careful study of all the available material which had been acquired by observation caused the great German mathematician and physicist, Gauss, in the thirties of last century, to form a theory as to the sequence and varied appearance of the phenomena of terrestrial magnetism at a certain moment of time according to the geographical latitude and longitude. It thus became possible to construct three different maps, of which two show the direction of the force, and the third its strength. The reason why two maps are necessary for direction is because the direction must be given both in relation to the north and to a south geographical line, and in proportion to the horizontal plane of a place. The direction of the terrestrial magnetic force in relation to the north-to-south line can be observed by the help of the compass, which, as we know, generally points somewhat east or west of this same north. This divergence is called the variation of the declination. On a magnetic map lines are drawn which show the direction of the magnetic needle at every point of the Earth's surface.

The magnetic dip needle used on the sledge journey to the North Magnetic Pole.

AMUNDSEN LANTERN SLIDE 014: FM/JFO

These lines, which are called magnetic meridians, converge at two points – the north magnetic pole, on the Arctic coast of North America, and the south magnetic pole, in the interior of the Antarctic continent. Each of the lines indicates, as will be understood, the direction one would go if he followed exactly the direction indicated by the north or south end of the magnetic needle. In the first case, one would at length arrive at the north magnetic pole; in the other, at the south magnetic pole.

If a magnetic needle be placed so that it can turn on an axis through its centre of gravity – exactly like a grindstone – the needle will of itself adopt a diagonal position when the plane of revolution is identical with the direction which the needle of a compass indicates. An instrument of the kind is called an "inclitorium," and the angle which the dipping-needle forms with the horizontal plane is called the magnetic inclination of a place. Here, in our parts, the north end of the needle points down towards the earth; in Australia, on the contrary, it is the southern end which dips. At the north magnetic pole the dipping-needle assumes a vertical position with its north end down; at the south magnetic pole it assumes a vertical position with its south end down. The inclination, then, at both their points in 90°, and decreases according as the distance becomes greater from them. On a series of points within the tropical zone the inclination is 0°; that is to say, the dipping-needle places itself exactly horizontally, and that line which we may imagine as drawn through all these points is called the "magnetic equator". It is situated partly above, partly beneath, the Earth's geographical equator.

The force of terrestrial magnetism works, as will be understood, with its whole strength in the direction given by the dipping-needle, and it may be asked, how great is this force in the different places? In order to discover this we must imagine the force dissolved into two parts, one part working horizontally, and one part working vertically. It is evident that it is the horizontal art of the force which causes the needle to take a set position, and if we know all about this force – "horizontal intensity," as it is called – and at the same time know the inclination, it is easy, by a simple calculation, to find the collective strength, the total intensity. For the determination of horizontal intensity two methods are adopted, either each one alone or preferably, for the sake of comparison, simultaneously. One method consists in placing a magnetic bar by the side of a needle at a given distance from it, and observing how many degrees the needle moves away from its original position. It is clear that the weaker of the horizontal intensity the greater the oscillation of the needle, and when the strength of the magnetic bar is known, it is possible, by the aid of the angle of oscillation and the distance, to calculate the horizontal intensity.

Inclination readings on April 28, 1904. Photo: NB

The magnetic instruments in use in winter. Photo NB

The other method is to note the time of oscillation of a magnetic bar suspended by a thread in such a manner that it can revolve in the horizontal plane. When the magnet is allowed to be at rest, it sets, under the influence of horizontal intensity, in the direction of the needle. Brought out of equilibrium by a little push, it will swing backwards and forwards, and the stronger the horizontal intensity, the sooner it will come to rest again, or, in other words, the shorter will be the time of each individual oscillation. When the strength of the oscillatory magnet is known, and observation is made of how many seconds are necessary for an oscillation, the horizontal can be calculated.

Maps are constructed to give an idea of the value of horizontal intensity, expressed in so-called electric units, on the different parts of the Earth. A line passes through all the places where the horizontal intensity is the same. The horizontal intensity decreases towards the magnetic poles. It is, therefore, matter of consequence that terrestrial magnetism here, where the inclination is 90°, acts with its whole strength vertically downwards, and thus cannot have any effect in a horizontal direction.

Although the magnetic maps are very dissimilar, they are alike in one respect, namely, that the magnetic poles are the points of mark on the surface of the Earth, and it is obvious that magnetic investigations just at these points, or in their immediate vicinity, must be of the greatest interest to science of terrestrial magnetism. The Gauss theory by no means solves all the riddles presented by the phenomena of terrestrial magnetism, but continual efforts are being made to complete these riddles by the collection of as reliable and comprehensive observations as it is possible to procure.

The magnetic work of the Gjøa Expedition is intended to be a contribution to this object. But the difficulties were not small. The very fact that horizontal intensity, as we have heard, becomes, in the vicinity of the magnetic poles, so infinitesimally small, renders necessary extraordinary precautions for the determination of this itself, as well as of the variation. The Gjøa Expedition's equipment of instruments was calculated for this purpose. The magnets, fourteen in number, were chosen with great care in Potsdam just before our departure. The inclination we were able to determine by the help of three inclinatoria of varying construction, and for the determination of the declination we had two different instruments.

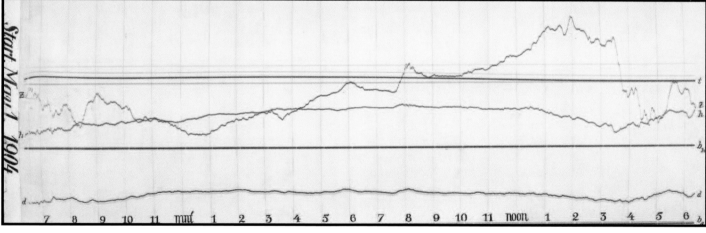

Automatic magnet readings from the Gjøa expedition. Photo NB

The "Villa Magnet" – the magnetic observatory - in summer time. Photo NB

Added to these were a set of self-registering variation apparatus; that is to say, three instruments permanently erected in a dark room, each instrument containing a small magnetic needle, two of the latter being suspended by a fine quartz thread, the third oscillating on a fine bearing in such a manner that the needle with its movement followed the declination, the second the horizontal intensity, and the third the inclination, even its minutest changes. Each needle was provided with a looking-glass, which reflected the light from a lamp on to a drum covered with photographic paper, which, by means of clockwork, made one revolution during the course of twenty-four hours. It was arranged so that the reflection from each of the three needles struck the drum at different heights, and caused a little dark spot; but when the drum with its paper revolved, each of these spots was continued, forming a consecutive dark line. There were thus three dark lines across each other on the paper, when after the lapse of twenty-four hours it was taken off.

After what we have heard, it will easily be understood that it would not have done to select the pole itself for a permanent observation station, even had we known beforehand its exact situation, and could have foreseen that it would keep immovable on one of the same spor. Advised by Prof. Adolf Schmidt, I therefore decided to make the base station, where the instruments for variation were to be erected, at such a distance from the pole that the inclination would be about 89°. This requirement was fulfilled by Gjøahavn, which accordingly became our headquarters. We constantly made excursions hence to adjacent part of the country, and right in to Boothia Felix, where I succeeded by the help of declination in absolutely proving what of late had been assumed on theoretic grounds, namely, that the magnetic pole has not an immovable and stationary situation, but, in all probability, is in continual movement. In what manner this movement take place our considerable amount of material acquired by observation will, when it has been worked out, give instructive information.

The magnetic observations were kept going day and night, without interruption for nineteen months. Meteorological observations were also taken the whole time. Prof. Mohn had equipped the expedition with a complete set of meteorological instruments, and made it his business that the meteorologist of the expedition should receive the best instruction. The meteorologist, Dr. Aksel Steen, was my magnetic counsellor at home in Norway, before the departure of the expedition, and many a good bit of advice did he give me. The astronomical equipment was for the greater part due to Prof. Geelmuyden.

Amundsens protocol for studies in vertical intensity in Gjøa Haven. Photo NB

Gustav Juel Wiik in the entrance to the magnetic variation house. Photo: NB

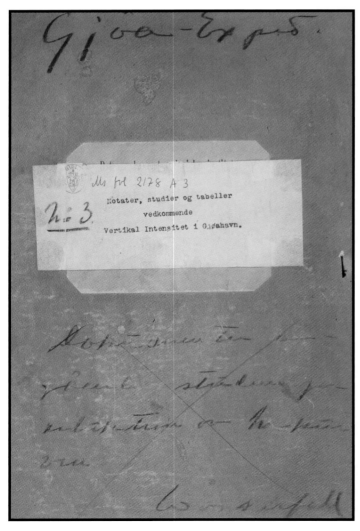

The Eskimo came and went now as often as they liked, and in a short time became quite at home with us. Towards Christmas they all disappeared, with the exception of an old man, Teraiu, with his wife, Kaijoggolo, and little son, Nutara. They came and lived with us during the whole of the coldest part of the winter, the rest of the tribe having gone westward to capture seal.

Christmas was now approaching with rapid steps, and countless preparations were made. The days had begun to be shorter and the cold sharper. Then came Christmas Eve, the first on board the Gjøa. The weather was splendid, absolutely still, and sparklingly bright. The thermometer -40° Fahr. (-40°C). And what a Christmas Eve it was out here!

Was not heaven itself sending us a greeting? The most glorious aurora we had yet seen lighted up the entire sky, in chasing rays from the horizon towards the zenith. The rays seemed to be racing on another, racing to see which would be the first in the wild chase. Then they all suddenly unite, as if at a given signal, and change into the shape of a sort, delicately-formed ribbon, twisting in light and graceful movements. It is as if the unquiet beams had now sought rest. Are they, perhaps, thinking of something new? Then suddenly the beautiful ribbon is, as it were, torn in many pieces. Again begins the chase, again the wild flight. It is difficult to imagine what the next step will be. It seems as if the zenith would now be chosen as the central point for the whole movement. And so it is. Suddenly, as if by magic, the most glorious corona streams forth from it.

The first Christmas in Gjøa Haven. From the left Helmer Hansen, Roald Amundsen, Peder Ristvedt, Adolf Lindstrøm, Gustav Juel Wiik and Anton Lund. Photo: NB

Christmas goes, the New Year comes. The many holidays have already begun to tire us, and we take up our work again with pleasure. The first item on our programme is the equipment for my approaching sledge journey to the immediate area of the magnetic pole. The original plan was that I should make this expedition with one companion and provisions for three months, supported by a relieving expedition under Lieut. Hansen with one man. There were consequently four of us who were obliged to have their things in order by a certain date. In one thing there was a general consensus of opinion, namely, that Eskimo fur garments were the most suitable for the climate. We had, therefore, taken time by the forelock and bartered with the Eskimo for the lightest and finest reindeer-skin clothing we could get. After many small trials, too, we all agreed that snow huts were far superior to tents when the temperature was below -22° Fahr. (-30°C).

I therefore started a class, with old Teraiu – the Eskimo who stayed with us, with his family – as teacher. We all four joined, and now built a snow hut regularly every forenoon. Sometimes one of us was master builder and the other masons, sometimes the other. Old Teraiu, who could not understand what we were building all these huts for, shook his head pensively, evidently in the conviction that we had taken leave of our senses. Sometimes he would throw out his arms to indicate the overwhelming number of houses, and exclaim, "Iglu amichjui – amichjui – amichjui!" Which means, "This is a dreadful lot of houses." But in this, too, we arrived at what we wanted: we became at last good snow builders.

Lindstrøm learning how to build an igloo. Photo: NB

On February 29 we took our sledges up on to the heights in order to be ready for a start the next morning. The day for beginning of our sledge-journey broke clear and still. The temperature was not exactly summer, the thermometer reading nearly -64°Fahr. (-53°C.).

Photo: NB

The first departure for the North Magnetic Pole on March 1, 1904. The attempt lasted only four days due to cold weather and lack of experience in handling dogs and sledges.

AMUNDSEN LANTERN SLIDE 012: FM/JFO

One sledge had a team of seven, mostly young dogs, for we had lost the others during the course of the winter from one or other mysterious disease: the other sledge was hauled by three men. We found it difficult to make any way; the sledges ran badly. The snow in this severe cold was like sand, and advance very heavy. After terrible labour we made 4 miles the first day. Before we could go to rest we had to build our house. Thanks to the many huts we had built before that winter, we did this fairly quickly – in about an hour and a half. The temperature, which had sunk to about -70°Fahr. (-57°C.), did not tempt us to be out longer than was absolutely necessary. As soon, therefore, as we had finished the hut, we went in and walled up the entrance with a large block of snow. The cooking apparatus was set going, and it was soon warm and cosy in our little snow-house. In spite of the low temperature – about -77°Fahr. (-62°C.) – the lowest we observed, we spent in all respects a comfortable night. The next day, after ceaseless toil from morning to evening, we managed to cover 3.5 miles. I realized now that this sort of thing was not good enough, and decided to make the depot where we were, return to the vessel, and wait for warmer weather.

On March 16 I again made another attempt to move this depot somewhat farther out. It was on this trip that we first met with the Nechjilli Eskimo, and accompanied them home to their snow-huts, which lay among the pressure ridges in Rae strait. Our first meeting with this tribe was thoroughly friendly and hearty. Their camps consisted of sixteen snow-huts, inhabited by about a hundred people. In appearance and dress, they were exactly like our former friends the Ogluli Eskimo.

When my companions and I were about to begin to build our house of snow, they all came and gave us to understand that they wished to help us. We gladly left the work to them, and after the lapse of half an hour our hut was completely finished. The following morning occurred a scene which very clearly shows in what respect the whites are held among these savages. From our earlier Eskimo friends, the Ogluli Eskimo, we had learned that the word "miki" meant a dog. As all our new dogs were young and not up to much work, I asked one of our new friends – a man called Attikleura, who appeared to be the chief of the tribe – to lend me his dogs the next day. He thought a good deal when I asked him to do this, looked at me, and smiled faintly, but made no answer. I, however, did not give in, but repeated my request. He nodded his head, and we did not mention the matter again, as I now considered it settled. When I came out of the hut in the morning, Attikleura's little son was standing near the door. I did not take much notice of him, but went to his father's hut to ask what had become of the dogs. I naturally used the word "miki" which I had learned.

He looked at me in astonishment, and made me understand that I had got his "miki". As I persistently denied this, he made signs to me that we should go out. He went straight over to his little boy, pointed to him, and said, "Ona mikaga," which to say, "Here is my boy." Now everything was clear to me. "Miki" did not mean with this tribe "dog," but "child." So great was then their fear of us that he had without demur given his son away. I let him understand that I had made a mistake; the whole thing ended by hearty laughter on both sides.

Hunting party consisting of Talurnakto, the Owl and Peder Ristvedt.
Photo: NB

Winter in Gjøa Haven.
Photo: NB

After two days' march we came across, at Matty Island, a small camp, consisting of six huts. These belonged to some Ischuachtorvik Eskimo, as they called themselves, who were from the east coast of Boothia Felix, near the place where Ross wintered in the Victory. These people made a very bad impression on me, and I said to my companion in the evening that we had better lash everything securely on the sledges, and let the dogs sleep near them. In the morning when it was time to start we missed a saw, and axe, and a knife. I made the Eskimo understand that they must return the stolen articles, but they pretended that they had no knowledge of the matter. After addressing myself to them

two or three times in vain, I grew tired of it, and got out one of our carbines. I then explained to them as well as I could that I knew who the thieves were, and that I would shoot them if the articles were not given back. This worked. The things were returned in a hurry. I did not dare to make any depot in the neighbourhood of these thieves, but retraced my steps, and confided everything to the care of our new friends, the Nechjilli Eskimo. I was never disappointed in the confidence I placed in these people; they were what they appeared to be from the first moment – thoroughly honest. Quite a crowd of them joined company with us, and returned to the Gjøa, staying with us for a few days.

The camp at the North Magnetic Pole.

AMUNDSEN LANTERN SLIDE 016: FM/JFO

On April 6 I started off with Sergeant Peder Ristvedt to make magnetic investigations in the vicinity of the pole. We were equipped for three months, but our nine dogs were not equal to drawing the heavily loaded sledges. We had a couple of Eskimo with us who were going out to capture seal. It was a lovely day, and curious as it may sound, felt quite summer-like with a temperature of -22°Fahr. (-30°C.). We had, of course, been used to a much lower temperature during the two preceding months, February giving an average of about -45°Fahr. (-43°C.). This was the reason why we perspired as if we were in the tropics that day with its -22°. We had to throw off garment after garment, and only stopped when modesty demanded it of us.

This sledge trip was not very successful. An injury to my leg, which I incurred, kept me lying in my bag for a week. I had, however, the satisfaction of getting close to the pole as was necessary. We had been obliged on our way to cache one of our sledges, and provisions for a month, in order to hasten our advance. This was, unluckily, in the neighbourhood of the Ichjuachtorvik Eskimo hunting grounds. When we came back to fetch our things, everything, with the exception of 10 lbs. of pemmican, had been stolen. We were thus obliged to return home after only two months' absence.

Roald Amundsen and Peder Ristvedt arrived at the North Magnetic Pole on May 17, 2004. The Norwegian National Day was celebrated with a festive meal, cakes and cigars.

AMUNDSEN LANTERN SLIDE 013: FM/JFO

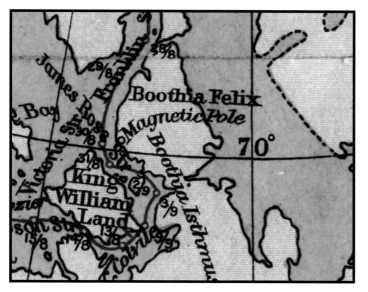

The North Magnetic Pole area. Photo FM

Godfred Hansen aboard the Gjøa.

Amundsen or Ristvedt at the North Magnetic Pole.

In the beginning of June, large numbers of Eskimo appeared at the ship with blubber and skins of seals for sale which they had caught during the course of the winter months. We paid them in wood and iron. In the middle of July most of them left us again, to hunt reindeer and catch salmon in different directions. In the summer of 1904, Lieut. Hansen went a rowing expedition with one man to Cape Crozier, about 100 miles distant, to put down a large depot. The latter was for use in his sledge-journey to the east coast of Victoria Land, planned for the spring of 1905. Gustav Wiik had all this time had sole charge of the magnetic observations of the station, and had done excellent work. The summer was short and cheerless.

The vessel slipped the ice on July 22. Of birds of passage we saw swans, geese, loons, ducks, eiders, and many small birds. The ptarmigan came in March and went in November, the only stationary animals were the Arctic fox, the stoat, and the lemming. The vegetation was rich, and large tracts were to be seen quite covered with flowers. There were butterflies, flies, and some other insects, not to omit several milliards of gnats. The winter set in somewhat earlier this year than the preceding one, and the ice formed a week sooner. The reindeer, of which there had been great numbers the previous autumn, were this year very seldom to be seen.

A group of Netsilik Inuit visits the Gjøa to trade.

AMUNDSEN LANTERN SLIDE 017: FM/JFO

The crew in Inuit clothing. Photo: FM

The crew in Inuit clothing from the behind. Photo: FM

Gustav Juel Wiik in Inuit clothing. Photo: FM

AMUNDSEN LANTERN SLIDE 019: FM/JFO

The whole of our winter provision thus consisted in 1904 of only twenty deer, and these had been shot inland, whereas, in 1903, we could have killed as many as we liked quite close to the vessel. However, the Eskimo, who had spent the summer reindeer-hunting in Northern America, brought us a quantity of venison, and from other quarters we procured salmon, cod, and trout, so that we were well provided for the next winter too.

In the middle of October the Eskimo returned from their summer excursions, and then visited us in great numbers, but went off again to fish before the darkest part of the winter set in. Towards Christmas they returned to the vessel, and we had the pleasure of their company for nearly two months.

A Netsillik Inuit with his salmon spear.

AMUNDSEN LANTERN SLIDE 022: FM/JFO

Godfred Hansen, Gustav Juel Wiik and Anton Lund.
Photo: NB

Roald Amundsen, Helmer Hansen and Peder Ristvedt in the aft saloon of the Gjøa.
Photos of John Franklin and Fridtjof Nansen in the background.

AMUNDSEN LANTERN SLIDE 030: FM/JFO

On November 20 we had a visit from an Eskimo family of a quite strange tribe. They proved to be Kinepatu Eskimo from Chestefield Inlet, near Hudson Bay. The man's name was Atagala. He knew English sufficiently to explain that near where he lived two large vessels were lying. For an old Mauser rifle and four hundred cartridges he undertook to take a mail down to them and return with an answer, about 1500 miles. On May 20, the next year, a sledge-team of ten dogs swung into our harbour. It was Atagala. He brought us mail from the Arctic, as ship belonging to the Canadian government, which was wintering at Cape Fullerton, in Hudson Bay. She had originally been the Gauss, and was built by the German South Polar Expedition, but was now out to inspect and choose suitable spots for small garrisons. Major Moodie was in chief command, and Captain Bernier in command of the ship. An American whaler, the Era, was also wintering at the same place. Captain Comer, of the Era, and Major Moodie sent me ten sledge-dogs, as I had written to the former, telling them that the greater number of our dogs had died in the course of the first winter.

Atagala (Artung-e-lar) and friends. Photo: FM

Captain George Comer (1858-1937). Photo: FM

Captain Joseph Bernier (1852-1934). Photo: FM

Editor's note:

Captain Comer, of the *Era*, describes the communication with Roald Amundsen in his diary:

March 18: "This evening a sled arrived from Chesterfield Inlet to trade. They brought a letter from a ship which is making the Northwest Passage. Gjoa is the way her name is spelt, Captain R. Amundsen. This letter leaves them all well, a crew of seven men, and they were in lat 68'38 north, long 96' west, frozen in. They have accomplished their work and expect next summer to push on towards Bering Strait. The man is to return with an answer." March 20: "I received a note from Major Moodie regarding the Norwegian ship from which he had a letter saying that her captain would like very much to have eight dogs sent to him. I wrote back saying I would send the dogs but there should be no pay for them". March 21: "I received a note from Major Moodie, declining my offer to take the dogs as a gift to the Norwegian captain. It looks as though Major Moodie wants the honor or glory of furnishing the dogs but I do not intend to have it said that I had to be paid in order to help a person in need – that is not American." March 23: "I have written a letter to Captain Amundsen of the exploring vessel Gjoa which the native Artung-e-lar will take with him when he returns." March 24: "Have made arrangements with Major Moodie to the effect that he can buy five dogs of my natives and send to the Norwegian captain and that I would send five, so in this way we may both share in the pleasure of helping him." March 26: "Artung-e-lar the native and his party got away to go to Baker Lake and from there to the Norwegian vessel. The major sent over here for the ten dogs, five of which he will pay my natives for and the other five which I have sent as a gift to the Captain of the expedition for his vessel's use. The man expects to reach there the first of June."

The Captain of the *Arctic*, Joseph Bernier, wrote the following in his memoirs about the long distance communication with Roald Amundsen:

"It is with great pleasure to me to recall many hours spent with that remarkable man Roald Amundsen, who has to his credit greater achievements in polar work than anyone else. We met on numerous occasions and paced the deck many hours discussing arctic problems.

While he was wintering in Gjoa Harbor, King William's Land, and I was in command of the D.G.S. Arctic at Fullerton, in Hudson Bay in 1905, I sent letters to him on March 26th, by the Eskimo Ahteegila and all the latest world news, especially news relating to exploring expeditions of which there was a large budget at that time. Later I received the following reply written on a sheet of squared paper.

Amundsen's reference to R.M. Donaldson's who was with me at Fullerton was due to my inclosing Donaldson's report to him, which is given below. Donaldson had been on the Neptune with Commander A.P. Low in 1904, and had incidentally called at Beechey Island and Port Leopold.

"The Neptune arrived at Beechey Island August 15th, 1904. We there secured a record attached to the Franklin Memorial Monument. Our Commander A.P. Low, took this record back to Canada with him to be forwarded to your people, leaving a record of our visit attached to the same place. Your record was tied first above the small Marble tablet, and had an inventory, not being touched previous to our visit. … "

Capt. J.E. Bernier
Master of the D.G.S.
Arctic,
Fullerton,

Gjoa Harbor,
King William's Land
22 May, 1905,

Dear Sir,
Your kind letter of the 26th March dispatched by the native "Atangala" – came me in hand – together with a lot of photos and news – the 19th inst. I received it – as you can imagine you – with the outmost pleasure. I did not know any of these news you send. All my comrades here are of course also in high state of delight. I send you my most hearty thanks for your kindness. Your information about the American Whalers to the westward are very important for me as I did not know it before. The report of R.M. Donaldson of the R.N.W.M.P. was of high interest to me. I am very glad to hear that our news from that time already have reached our relations. The depot of Port Leopold was put in a very good position, but I hope we shall get away without it. Will you please thank Mr. Ben Kuilird of Skien for his good wishes. – Both my comrades and myself send you our best compliments and wishes for your fortune in the Arctic.

I am, Dear Sir, Yours Very Sincerely,

Roald Amundsen,
Commanding the Norwegian Gjoa Expedition.

Son of the Vikings Navigates the Northwest Passage.

Capt. Roald Amundsen Achieves Undying Fame—Success Crowns His Efforts Where Sir John Franklin and Others Have Failed—Location of Magnetic Pole Determined.

ALL who know the story of the search for the Northwest Passage will have no doubt that Capt. Roald Amundsen and his little vessel, the Gjöa, have earned a conspicuous place in the last chapter of the book. It is not that Amundsen has made an original discovery or accomplished one of the most wonderful feats of navigation. In fact, the time has been ripe for years to do just what he has accomplished.

His feat is, none the less, very remarkable. He had the boldness to conceive, the courage to attempt, and the good luck to achieve the first voyage by a single vessel through the Northwest Passage; and it is a very notable fact that after 300 years of the most strenuous effort to find the Passage and to make the journey—persistent effort that ended practically with the Franklin search expeditions about a half century ago—it was left at last for a sloop of 47 tons, 70 feet long, 20 feet beam, manned by eight men, and propelled by a small petroleum engine to make the passage. The Gjöa is now in Winter quarters near the delta of the Mackenzie River, which is visited by whalers every Summer. Amundsen reports that his men are well, his ship is all right, and there is no doubt that by the time the whaling season opens, next Summer, the little vessel will be on her way to Bering Sea and the Pacific Ocean.

We knew before Amundsen sailed from Christiania, on June 16, 1903, that, after he completed his magnetic work in the neighborhood of the north magnetic pole, he intended to try to make the Northwest Passage and come home by way of Bering Strait. We knew the exact route by which he expected to make this journey, and the route has been known to every student of polar exploration since the records of the ill-fated Franklin expedition were recovered.

While Sir John Franklin was dying on his ship a small party of his men discovered this route and linked it with the land explorations of Simpson and other famous discoverers who made the maps of the northern edge of our continent in the early part of the last century.

These land explorers had followed the coast hundreds of miles to the west as far as Cape Barrow, the most northern point of the continent. Mr. Elson had traced the northwestern coast of Alaska from Bering Strait to Cape Barrow, so that the whole northern coast of America was outlined. The explorers, looking northward, had seen islands here and there out in the Arctic Ocean, and they found that the floe ice moved off the land in Summer, leaving channels of open water along the mainland.

What the Franklin party discovered was a way to reach these channels along the mainland. How they found the Northwest Passage that Amundsen has now triumphantly followed may be briefly told.

On May 24, 1847, Graham Gore, First Lieutenant of the Erebus, with another officer and six men left their ships and started southward. They reached Point Victory, on King William Land, and went onward till they saw the coast of North America, the charts of which were in their hands. The Franklin expedition had been sent from England for no other purpose than to find the Northwest Passage.

The little party realized that the long-sought-for passage had been discovered, and could actually be accomplished, if they might only force their ships through the short ice barrier that intervened between them and the open water. They deposited a record of their discovery, and then hurried back to their ships to impart the joyful tidings to their comrades. Then found the expedition plunged in the

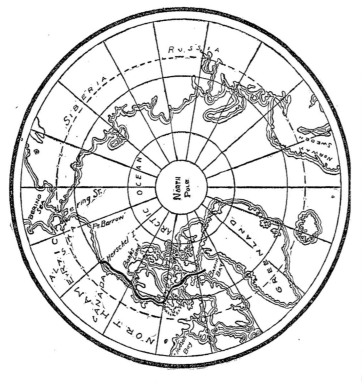

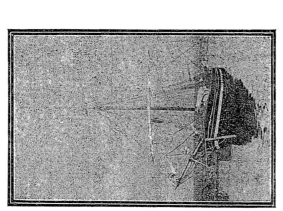

The Gjöa, with which Amundsen Made the Passage.

England he declared that "there is no Northwest Passage."

A most remarkable fact that persisted for 150 years after the discovery of America was the faith of Europe that America was merely a geographical dependency or "Tartary," and at any rate, whatever

gator, through Bering Strait into the Arctic C and finally reached the northeast coast of Land, where he was frozen in for two year his supplies were nearly exhausted. Aband their vessel, the party finally reached the Res further east, were transferred later to the Phe and taken through Lancaster Sound to Eng They had the satisfaction of being the first m cross between the Pacific and Atlantic Ocea the north of America. They had found conti sea all the way and had discovered a Northwest sage; but it took three ships as well as som sledging to get them across. They had proved i sible to pass from sea to sea, but by exposure to dangers that from that day no other navigato attempted to follow this route.

+ +

Amundsen is the second to make the North Passage, but he has taken his ship through him, and his success is far more brilliant and able. He has proved that a single ship may between the Atlantic and Pacific by a route from King William Land to Bering Strait is ably available nearly every Summer. It is do however, that, save in very exceptional seaso vessel could make the entire journey between Bay and Bering Strait in a single season.

It is well known that the main purpose Amundsen expedition was to make a magnetic of the region surrounding the North Magneti and to relocate the pole if, as is probable, Ross. The information about his magnetic thus far received is too meagre to be discusse profit, but from the two letters he sent to H Bay it appears to have been very successful. surveys he had in view are of great importance scheme of worldwide investigation now unfoldi wegian explorer and his seven comrades wil the small expedition a unique and a very prom place among successful polar enterprises.

CYRUS C. ADA.

Editor's note:

The letter Roald Amundsen wrote to Captain Comer and a photo of "Atangala" were printed in a large article in the New York Times on December 10, 1905 – more than eight months before the *Gjøa* arrived in Nome.

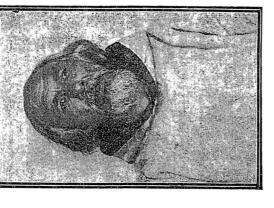

Eskimo Messenger Who Brought Amundsen's Letter to Captain Comer.

Group of Eskimo Women at Cape Fullerton. (From a Photograph Given by Amundsen to Capt. Comer.)

Letter from Captain Amundsen to Captain George Comer, of the American Whaler *Era*, of New Bedford, Mass.

---

them all when they finally abandoned their ships and sought the mainland.

It is this Summer channel along the coast that Amundsen has followed westward; and the Franklin party not only pointed out the short cut to the channel, but the fate of its ships gave a warning as to the channels which he fully improved. From the two letters he sent by messenger to the Canadian Government party in the north of Hudson Bay, a while ago, it is evident that he kept the Gjöa's Winter quarters away from the shores, where she would likely be crushed or imprisoned by heaped-up ice. When his magnetic work was done and the water channels opened along the coast, the Gjöa, as well as her commander, was ready to go on.

Our map shows the track of the Gjöa as she entered Lancaster Sound from Baffin Bay and threaded the channels leading westward till she reached the region where Amundsen made his magnetic surveys. This region is roughly inclosed with a circle of X's. In this area Amundsen spent nearly two years. His last magnetic work was done on King William Island, not far from where Lieut. Gore solved the question of the Northwest Passage; and it was here that the Gjöa started on the journey which, next Summer, will be acclaimed as the first voyage by one ship between the Atlantic and the Pacific to the north of this continent. The map also shows Herschel Island, just a little west of the present Winter quarters of the Gjöa, whence Amundsen made his sledge journey south to Eagle City, one of our settlements in Alaska.

Those will best appreciate his success who have read of the prodigious effort and the enormous treasure that were expended for three centuries to find the Northwest Passage. The literature of the voyages for the discovery of the North Pole is scarcely more voluminous. The writer has just counted in the library of the American Geographical Society eighteen books on various expeditions that were fitted out solely for the search for the Northwest Passage; but many of the seekers for this elusive channel never wrote a book, and among them was Henry Hudson, perhaps the most illustrious of them all, who was set adrift in a small boat to perish in Hudson Bay while he was seeking the passage.

For many generations the purpose of these voyages was to find a navigable short cut from Europe to the lands of Asia, that were fabled to be enormously rich. Sebastian Cabot sailed up the Canadian coast in the hope of finding the famous China passage. He reached 67 degrees 30 minutes north latitude, and seeing open water to the northwest he firmly believed in the possibility of taking his vessel right through to China by this polar route, which would have been only about a third as long as a route to Asia by way of a Panama Canal. But his faint-hearted companions compelled him to return.

The only purpose William Baffin had in view when he sailed up the west coast of Greenland to Smith Sound was to find the Northwest Passage. He discovered two broad openings extending westward— Jones Sound, obstructed by ice, and Lancaster Sound, which he cautiously penetrated. On his return to

America was, it was an impediment in the path to China and must be circumvented if there was any way to do it.

But the hunt for the Northwest Passage was not given up for a century after all hope was abandoned that, if found, it would provide a new route to China. The quest for a commercial short cut to Asia was over, but there remained the spirit of daring adventure and the determination to see if there was such a thing as the Northwest Passage. It was England that renewed the search in 1818, with the far nobler purpose of completing the geographical survey of the western hemisphere and adding to the sum of human knowledge. No explorations ever called for a higher degree of courage, devotion, and physical stamina than those in the archipelago north of our

continent which began with John Ross in 1818 and ended with the Franklin search expeditions about 1857.

It is a curious fact that John Ross, who spent four Winters in those frozen seas, persisted in the idea that there was no Northwest Passage. He asserted that the Province of Boothia connected America with the north pole, and even declared, as proof of his contention, that he had found a difference of thirteen feet between the levels of the seas to the east and west of Boothia.

The loss of the Franklin expedition of 219 men and the efforts to clear up the mysterious tragedy ended for nearly fifty years the exploration of the great archipelago north of our continent. It was not revived till Sverdrup recently added some large islands to the Parry group and Amundsen went to Boothia to make his surveys in the region of the North Magnetic Pole. Only one result of the great work of the Franklin search expeditions need be mentioned here. This was the discovery of another Northwest Passage, first known to the world, though the more southern passage of the Franklin party was found several years earlier.

McClure, in 1850, pushed his ship, the Invest-

[Handwritten letter]

Gjöa Harbour, King Williams Land.
Lieut. Nov. 29, 1905.

Captain Gorg Comer
Master of the American Whaling Schooner Era.
Fullerton.

Dear Sir!

Your kind letter of the 22nd March reached me on the 19th inst. I thank you very much for it. — It is kind of you to offer to take messages with you from Pipuke Bay. I'm sure some natives leave for their place you shall hear from me.

Your informations about the American whalers to the westward are very interesting and I hope to meet with them. — I thank you kind. Ready for the 5 dogs you have sent me, but — as the sledge parte, which I was to use them, already started on the 2nd April — I am, and have them, as I have very nearly no dogfeed left. I obtain one of a good governance of your kindness and leave the others back gorly Atangala — the natic — holy many thanks for his assistance. — I am very glad to hear that you are successful in taking whales and I wish you still more luck to. Bring my comrades and I are with good health and send you our wishes for your future success and will had compliments. Robert m. Bertie.

Yours very sincerely, Roald Amundsen
Com. the Norwegian Gjöa expedition.

During our seventeen months' intercourse with the Nechjilli Eskimo we became by degrees so intimate with some of them that they little by little lost the mistrust they usually have for strangers, and showed us complete confidence. We, however, never really acquired their language, and, consequently, could not thoroughly understand their life.

What I have to tell about them, however, is based partly on careful observation, and partly on information from the Eskimo themselves, and this being the case, I venture to think that my information regarding one of the most interesting and least-known races of the world is correct. What adds greatly to the value of these searches in the series of splendid photographs taken by Lieut. Hansen during our sojourn in those parts.

"Kabloka was too much of a Mongolian to be handsome but she captivated everyone with her child-like innocent ways".
– R.Amundsen. Photo: NB

Inside an igloo. On the left is a blubber lamp, cooking equipment and a drying rack for clothes. Photo: NB

"The Owl" has captured a trout. Photo: NB

Praederik and his wife Draga in their igloo. The blubber lamp on the left is drying the clothes on the rack. Photo: NB

Nechjilli, which the Nechjilli Eskimo looks upon as their home, are the banks of the great Willersted lake on Boothia isthmus, and of the little bit of river which flows from the lake into the sea. Unfortunately, we never had the time to pay them a visit, but from the Eskimo's often repeated descriptions I know what the country looks like, and what their life is there. From the time the ice breaks up in June or July to January or February the next year, it is here that they live – in summer in their tents, and, when the snow falls, in their snow-houses. Often in transition periods, from winter to summer and summer to winter, when the snow – as it is in the month of June – is too waterlogged to be used for the building of entire snow-huts, they are obliged to use a construction the walls of which consist of snow and the roof of skins, a combination of snow-hut and tent; or, as often happens in September, when the cold strikes in and the lakes freeze before the snow comes, they are obliged to construct a building of ice with a skin roof.

Inuk woman. Photo: NB

Two young Netsilik archers. Photo: NB

Inside an igloo. Photo: NB

A Netsilik family. The father is carrying a snow shovel. Photo: NB

When an Eskimo is about to build a snow house, he is always careful first to consult his "hervond." This is simply a stick of straightened horn taken from the antlers of the reindeer. At the lower end it has a ferrule of musk-ox bone, and at the upper a handle of reindeer bone. It is about a yard long. With his keen glance he now scans the country, and at the place which pleases him best thrusts his "hervond" into the snow. He does this in order to find out its quality, for it is as important for an Eskimo to find good snow for his building as it is for a bricklayer to have lime for his stone. A very long experience is required in order to test the snow in this manner, and, when several Eskimo are together, it is a task generally left to the oldest ones. The most suitable snow is that of a solid and compact kind, with a superincumbent layer of loose snow, about a foot in depth. Nor must the underlying snow be too hard, or it will be difficult to cut out the blocks. The site once chosen, the upper loose snow is shovelled away, and is laid round the spot where the house is to be. When the underlying hard layer is laid bare, the builder begins with his knife – which is usually long-bladed and long-handled – to cut out and build up the blocks. The house is constructed from inside, and the blocks are cut exclusively from the building site: it is seldom that an Eskimo has resort to the snow outside. The blocks are cut out of snow with a high edge, and that is the reason why the site can contain sufficient material. The hut is built spirally, in such a way that the succeeding block is always supported on a preceding one, and in shape much resembled a large beehive. Our greatest difficulty was always when we had to decrease and build the roof. The blocks are then placed in a very inclined position, one may almost say rocking. But the Eskimo are born to this way of building. Where one of them puts the block there it stays, even if it forms an angle of 45° with the horizontal plane. The structure is completed by a little, dexterously placed, plug of snow in the apex of the roof. After the house is up, there will be a mass of refuse snow lying inside it. With this the sleeping-bench and fireplace are made. Meanwhile, the lady of the house has not been without occupation outside. The loose snow, which was shovelled away at the beginning, she uses to caulk all the holes and cracks with, and if she has any to spare she throws it over the entire house, which helps a very great deal in making it warm and draughtless. When all is finished inside, an aperture is cut in the wall of the same height as the bench. The man comes out and the woman takes his place. First of all, the large watertight kayak-skin is handed in and is spread over the entire bench; then comes the turn of all the reindeer-skins – soft, large, and warm; then the rest of the effects, such as coking-utensils, a drying-grill, blubber for the lamp, and a number of other things which the Eskimo find indispensable. When all this is done, the housewife is called in. It will be asked, what was this immured lady doing inside the hut? Perhaps it will not be indiscreet of me to poke a little hole in the wall and peep in. In the name of knowledge everything is permissible, so with a "ski" staff, which I happened to have with me, I made a hole in the wall and opened a way into the sight of this mysterious interior.

The first thing she does is to put the lamp in place and make a fire. After that she fills the cooking-pot with snow, and hangs it over the flames to melt into water for her thirsty husband. As soon as she is satisfied that the lamp-flame is burning to its greatest extent, she turns her attention to arranging other things, the sleeping-bench is levelled and flattened, reindeer-skins placed in order on it, and everything made as comfortable and cosy as possible. All being arranged, she seats herself before the fireplace and seems to be particularly anxious to make the fire burn as brightly and give out as much heat as possible. Now I understand why it is she is walled up in this house – in order to warm it and make the blocks of snow sink, so that the whole will form a close and compact wall. But she will certainly not succeed in this is if I continued at my peeping, so I fill it up again and take myself off. Meanwhile, the man has built the passage, 9 to 12 feet in length, which leads into the house. But he will certainly not dare to make a hole in the wall and put it in communication with the interior of the house before he receives higher orders from his better half. He amuses himself meanwhile with his friends, who are in a similar situation, and whiles away the time in joking and conversations. They are a fine group of men who are standing there, ranging tall, from 5 feet 9 inches to 6 feet, though there are some short ones among them. They are powerfully built, the life they lead inducing all-round development. The ladies' pellucid voices are now heard, and the expectant husbands can complete their structures by knocking a hole through the wall from the passage to the hut.

Let us now pay a visit to one of these camps, and see what Eskimo life is here in these burrows of snow immediately after their construction. The huts are of different sizes. Some people like them high, some low. The circumference is from 30 to 45 feet, according to the size of the family. It is the month of January, and the cold is severe. They, therefore, live two families together, so as to be warmer. The members of the family have just assembled after the building operations and a long day's sledging. The housewife sits in her accustomed place and croons her monotonous chant, consisting of four words and as many notes, which are repeated in varying forms. These sounds, when they are repeated often enough, we found unendurably monotonous. Politely to request them to be quiet was of no use; but we found another most effective means, namely, to give a vocal performance of our own at the same time. Then we had peace, for our many tones, no doubt, sounded as awful to Eskimo ears as their four did to ours. Well, this was not very polite on a first call, but, anyhow, they were not offended.

The first thing an Eskimo does when he enters his hut is to take off his outer coat and beat all his clothes quite free from snow. This he does so that the latter shall not have time to melt and wet his clothes. If he intends to be in the whole evening, he takes off his other outer garments. If any of them have become wet during the course of the day, they are thrown to the lady of the establishment, who puts them up on the grill to dry. His hunger has now to be appeased, and the most tempting pieces of meat and fish are brought out – of course frozen stiff. But this does not affect the Eskimo in the least; once down it melts soon enough, and enormous quantities disappear. Their knives are their only eating implement, but these they handle with dexterity. They hold the piece of meat fast with their teeth and the left hand, and with lightning rapidity pass the knife right under the noses, and cut off a piece of meat so close in to their lips that one is astonished that the latter do not go too. One large bit of blubber after the other goes the same way.

The family having thus finished this important business, a nap will possibly be to their taste, and the entrance is carefully bricked in from the inside. They now proceed to undress till they are quite naked, and then sleep the sleep of the just under large coverings of reindeer-skin shared in common, possibly till late the next day. This, however, depends upon whether they have enough food. If the man intends to live here for any length of time, he chops himself a window the following day out of the ice on the nearest fresh-water pool, and inserts in the wall immediately above the entrance. His dame can then see to do her homework by daylight. She has plenty to look after. She sits by the fire, which is her accustomed place, with her legs tucked up under her, and watches the flames and her offspring, who are running in and out playing. She smiles and looks absolutely happy. Probably it is the two small physiognomies, encrusted with soot and train-oil, which call these pleasant thoughts. It is not so long since the youngest left her hood, where children are carried till they are about two years old.

Their play grows less by degrees, and the youngest one goes up to his mother and looks inquiringly in her face. She knows her boy, she does. The children here are not weaned so quickly, and mother's milk is to their taste long after they begin to walk. I have even seen boys ten years of age lay their arrows aside and take part in the repast.

But see, here comes a friend, of the same sex, of course. She has come to pass the time of day; is bored, perhaps, in her own hut. It is Alo-Alo, a young and attractive woman. The sharp cold has given her a fresh colour, and the pretty brown eyes with the blue whites look very much as if they could hide something behind them. Out of her hood sticks up a little wondering face; it is her year-old son "Akla," or the brown bear. Conversation is soon in full swing, and the two women seem to have a great deal that is amusing to tell one another. Suddenly the baby in the hood begins to move, and with incredible rapidity and quite unparalleled adroitness changes place from the hood to his mother's lap. He has his wishes complied with, and is going to be put back in his warm, cosy place, when his mother discovers that he is more than usually dirty to-day. The washing process which then takes place must be very practical when water is scarce. She licks the child clean, and then puts him back. If it has been a fine day, the men have been out on the ice to capture seal, and are now coming back in the dusk. They seldom return home empty-handed, but have a seal or two with them, which are then handed over to the housewife, who has to see to their partition. The entrails, which are the greatest delicacy they know, go to the one who has caught

Roald Amundsen and the Inuit Talurnakto and the Owl. Photo: NB

the seal; the rest is divided among all. After supper they often require a little diversion in the long winter evenings. They then assemble in the largest hut, and spend a few hours together, singing and dancing. These huts are often quite handsome structures, and I have seen them 14 feet high and 25 feet in diameter. On these occasions the women all sit round in a circle and begin their monotonous chanting, the men entering the circle one by one to perform a kind of solo dance, beat a frame covered with thin tanned reindeer-hide, and scream something perfectly dreadful. What astonished me most at these festivities was the singing of the women. I had always thought that all their tunes – or rather variations on the five notes – were impromptu, but here I had certain proof that they really were songs, for I heard as many as twenty women singing together at these gatherings for a whole hour at a time, without any of them falling out of the melody. In my opinion this almost points to musical gifts.

The next evening the magician of the tribe will perhaps give a representation in the same hut. This is a very serious affair – the only performance we never had an official invitation to. We tricked them all the same, and found out what went on. The hut is made almost dark, only quite a little flame being allowed to burn, which, of course, made things the more mysterious – complete darkness would be too dull. The magician and his assistant (usually his wife) take their places on the bench, and the company sit at the other end of the hut. Absolute darkness broods over the performers. The two now begin to utter loud howls, and, on the whole, lead one to suppose they are killing one another. After this farce has been going on for half an hour the noise grows less, and by degrees everything becomes quiet.

The light is made stronger, and, to the apparent surprise of everybody, the magician now exhibits two holes in his coat, which, before the light had been subdued, was quite whole – one hole in his chest and the other in his back, and they go to prove, of course, that during this turbulent scene he has run himself through with his spear. Judging by appearances, the Eskimo all take this very seriously; but when later I joked with them about it they laughed and said that the whole thing was nonsense.

Any real sign of astonishment these people seldom show. One of the few times that I can remember seeing any trace of this was when I sent a messenger to the ship – I was then in camp about 10 miles away taking magnetic observations – with a letter in which I asked for a certain quantity of ammunition. When he returned the next day and I told him before he gave me the consignments that I knew how many cartridges he had with him of each kind, and that he might count them himself, he was astonished to see that I was right, and much impressed by the use we put our writing to. They often amused themselves later by scribbling some strokes on a bit of paper and giving it to us. We always pretended to be highly astonished, and read it out loud; this greatly amused them. Family life gave us the impression, as a rule, of being happy, though I know of cases where the husband ill-treated his wife. The male sex being so much more numerous than the female, it was not unusual to find marriages where the wife had two husbands. The reverse relationship I never met with. In general, the husband was spokesman and the wife obeyed blindly, but elderly widows were sometimes personages of great influence.

Umiktuallu kills his foster-son. Photo: FM

The religious opinions of the Eskimo were like our own in that they had an understanding of a good and an evil being, of punishment and reward. If a man had behaved as he should in this life, then he would go to the hunting-fields in the moon; and had he been a bad man he must go under the earth. During the whole of our stay among them there only occurred, as far as I know, four births and two deaths. The latter, in both cases, being suicide. It is not considered to be wrong; but is, however, only resorted to when the pain in an illness is to great to be borne. The way in which they do it is, I think, peculiar to them alone. A sealskin thong is stretched across the hut 2 feet above the floor. The sick person is left alone in the hut and the others go outside; they however, have peepholes in the wall, through which they follow events. The sick person now kneels down and endea-vours to suffocate himself by pressing his throat against the strained thong. If the unfortunate person is unable to do the business for himself, or it seems to be taking too long, one of those outside comes in and expedite matters by pressing his head down on the thong. Fighting with closed fists occurs now and then, and murder is not unknown. It thus happened in the summer of 1904, at the station, that a boy twelve years of age accidentally shot another boy of seven in a tent. The father of the boy who was killed immediately seized the other, who, for that matter was his adopted son, and dragged him out of the tent and stabbed him to death. Their dead they sew up in a reindeer-skin, and lay them on the ground. A few articles, such as a bow, spear, arrows, and other things, are placed beside them. We found many an interesting object in this manner.

A Netsilik burial.

ＡＭＵＮＤＳＥＮ　ＬＡＮＴＥＲＮ　ＳＬＩＤＥ　０２４：　ＦＭ／ＪＦＯ

On April 2, Lieut. Hansen and Sergeant Ristvedt started on their sledge-journey to chart the east coast of Victoria Land. They had two sledges, twelve dogs, and equipment for seventy days. The provisions were measured as shortly as possible so as to reduce weight. All the same, it is very necessary on a long journey of the kind that everything should be carefully planned so as really to hold out the requisite time. The depot, which had been made the year before, had been entirely spoiled by bears, but Lieut. Hansen and his companion shot bears, seals, and reindeer, and thus spun the journey out for eighty-four days. Excellent work was done. The east coast of Victoria Land was charted right up to the 72nd parallel. The land, formerly seen by Dr. Rae, at the south end of Victoria Strait, proved to be a group of over a hundred small low islands. These were charted on the way back. An interesting event from this journey was the meeting with another unknown Eskimo tribe, the "Kiilnermium Eskimo," whose hunting-fields extend from the Coppermine River eastwards. These Eskimo, like the others mentioned, have no connection with civilization. We, of course, received our bold companions with flags waving on their return, and a feast to commemorate it.

On June 1 we dismantled the observatory containing the magnetic self-registering instruments. For nineteen full months Wiik had kept this going, and had done work which will, without doubt, be rich in results.

Peder Ristvedt at their furthest point during Ristvedt and Godfred Hansen's sledge journey along the coast of Victoria Land.

AMUNDSEN LANTERN SLIDE 015: FM/JFO

On August 13, at three o'clock in the morning, we continued our way westwards, and I am not sure that the little brown-eyed people in there on the beach were quite cheerful that morning. Hardly, for they were losing several rich and great friends. They waved long to us – probably a farewell for life; and if some traveller, many years later, pays this place a visit, the numerous tent-rings will remind him of the many happy days the Gjøa Expedition spent here with their friends, the Nechjilli Eskimo. The day afterwards we stopped at a place called by the Eskimo, Kamiglu. Here we took an Eskimo boy named Manni on board.

He won us one and all by his openness and honesty; and even the cook, who hated Eskimo had, I think, a warm feeling somewhere at the bottom of his heart for him. It was my intention to bring him home and show him a little of the world he could never have imagined, and to send him back again, in the event of his wishing it; but he was accidentally drowned at Herschel Island. After passing through narrow and shallow waters we came out, on August 21, in Dolphin and Union Straits. Now we could breathe! On the forenoon of August 28, we sighted a sailing-ship. It was a proud moment for us all when we hoisted our flag and bore down on the American.

The Gjøa decorated with flags to celebrate the return of Hansen and Ristvedt. Photo: NB

Editor's note:

"At 8 a.m. my watch was finished and I turned in. When I had been asleep some time, I became conscious of a rushing to and fro on deck. Clearly there was something the matter, and I felt a bit annoyed that they should go on like that for the matter of a bear or a seal. It must be something of that kind, surely. But then Lieutenant Hansen came rushing down into the cabin and called out the every memorable words: "Vessel in sight, sir!" He bolted again immediately, and I was alone.

The Northwest Passage was done. My boyhood dream - at that moment it was accomplished. A strange feeling welled up in my throat; I was somewhat overstrained and worn - it was weakness in me - but I felt tears in my eyes.

The words were magical. My home and those dear to me there at once appeared to me as if stretching out their hands - "Vessel in sight!".

I dressed myself in no time. When ready, I stopped a moment before Nansen's portrait on the wall. It seemed as if the picture had come to life, as if he winked at me, nodding, "Just what I thought, my boy!" I nodded back, smiling and happy, and went on deck.

'Vessel in sight' ... Vessel in sight."

- From Roald Amundsen's diary

The Gjøa meet the first ship, the Charles Hanson of San Fransisco, after having sailed through the Northwest Passage. Photo: NB

The Gjøa's route from Gjøa Haven to King Point. Photo FM

On September 3 we were stopped by the ice at King Point, and soon after that were beset for a third winter. However, we were in high feather all the same; on the shore lay the finest driftwood that could be desired, the sea was full of fish, and not far off there were hares in thousands. On the shore, some fathoms in past us, lay the nipped whaler the Bonanza. The first thing we did was to build ourselves a house of drift timber, and after that the observatories were put up.

The Gjøa frozen in at King Point. In front the driftwood house built for most of the crew. The wrecked whaler, the Bonanza, to the left. Photo: NB

Settling in at King Point. The Gjøa, the wrecked whaler the Bonanza, and a group of Inuit around the bonfire. Photo: NB

The Inuit at King Point had guns and used machinewoven cloth in their tents, as opposed to the Inuit at Gjøa Haven. Photo: NB

From October 20 to March 12 I was out travelling with the Gjøa's mails, Lieut. Hansen having command on board meanwhile. This winter was exceedingly severe and disagreeable. On my return everything was in the best order; but on March 26 Wiik became ill and had to take his berth. He died on the 26th. It was a hard blow to lose a comrade so near home. It was not until May 9 we were able to bury him, the ground up to then being too hard frozen. In the mean time his coffin stood in the dwelling house on shore, which we gave up to it, nailing up the door. Later on we put up a large cross with an inscription on it at the north end of his grave, and when the flowers came, decorated it with them. It is situated on a very prominent point, and will be a landmark for the numerous ships which pass by it.

Inuit graves on Herschel Island.

AMUNDSEN LANTERN SLIDE 031: FM/JFO

AMUNDSEN LANTERN SLIDE 029: FM/JFO

Jimmi, who escorted Amundsen on the postal expedition to Eagle City.

AMUNDSEN LANTERN SLIDE 028: FM/JFO

Kappa, Jimmy's wife.

The magnetic observatory at King Point was used as Gustav Juel Wiik's final resting place. Photo: NB

Editor's note:

When all was ready for the winter, the next step was to get the news to the Times of London which was willing to pay good money for the exclusive story. The nearest telegraph office was in Fort Egbert outside Eagle City, Alaska which was a 500 mile sledge trip away over the Brooks range of coastal mountains.

From Eagle City, Amundsen sent a long telegram to Nansen costing over $700, but he had to send it collect, as the conquerer of the Northwest Passage had no money. As a result, a Major Glassford of the US signal corps decided it was his right to divulge the contents of the telegram to the local press in Seattle. The scoop was lost, and the Times refused to pay the much needed fee for the story. Nansen also refused to pay the telegraph fee on account of Glassford's violation of trust. While in Eagle City, Amundsen boarded with the Frank Smith family, who lived in the Northern Commercial CO. mess house. He gave speeches to the residents and waited for mail from home, before returning to the *Gjøa*. The main street in Eagle City is now named Amundsen Avenue.

On March 12 1906 he arrived back at Herschel Island, having traveled over 1000 miles by ski and dog sled.

He brought news to the men of Norway's new found independence and adopted King. At this point Wiik was seriously ill, apparently with pleurisy (or appendicitis), and died a few days later.

The spring was a cheerful time. The continual passage of Eskimo and whites made the time pass quickly. On July 2 we got out of the ice, and brought up under the Bonanza, so as to avoid the ice which was drifting backwards and forwards in the land lead.

On July 11 two of the American whalers came to our place to collect driftwood, and the same evening we stood out. We took a last farewell of our comrade whom we were leaving behind us out there, and dipped our flag as a last mark of honour to him as we passed under his grave. Already at Herschel Island we were stopped by the ice, and were kept there a whole month. After many narrow passages and abrupt turns, we stood down Behring Strait on August 30. The day afterwards we went into Nome, a gold-digging town in Alaska. The reception we received and the enthusiasm our enterprise had aroused there we shall never forget.

On September 5 the Gjøa set sail southward under Lieut. Hansen's command for San Francisco, and on the 7th I left with the magnetic instruments for Sitka, in order to conclude our work. On October 19 we met again in San Francisco, where we confided the vessel to the hands of the American navy. There rests the old Gjøa, and greatly does she need it.

The Gjøa on arrival at Nome on August 31, 1906. Photo: NB

The citizens of Nome's honorary breakfast for Roald Amundsen and Godfred Hansen. Photo: NB

Photo of the crew of the Gjøa on the arrival at Nome includes the extra crew members Ole Foss and Beauvais hired at Herschel Island.
Photo: FM

The Gjøa is pulled on shore in San Francisco. Photo: FM

Before Roald Amundsen's lecture, the President of Royal Geographical Society, made the following introduction:

I shall say little on the subject of Captain Amundsen's very remarkable explorations, as the paper will speak for itself, and you will hear what highly competent experts think of these explorations when we come to the discussion, which, I am glad to say, will be joined in by his Excellency Dr. Nansen, by Admiral Sir Vesey Hamilton, by Sir Allen Young, and a number of other well-known Arctic authorities. But it strikes me as extraordinary that only seven men should start away in a very small vessel and live a number of years in the Arctic Regions, and do the remarkable work they have done. I must say a few words about Captain Amundsen's preparation for this work, and the foresight he displayed. Many years ago he went on a sealing expedition into the Arctic Regions for no other purpose that to prepare himself for his recent work. Later on, as he advanced in his ideas and felt that examinations into the conditions around the magnetic pole was to be the main object of his explorations, he went to Hamburg, where he put himself under the tuition of Dr. von Neumayer, one of the greatest living authorities on magnetism, and he devoted a long period to studying the subject, and it is typical of Captain Amundsen's character that his first step in the present expedition was to purchase and select his magnetic instruments. As another means of preparation for Polar work, he went as first officer in the Belgica to the Antarctic Regions, and remained there for two years. In conclusion I must point out that, as an incident in his recent explorations, Captain Amundsen passed through the Northwest Passage in the first vessel that has ever sailed through it. I wonder what would have been the effect a century ago if it had been announced that someone was going to address a meeting describing his voyage through the Northwest Passage? I do not think the Albert Hall would have sufficed if it has existed in those days. I now call upon Captain Amundsen to read his paper.

After the lecture there was a list of speakers:

Fridtjof Nansen (1861-1930). Photo: FM

His Excellency Dr. Nansen: The way in which you have received my compatriot, Captain Amundsen, shows a hearty appreciation of the deed he has done and the most interesting lecture he has given us here tonight. As Captain Amundsen has already pointed out himself, the fact that it has been possible for him to accomplish that great deed is due entirely to the work of British seamen. It is due to the enormous amount of work already done in that region by many British expeditions sent out in search of a Northwest Passage. But a Norwegian has been the lucky man to finish this quest for the Northwest Passage, and has been the first to pass through it with a vessel. It shows us a good example of the way in which British and Norse sailors work together. When we look back upon the centuries that have passed, it is in fact, a remarkable thing how the one has always succeeded the other. The first step in this direction is very long back. The first step in that exploration to the west was, in fact, the discovery of Iceland. That was made by people from this country, by Irish monks, in the beginning of the eight century; but not long after that came the Norse Vikings. They also discovered Iceland by an accident more or less, and I am afraid that they did not treat the Irish monks very well, because they all disappeared; but the Norsemen kept the ground, and from Iceland they discovered Greenland, and formed settlements there for several centuries, and from Greenland they were the first to discover America, Newfoundland and Labrador – that was about the year 1000. And on leaving those regions they sailed through Davis Strait, and sailed far north into Baffin Bay, and their settlements disappeared altogether. Then again come the English, who opened a new campaign in the year 1497 with Cabot's first famous expedition. And you go on westward always in quest for the same goal – the Northwest Passage – until the great search of the Franklin Expedition. Then come the Norsemen again, and they finish; and it is a strange thing to remember that both these great quests if this seafaring nation, the Northeast Passage and the Northwest Passage, have been made by two Scandinavians – the Northeast by a Nordenskiöld, and the Northwest by an Amundsen. But the fine thing is the way you are able to appreciate what little we have done, and I think we may say we belong to the same race; and of these series of gallant achievements we may say with Tennyson

–"On equal temper of heroic hearts
Made weak by time and fate, but strong in will
To strive, to seek, to find, and not to yield."

We have here to-night the last representative of man, and a very good representative indeed. I knew Amundsen before he started, and I have seen preparing for his expeditions. He mentioned my name in his paper, but he said far too much about me, because what little I was able to do was only of slight importance. He was the man who planned the expedition, and he has learnt the secret of success in Arctic expeditions – that is, in the planning first and then in the preparation. The way in which he prepared the expedition is very characteristic of the man. As our President has already pointed out, the first thing he did was to learn to make his scientific observations, and the next thing was to buy scientific instruments, and the third thing was to buy the ship. It is generally the opposite way with explorers; they go first for the ship, and when they get that they try and get as little scientific training before they start. He has carried out his expedition with the same thoroughness that he prepared for it. He could have done the Northwest Passage long before he did, and for many a man it would have been too tempting to make the Northwest Passage, knowing it would be appreciated by the public, instead of making scientific observations, which, I am afraid, very few of the public and of you appreciate as they ought to be appreciated. Amundsen came on his voyage to the Harbour, where he stayed for two years. The sea to the west was open, the Northwest Passage was open to him, but he stopped for two years and did what he had come to do – make his magnetic observations in the neighbourhood of the magnetic north pole; and then, when he had finished this part, he was fortunate enough to take the Northwest Passage. In my opinion, when we want to send out a man to an unknown region where new explorations is to be done, he is the sort of man we should send; he knows what is of importance and what is not; he knows not to do sensational things when he has good work to do, but he can appreciate sensational things at the same time, as he has shown us. And we may see him start again on a new exploration, and I feel certain, next to his own country, he will have many wellwishers in this country, and I believe we shall all of us join in the words of Browning, and say –

"Greet the unseen with a cheer!
Bid him forward, breast and back as either should be,
'Strive and thrive'! cry 'Speed – fight on, fare ever
There as here!'"

Sir Richard Vesey Hamilton (1829-1912). Photo: FM

Admiral Sir Vesey Hamilton: I am sorry it has not fallen to the lot of someone more capable than myself to give expression to the very high opinion we have of the wonderful work done by Captain Amundsen and his seven followers. I do not think an Arctic expedition did so much with such small means, and the character he gives his men is something admirable. One of the reasons of the success of the expedition was that every man had his heart thoroughly in it; therefore, instead of seven men we may say there were fourteen or twenty-one. With regard to the magnetic observations, I see somebody here who knows a great deal more than I do about them, and so I shall skip the greater part of them. The vessel was probably the smallest vessel that has ever navigated the Arctic ice, even in the days of Baffin. I am perfectly sure none of them had so few men. One thing particularly striking is the contrast between the Eskimo of the north coast of America and the Eskimo of the Labrador Coast and of Greenland. That in itself would form an interesting subject of inquiry. It was very interesting to me to hear the lecturer's observations about Beechey Island, because your late President and I went ashore there. I have had the experience of three Arctic winters and five Arctic summers, and I can say that nothing I have heard of surpasses the work of Captain Amundsen. In every way "Tis not in mortals to command success, but we'll deserve it." And Captain Amundsen has deserved it. It is great thing when a general not only looks ahead, but looks astern. With regard to the dogs, all I can say is, I have had 2000 miles' travelling with dogs, and I am sure if Job had been there his patience would have been exhausted. I think I need to say no more. The enthusiastic manner in which you have received Captain Amundsen's lecture shows the great interest you felt in it, and I am sure I am not taking too much upon myself when I assert that everyone here present will look forward to the full results of the voyage with great interest.

Sir Allen Wiliam Young (1830-1915). Photo: FM

Sir Allen Young: I think we cannot be too grateful to Captain Amundsen for the most interesting narrative he has given us tonight, and especially when we consider the results of the expedition. One point which Dr. Nansen made was greatly to the credit of Captain Amundsen – that when he arrived at the point of the hemisphere at which the Passage was open to him, with every prospect of going through in one season if he had intended to do so, he abandoned all idea of that, and determined, in the cause of science, to remain for eighteen months in the neighbourhood of the magnetic pole in order to make further observations on the inclination and horizontal force, with the object of determining any variations in the position of the pole itself. No doubt the scientific results will be very valuable when they have been carefully worked out, especially, we hope, they will indicate if there is any variation in the position of the north magnetic pole. It was suggested by Ross in 1831 that those poles supposed to have an area of about 50 miles in diameter, for which there is no apparent horizontal force. The most marvellous part of this journey was that it was completely without check. In 1858 I was navigating with Sir Leopold McClintock, and our object was to get round to King Williams Land, but we were checked about 25 miles down by a solid barrier of ice. Then we tried the alternative way of going round by Port Leopold, and after several attempts we succeeded in getting there; but we were again faced with ice, so we had to go back and find our winter quarters on the east side.

Now, it seems to me that Captain Amundsen went straight down, and I think the way in which he escaped and got through was most marvellous. Captain Amundsen, however, did not neglect the opportunity of making geographical discovery, for he sent a travelling party under Lieut. Hansen to Victoria Land, which successfully filled in the gap between Collinson's furthest up, Gateshead Island in 1853, and the discoveries of McClure in 1853, and added to our knowledge of the western shore of McClintock Strait, which can now be mapped out on both shores. I should like to ask Captain Amundsen if he was able to gather knowledge, retained by tradition among the Eskimo or from information by some of the older natives, of the ultimate fate of the crews of Sir John Franklin's ships, or if he found any relics or papers which could throw additional light upon the disastrous return of those gallant men, or the actual position of either of Franklin's ships in which they ultimately sank or were driven on shore after being abandoned. Well may all, and especially those who have had experience of Arctic seas, offer their heartiest congratulations to Captain Amundsen.

Captain Ettrick W. Creak (1835-1920) Photo: FM

Captain Creak: I think I will begin by saying that I entirely endorse everything that has been said about the gallant and sailor-like conduct which characterized the work carried out by the expedition. It seems perfectly marvellous to me that a vessel of this size should have been taken across the Atlantic, up Davis Strait, through Behring Strait, and then on to San Francisco. I think it is a sort of passage that will stand as a record. The chief object of the expedition was to make a magnetic survey of the region of the north magnetic pole, which had been approximately found by Ross in 1831, for there had been a controversy going on upon the question of its movements for years past. Some people, who thought they knew something about the matter, depicted the magnetic pole as a sort of wandering Jew going about the Earth and not knowing where to stop. Great mathematicians had been at work, but they never gave a fairly satisfactory solution. This expedition was therefore planned to determine existing conditions during two years. Nothing but observations would do it. Captain Amundsen, having arrived at Beechey Island – a position where there came the parting of the ways – had a momentous question to decide, to turn northward or southward. Fortunately he had an excellent sign-post which came to his assistance in his magnetic instruments. Theorists said go north, but the magnetic instruments said go south.

Amundsen obeyed his excellent mentor and went south down Peel Sound. Off Prescott Island his compass became useless. Nowadays we hear of a mass of 18,000 tons of steel and iron, namely, the Dreadnought, being steered across the Atlantic, guided by the compass; why should not this wooden ship be guided by the compass? You must remember this – that the Gjøa had fittings of iron. If she had one degree of error to start with, by the time she reached Beechey Island she would probably have twenty-five or thirty, which would be quite enough to entirely destroy the action of the compass. The Dreadnought was taken over her ground with certainty, because as she proceeded the Earth's directive force on her compass grew stronger; with the Gjøa the directive force became less and less, and she lost it entirely close to the pole. But supposing the Gjøa had been entirely free from iron, it may be of interest to follow the behaviour of the compass when she was being steered geographically due south. In Peel Sound the compass would indicate a course about N. 30°W.; off Cape Colville, S. 40°W.; at Gjøahavn, south. Consequently in that short distance the compass north would – geographically – point in nearly an opposite direction, and be of little practical use as a navigational instrument.

Thus I have tried to explain why the compass is practically useless after we come to a certain point, due partly to the iron in the ship and partly to there being no force. Now, Captain Amundsen arrives and gets his ship moored, and he mounts his magnetic instruments. From what he has described, I gather he had a most splendid set. There were differential instruments which were going for nineteen months, which tell us for every moment of the day what the direction of the needle was and the changes in the force driving it. Probably the declination of the needle was changing 10° either way – 10° to the left and 10° to the right of magnetic north, and at about 7 o'clock in the morning, and at 1 or 2 o'clock in the afternoon respectively. Still more important were the excursions he made, so that he could give a most valuable account of all the magnetic conditions surrounding him. He certainly, so far as I can see, found out where the pole is for one epoch, but there is still some doubt as to whether it is a fixed point or not. That remains to be proved.

It will require years to get the observations into form, but I think we have every hope that eventually we shall be able to find out what magneticians have been wishing for for many years. We shall have found out where the magnetic pole is, and also what is going on there. I am also happy to learn that they made a series of meteorological observations. It will be interesting to know, also, what work has been done in connection with geology – I think Captain Amundsen had a geologist among his party. I should like to know whether he made any inquiry into the local magnetic disturbance of the region. The only other remark I can make now is, that I think it is very sad that Wiik has not lived to return to his native land after watching those instruments all those months, and witness the fruits of his labours. I will conclude by saying that Captain Amundsen and his comrades have accomplished the task they set out to perform, and that the whole of the expedition may be described as having been conducted with the highest enterprise, judgment, and courage.

May I add one more remark, and that is that this expedition was sent out entirely for magnetic purposes, but in addition to those magnetic purposes it has done good work for geography; cannot geographers do something for magnetic?

Admiral Sir Arthur Mostyn Field (1855-1950) Photo: FM

Admiral Field: Captain Creak has gone so very thoroughly into the question of the magnetic part of the observations, that really I am afraid that there is very little for me to say in the matter. I am sure the observations of Captain Amundsen, when they are worked out thoroughly, will be of the greatest service in improving our magnetic charts. We are sadly in want of those observations. It is only within the last year that we have had the south magnetic pole fixed satisfactorily. That is a very great advance, and I may say that the Admiralty are paying great attention at the present time to the question of magnetism. The officers are being specially instructed in the subject, and we are taking advantage of recent long cruises by a squadron going across the North Pacific, down the coast of North and South America, making continuous observations the whole of the way; also from Newfoundland and across the South Atlantic Ocean. So that we are making great progress, I am glad to say, in magnetic work, and these observations with regard to the poles, both north and south, will assist us very materially, and I am sure all magneticians will be very grateful indeed to Captain Amundsen for his labours. I can only say, with regard to Captain Creak's last remark, I quite second that, and I hope the explorers that the Geographical Society send out will bear in mind the needs of magnetism.

I will conclude by saying that, at the suggestion of the president of the Geographical Society of the Pacific, and with the concurrence of the President of the Royal Geographical Society, the name of "Amundsen Gulf" has been given in the Admiralty Charts to that part lying to the south of Banks Island, in commemoration of the voyage which has just come to such a successful conclusion.

The letter from the Geographical Society of the Pacific naming the Amundsen Gulf in the honor of Roald Amundsen. Photo: NB

63

The President:

The hour is late, and I feel sure, after what his Excellency the Norwegian minister and the other speakers have said, it will be quite unnecessary for me to add one word to express the intense admiration we feel for Captain Amundsen and his exploits. I will only. Therefore, ask you to join in a hearty vote of thanks to him.

Captain Amundsen: I speak English so badly that I hope you will excuse me if I thank you in only a few words. First, I should like to answer a few questions put by Sir Allen Young. He asked if I had any information about the Franklin Expedition; but I have none. The Eskimo did not know anything about the members, but I got some information about one of the ships. Two of the tribes found the vessel in the winter-time when they were out seal-hunting, and they took as much of the iron and wood as they could get from the ship, and of course, when the spring and the summer came and the ice melted away, the ship went down. Captain Creak asked if I had any geologists on board. Yes, I had one, but he had nothing to do, the land consisting of sand all the way. I should like to take this opportunity of thanking the Royal Geographical Society for the invitation to lecture here tonight, and for the great honour they have shown me; I thank you for the kind sympathy you have shown me during the reading of my paper.

Editor's note:

Roald Amundsen started to organize his lecture tour immediately after the arrival in Nome.

1520 Chestnut Street,
Philadelphia.

October 6, 1906

Ans. Oct 12

Captain Ronald Amundsen
c/o Norwegian Consul
San Francisco, Cal.

Dear Sir:

Confirming the telegram which I have just sent, I wish to invite you to address the Geographical Society of Philadelphia. The officers of the Society are hoping that you will sail for Europe from New York or Philadelphia and that you will arrange to address our Society when you come East.

You will have an audience of at least twelve hundred people and will have an excellent hall to speak in. The Society would like to give you a reception at the close of the address and I think you would enjoy meeting the active workers in geography who are members of our Society.

Although the funds of the Society are limited we will be pleased to pay your hotel expenses in Philadelphia and such travelling expenses as you may incur in accepting the invitation to address the Society.

Hoping that my telegram and this letter may reach you and that your answer may be favorable, and bespeaking as early reply as you can conveniently make, I am

Very truly yours,

Emory R. Johnson

President

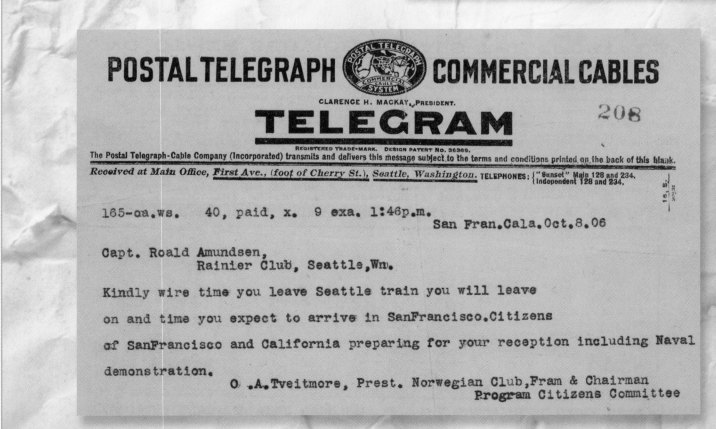

POSTAL TELEGRAPH · **COMMERCIAL CABLES**

CLARENCE H. MACKAY, PRESIDENT.

TELEGRAM

208

REGISTERED TRADE-MARK. DESIGN PATENT No. 36369.

The Postal Telegraph-Cable Company (Incorporated) transmits and delivers this message subject to the terms and conditions printed on the back of this blank.

Received at Main Office, First Ave., (foot of Cherry St.), Seattle, Washington. TELEPHONES: {"Sunset" Main 128 and 234, {Independent 128 and 234.

165-oa.ws.   40, paid, x.   9 exa. 1:46p.m.   San Fran.Cala.Oct.8.06

Capt. Roald Amundsen,
        Rainier Club, Seattle,Wn.

Kindly wire time you leave Seattle train you will leave

on and time you expect to arrive in SanFrancisco.Citizens

of SanFrancisco and California preparing for your reception including Naval

demonstration.

O .A.Tveitmore, Prest. Norwegian Club,Fram & Chairman
                    Program Citizens Committee

PARK HALL, CARDIFF.

C^APT. AMUNDSEN

WILL GIVE HIS

LECTURE

ON

TUESDAY, DECEMBER 3rd, at 8 p.m.

ENTITLED

HOW WE REACHED THE SOUTH POLE

The Lecture will be a vivid narrative of Capt. Amundsen's successful journey to the South Pole. It will be illustrated by **Lantern Slides and Kinematograph Films** taken during the Expedition.

THE CHAIR WILL BE TAKEN BY

THE RT. HON.

THE LORD MAYOR OF CARDIFF

Photo by Perlesck, Christiania.

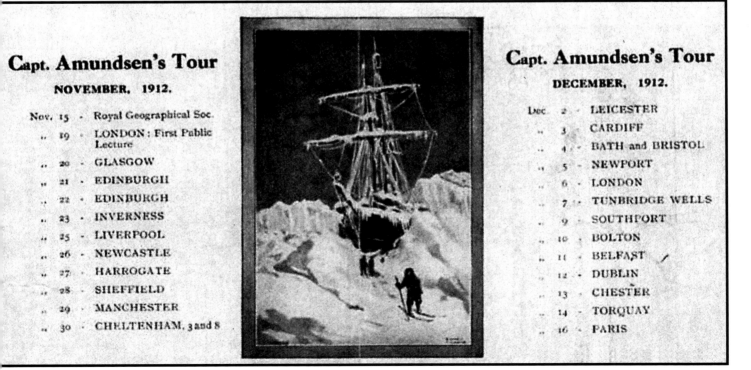

Capt. Amundsen's Tour

NOVEMBER, 1912.

Nov. 15	-	Royal Geographical Soc.
„ 19	-	LONDON: First Public Lecture
„ 20	-	GLASGOW
„ 21	-	EDINBURGH
„ 22	-	EDINBURGH
„ 23	-	INVERNESS
„ 25	-	LIVERPOOL
„ 26	-	NEWCASTLE
„ 27	-	HARROGATE
„ 28	-	SHEFFIELD
„ 29	-	MANCHESTER
„ 30	-	CHELTENHAM, 3 and 8

Capt. Amundsen's Tour

DECEMBER, 1912.

Dec. 2	-	LEICESTER
„ 3	-	CARDIFF
„ 4	-	BATH and BRISTOL
„ 5	-	NEWPORT
„ 6	-	LONDON
„ 7	-	TUNBRIDGE WELLS
„ 9	-	SOUTHPORT
„ 10	-	BOLTON
„ 11	-	BELFAST
„ 12	-	DUBLIN
„ 13	-	CHESTER
„ 14	-	TORQUAY
„ 16	-	PARIS

Photos: FM

The Norwegian South Polar Expedition

Presentation at the Royal Geographical Society,

London, November 15, 1912

While the struggle for the North Pole covers hundreds of years, the struggle for the South Pole is of comparatively recent date. About 1900 we find several expeditions – English, German, French, Belgian, Scottish, and Swedish – working hand-in-hand in order to withdraw the veil and lay open the great mysteries of the Antarctic. The object of several of these expeditions was of course scientific, but I believe I may say that the pole itself loomed behind as the ultimate goal.

My time tonight does not permit me to review all the expeditions that have contributed to increase our knowledge of the great unexplored section of the Antarctic continent. I shall mention only the expeditions which earlier have done work in the region, where we had to look for our starting-point. Our goal being to reach the South Pole, we first of all had to push forward with the ship as far south as possible, and there build our station. The sledge journey would be long enough, anyway. I knew that the English would go to their old winter quarters in McMurdo Sound, South Victoria land. The newspapers had stated that the Japanese had

reserved King Edward VII. Land. Thus there was nothing else for us to do, but to build our hut on the barrier itself, as far from these two expeditions as possible, in order not to be in their way.

The great Antarctic barrier or the Ross barrier as it's called, between South Victoria Land and King Edward VII. Land, has an extent of about 450 geographical miles. The first who met with this enormous glacial formation was Sir James Clark Ross in 1841. He, naturally enough, did not take the risk of running his two sailing vessels, Erebus and Terror, close under the mighty 100-feet high icewall, which barred his progress towards the south. But he examined it as well as circumstances would permit at a reasonable distance. These observations made it clear, that the barrier was not a straight, steep icewall, but was broken at intervals by bights and small inlets. In the chart of Ross we shall notice an imposing bay-formation in 164° W and 78° 30′ S.

The next expedition to sail down to these regions was the Southern Cross expedition in 1900. It is interesting that this expedition found this bay in the same place, where Ross saw it in 1841 – sixty years earlier. It is interesting, that this expedition succeeded in landing in a little bay – Balloon bight – some miles to the eastward of the big one, and from there climbed up on the barrier, which up to this time had been considered inaccessible and invincible hindrance for an advance towards the south.

The Southern Cross Expedition (British Antarctic Expedition, 1898-1900) was led by the Norwegian Carsten Borchgrevink (1864-1934). The expedition was the first to winter on the Antarctic mainland.
Photo: FM

The Erebus after the collision with the Terror on March 13, 1842.

AMUNDSEN LANTERN SLIDE 043: FM/JFO

In 1901 the Discovery steamed along the barrier and confirmed in every respect what the Southern Cross expedition had observed. The expedition also succeeded in discovering land in the direction mentioned by Ross – King Edward VII. Land. Scott also landed in Balloon bight and observed, like his predecessors, the big bay formation to the west.

In 1908 Shackleton in the Nimrod followed, like his predecessors, the barrier and arrived at the conclusion that disturbances in the barrier had broken away the shore-line of Balloon bight, merging that indentation into the bay to the west. To the big newly formed bay he gave the name "Bay

of the Whales." But his original plan of landing here was abandoned – the barrier in this place looking too dangerous as a foundation for winter quarters.

When the two charts are compared, it was not difficult to decide that the bay put down on the chart by Ross and the Bay of Whales was one and the same. Though some few pieces had broken off here and there, this bay had remained constant for about seventy years. It was an obvious conclusion that the bay was no casual formation, but owned its existence to subjacent land, banks, etc. This bay we selected as our basis of operation.

Robert Falcon Scott (1868-1912). British Royal Navy Officer and expedition leader of the Discovery Expedition (British National Antarctic Expedtion, 1901-04). Photo: FM

Ernest H. Shackleton (1874-1922) on the Nimrod Expedition reached their farthest south at 9 am on January 9, 1909: 88°23' S, longitude 162°- just 97 miles from the South Pole. Photo: FM

Borchgrevink's chart from the Southern Cross Expedition shows the Bay of Whales. Photo: FM

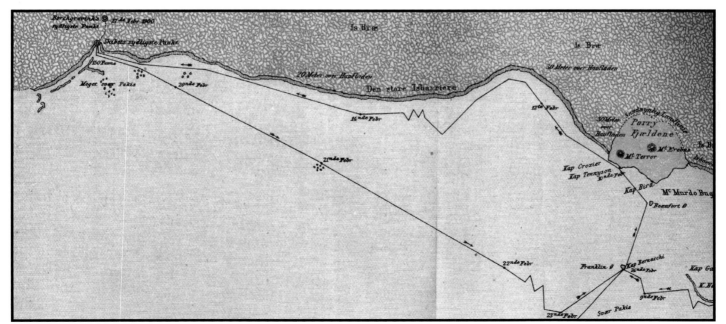

AMUNDSEN LANTERN SLIDE 037: FM/JFO

Roald Amundsen participated as first mate in the Belgica Expedition, 1897-99, the first expedition to winter in the Antarctic.

It is 350 nautical miles (650 kiloms.) from the English station in McMurdo Sound, and 100 nautical miles (185 kiloms.) from King Edward VII. Land. It therefore seemed to us that we were at sufficient distance from the English sphere, and need not to fear that we should come in their way. The reports of the Japanese on King Edward VII. Land were rather vague, and it seemed to us that a distance of 100 miles was more than enough.

On board of Nansen's old well-known vessel, the Fram, we left Norway on August 9, 1910. We carried on board ninety-seven fine Eskimo dogs from Greenland, and provisions for two years. The first port we touched was Madeira, where we finally made everything ready for the long voyage to the Ross barrier.

It was no short distance we had to cover – about 16,000 nautical miles (29,600 kiloms.) – from Norway to the Bay of Whales.

We had calculated that it would take us five months to make the trip. The Fram, which with good reason is said to be the most solid polar ship in the world, proved to be exceedingly seaworthy on this long voyage over pretty nearly all oceans. Thus we sailed through the north-east and south-east trades, the roaring forties, the foggy fifties, and the icy sixties without any mishap, and arrived at our sphere of work at the barrier on January 14, 1911. Everything had gone unusually well.

Editor's note:

INVOICE TO ROALD AMUNDSEN FROM THE SHIPYARD IN HORTEN, THE KARLJOHANSVERNS VERFT:

The Norwegian Navy's main base used to be located at Karljohansvern in Horten, 100 km south of Oslo. One of Norway's major shipyards was also to be found here, namely the Karljohansverns Verft. Before Roald Amundsen left for Antarctica in 1910, some adjustments and technical changes had to be carried out on the *Fram*. All this work was done at the shipyard in Horten. This invoice shows the detailed expenses for some of the upgrades on the *Fram* in the spring of 1910. The invoice adds up to NOK 27,656.10 (equivalent to NOK 1,431,178,- in today's currency). Roald Amundsen has certified the invoice with his own signature. Some of the items in the invoice include: adjustments related to the replacement of the steam engine by a diesel engine; a better ventilation system for the engine room; insulation of beams in the engine room; adjustment of the propeller to the shaft; installation of foundations for pumps and other equipment; additional piping for fuel, cooling water and bilge water; installation of an emergency inlet for the cooling water to the main engine; docking of the vessel for replacement of the stern tube; inspection of the outer layer of the hull; installation of a new windlass and motor for the anchors; panelling of the galley with zinc plating, and a new floor in the galley made of a coating of lead with ceramic tiles on top. Some of the acquisitions include: four tents, kites made for the trip, adjustments to compasses, two sets of signal flags, eight (expedition) telegraph flags and semaphore flags, six national flags, one jack, 100 dog harnesses, 60 tent pegs and four tent poles.

All the upgrades and adjustments to the *Fram* added up to a total of approximately NOK 100,000,- in 1910 (today's equivalent: NOK 5,000,000,-).

The Fram at the naval dockyard in Horten.

AMUNDSEN LANTERN SLIDE 155: FM/JFO

Framekspeditionen. Hr. kaptein Roald Amundsen.
til
Karljohansverns Verft.
19   Debet.

Arbeider utført utenfor anbud av 9/3 1909
i henhold til skriftlig eller mundtlig anmodning.

Ventilation av maskinrum, forstøtning av
bjelke i maskinrum, arbeider ved avløpsledningene
for begge motorer, netting rundt rækverk, forstøtning av vandtanker, vareror m.v., underlag for
centrifugalpumper, oljerenser, vifte m.v., pøse-
række, forskjellige hylder m.v., ombytning av
dæksstøtter i forreste salon, forandring av forreste lasteluke.

Taleførledning og telegrafledning, rørledning
til oljerenseren, parafinrenser, tragter og lygter,
efterset og reparert centrifugalpumpe, utført og
anbragt samlingskasse, kilespor i reservepropeller
samt tilpasset propelleren til akselen, excenter-
stang og skive til lubrikator m.v.   kr. 3 387,13

Drivning og kitning av den del av utenbords-
klædningen og dæk som ikke blev fornyet, likesaa
av de vandtætte skot. Skibmaning og eftersyn av
sluser i de vandtætte skot, eftersyn av ror og
vareror samt prøvning av vareror, eftersyn og repa-
ration av pumper, skrapning, oppudsning og maling " 3 334,59

Doksætning for eftersyn av akselhylsen   "   207,03

Avtagning av sinkhud, skrapning og brænding
samt eftersyn av klædningen utenbords m.v.   " 1 111,12
                                Overføres kr. 8 039,87

Framekspeditionen. Hr. kaptein Roald Amundsen.
til
Karljohansverns Verft.
19   Debet.

                                    Overført kr. 8 039,87
Ilandtagning av ankerspil, wincher, montert
nyt ankerspil og motor for dette, vandbeholder
m.v. for motor, transmissioner for overføring av
kraften fra motor til ankerspil, isolation av bjel-
ker m.v. omkring motor, huller med lok i dæk, man-
øvrehaandtak til dæk m.v.   " 3 083,91

Nyt ankerklys for b.b. kjetting   "   284,58

Ny sofa i messen med kronometerskap, indred-
ning av tidligere kulbokser til lugarer med pane-
ling, køier og møbler, borttagning av skillevægger
i indgangene agter, av skaper i arbeidsrum samt
derav følgende forbinding av skibssiderne samme-
steds   "   878,14

Sinkklædning av kabyssen samt av rummet for-
ut om st.b., belæg av bly med lerfliser ovenpaa
paa gulvet i kabyssen   "   460,97

Arbeider og anskaffelser som:
4 stk. telter, forarbeidelse av drager, dragefor-
søk, forandring av kompasser, 2 sæt signalflag,
8 felttelegrafflag og semaforflag, 6 national-
flag, 1 gjøs, 100 hundesæler, 60 teltplugger,
4 teltstokker, forandring av nathushjelm m.v. " 2 121,94

Faldrepstrap med repo   "   369,18
                                Overføres kr. 15 238,59

The receipts for the reconstruction of the Fram and the purchase of the diesel engine. Photos: FM

Framekspeditionen. Hr. kaptein Roald Amundsen.
til
Karljohansverns Verft.
19   Debet.

                                    Overført kr. 15 238,59
Forskjellige anskaffelser, hvoriblandt
ankerkjetting og pram   " 1 868,60

Forskjellige arbeider vedrørende maskineri,
rørledninger o.l. som: trustlager, trustaksel,
lense- og avløpsrør, nødindtak for kjølvand til
hovedmotoren, ledninger til Downtons-pumpe, drift
av pumper og vifte, dørk i maskinrum, uttagning
av gammel samt forarbeidelse og indsætning av ny
akselhylse, rørledninger for petroleumsovnene
m.v.   " 8 385,46

Transport- og ekviperingsarbeider   " 2 163,45
                                          kr. 27 656,10
                                          S. E. & O.

Rigtigheten heraf attesteres.

Horten 7 juni 1910

Roald Amundsen.

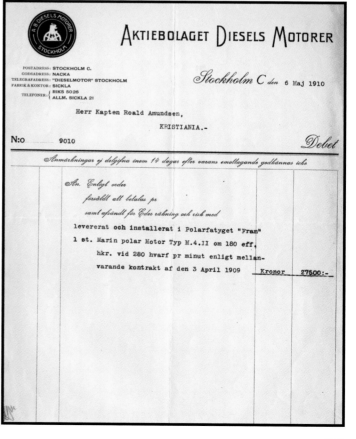

AKTIEBOLAGET DIESELS MOTORER

POSTADRESS: STOCKHOLM C.
GODSADRESS: NACKA
TELEGRAFADRESS: "DIESELMOTOR" STOCKHOLM
FABRIK & KONTOR: SICKLA
TELEFONER: { RIKS 5026
            { ALLM. SICKLA 21

Stockholm C den 6 Maj 1910

Herr Kapten Roald Amundsen,
                KRISTIANIA.-

N:o _____ 9010   *Debet*

Anmärkningar ej delgifna inom 14 dagar efter varans emottagande godkännas icke

*An. Enligt order
    försåldt att betalas pr
    samt afsändt för Eder räkning och risk med*
levererat och installerat i Polarfatyget "Fram"
1 st. Marin polar Motor Typ M.4.II om 180 eff.
   hkr. vid 280 hvarf pr minut enligt mellan-
   varande kontrakt af den 3 April 1909   Kronor 27500:-

*The Fram in
dry dock at Horten.
Photo: FM*

*King Haakon VII and Queen Maud of Norway visit the Fram on June 2, 1910. The expedition received from their Majesties the gift of a beautiful
silver jug, which afterwards formed the most handsome ornament of the Fram's table on every festive occasion.*

AMUNDSEN LANTERN SLIDE 153: FM/JFO

The King and Queen leave the Fram after wishing Amundsen and the crew a successful journey.

AMUNDSEN LANTERN SLIDE 154: FM/JFO

The Fram outside the Uranienborg, Roald Amundsen's home in the Bundefjord, south of Christiania. Photo: FM

On June 3, before noon, the Fram left Christiania (Oslo), bound at first for Amundsen's home in the Bundefjord to take on board the house for the winter station,

AMUNDSEN LANTERN SLIDE 150: FM/JFO

Roald Amundsen's dog Pan in the hill behind Roald Amundsen's home.

AMUNDSEN LANTERN SLIDE 152: FM/JFO

The dog house at Uranienborg.

AMUNDSEN LANTERN SLIDE 168: FM/JFO

June 6, 1910: Roald Amundsen and Pan in front of the Fram on the eve of departure.

AMUNDSEN LANTERN SLIDE 151: FM/JFO

Editor's note:

From Roald Amundsen's The South Pole:

On the afternoon of June 6 it was announced that everything was ready, and in the evening we all assembled at a simple farewell supper in the garden. I took the opportunity of wishing good luck to every man in turn, and finally we united in a "God preserve the King and Fatherland!" Then we broke up. The last man to get into the boat was the second in command; he arrived armed with a horseshoe. In his opinion it is quite incredible what luck an old horseshoe will bring. Possibly he is right. Anyhow, the horseshoe was firmly nailed to the mast in the Fram's saloon, and there it still hangs.

When on board, we promptly set to work to get up the anchor. The Bolinder motor hummed, and the heavy cable rattled in through the hawse-hole. Precisely at midnight the anchor let go of the bottom, and just as the Seventh of June rolled in over us, the Fram stood out of the Christiania Fjord for the third time.

Twice already had a band of stout-hearted men brought this ship back with honour after years of service. Would it be vouchsafed to us to uphold this honourable tradition?

Such were, no doubt, the thoughts with which most of us were occupied as our vessel glided over the motionless fjord in the light summer night. The start was made under the sign of the Seventh of June, and this was taken as a promising omen; but among our bright and confident hopes there crept a shadow of melancholy. The hillsides, the woods, the fjord all were so bewitchingly fair and so dear to us. They called to us with their allurement, but the Diesel motor knew no pity. Its tuff-tuff went on brutally through the stillness. A little boat, in which were some of my nearest relations, dropped gradually astern. There was a glimpse of white handkerchiefs in the twilight, and then farewell!

The crew of the Norwegian South Polar Expedition before departure. Standing from the left: Wisting, Rønne, Sandvig (left in Funchal), Schröer (left in Bergen), Kristensen, Bjaaland, Hanssen, Hansen, Johansen, Beck, Stubberud & Olsen.
Sitting in the middle: Nilsen, Amundsen & Prestrud. Front row: Nødtvedt, Gjertsen & Kutchin.
Photo: FM

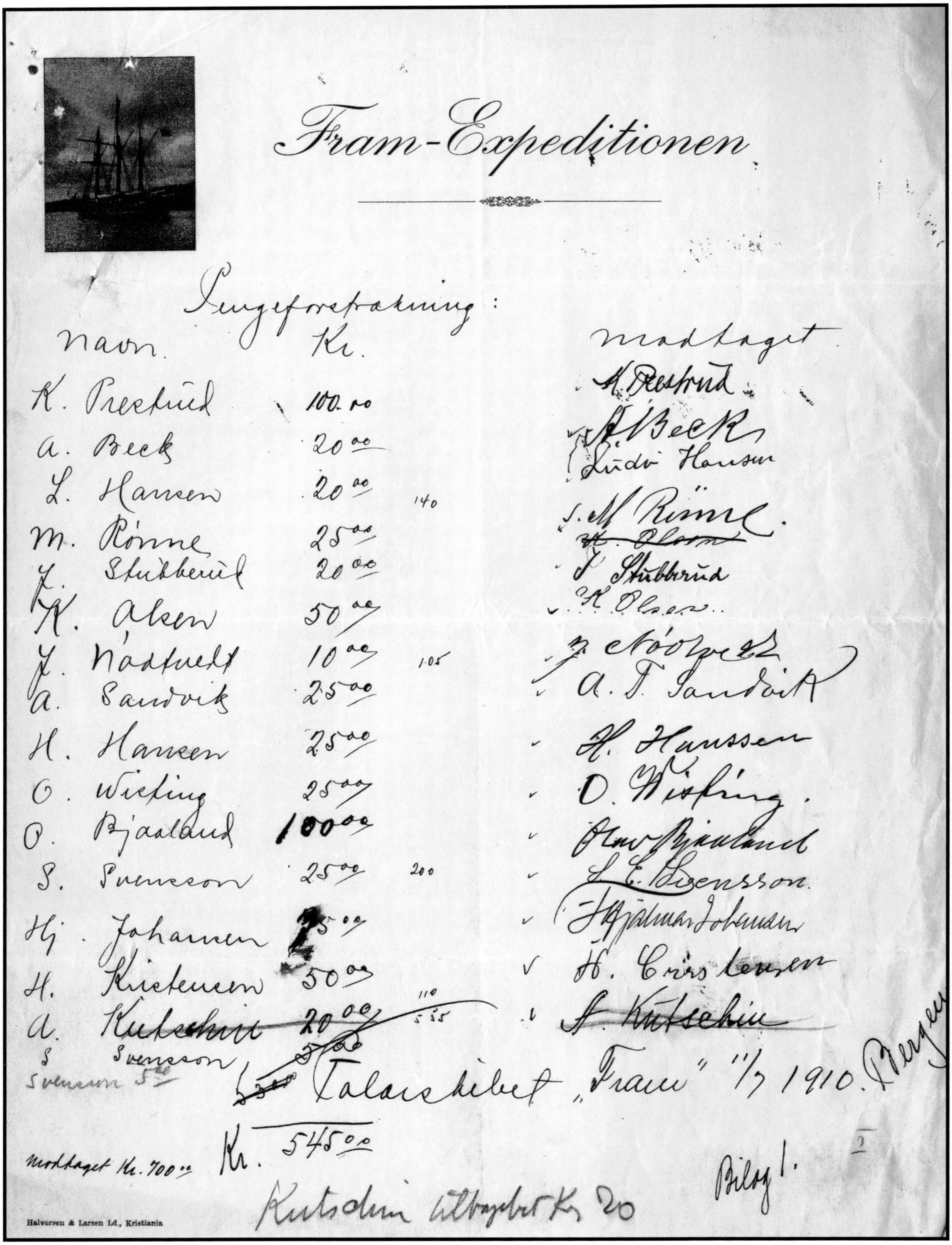

Fram-Expeditionen

Lønsforstrækning:

Navn.	Kr.		modtaget
K. Prestrud	100.00		K. Prestrud
A. Beck	20.00		A. Beck
L. Hansen	20.00		Ludv Hansen
M. Rönne	25.00	140	s. M. Rönne
J. Stubberud	20.00		H. Olsen
K. Olsen	50.00		J. Stubberud
J. Nödtvedt	10.00		K. Olsen
A. Sandvik	25.00	1.05	J. Nödtvedt
H. Hansen	25.00		A. T. Sandvik
O. Wisting	25.00		H. Hanssen
O. Bjaaland	100.00		O. Wisting
S. Svensson	25.00	200	Olav Bjaaland
Hj. Johansen	25.00		S. E. Svensson
H. Kristensen	50.00		Hjalmar Johansen
A. Kutschin	20.00	110 5 55	H. Kristensen
S. Svensson 5			A. Kutschin

Talarskibet „Fram" 11/7 1910. Bergen

Kr. 5455.00

modtaget Kr. 700.00

Bilag!

Kutschin Altbyebet Kr. 20

Halvorsen & Larsen Ld., Kristiania

A payment to the crew was made on July 11, 1910 in Bergen. Most of the crew members have signed the document. Photo: FM

Hjalmar Fredrik Gjertsen, first mate (1885-1958).
Amundsen lantern slide 234: FM/jfo

Knut Sundbeck, engineer (?-1967).
Amundsen lantern slide 235: FM/jfo

Alexander Kutchin, oceanographer (1888-1912). Photo: FM

Helmer Hanssen, ice pilot, member of the polar party (1870-1956).
Photo: FM

Jacob Nødtvedt, second engineer (1857-?). Photo: FM

Sverre Hassel, member of the polar party (1876-1928). Photo: FM

Olav Bjaaland, skimaker, member of the polar party (1873-1961). Photo: FM

Oscar Wisting, member of the polar party (1871-1936). Photo: FM

Hjalmar Johansen, member of the Edward VII Land party (1867-1913).
Photo: FM

Andreas Beck, ice pilot (1864-1914).
Photo: FM

Halvardus Kristensen, third engineer (1879-1919).
Photo: FM

Karenius Olsen, cook (?-?).
Photo: FM

Ludvik Hansen, ice pilot (1871-1955).
Photo: FM

Adolf Henrik Lindstrøm, cook
(1866-1939). Photo: FM

Kristian Prestrud, second officer, leader of the Edward VII Land
party (1881-1927). Photo: FM

Thorvald Nilsen, Captain of the Fram, second in command
(1881-1940). Photo: FM

Jørgen Stubberud, carpenter, member of the Edward VII Land party (1883-1980). Photo: FM

Martin Rønne, sailmaker (1861-1932). Photo: FM

The saloon of the Fram.

AMUNDSEN LANTERN SLIDE 157: FM/JFO

AMUNDSEN LANTERN SLIDE 162: FM/JFO

Thorvald Nilsen gathered a small audience in the harbour of Funchal.

Kristian Prestrud adjusting the chronometers in Funchal, Madeira.

AMUNDSEN LANTERN SLIDE 161: FM/JFO

In the rigging.

AMUNDSEN LANTERN SLIDE 160: FM/JFO

The foredeck of the Fram.

AMUNDSEN LANTERN SLIDE 170: FM/JFO

There are dogs everywhere, also on the bridge.

AMUNDSEN LANTERN SLIDE 174: FM/JFO

Editor's note:

From Roald Amundsen's The South Pole:

Fredriksholm, out on Flekkero, we had found room for perhaps the most important of all the passengers, the ninety-seven Eskimo dogs, which had arrived from Greenland in the middle of July on the steamer Hans Egede. The ship had had a rather long and rough passage, and the dogs were not in very good condition on their arrival, but they had not been many days on the island under the supervision of Hassel and Lindstrom before they were again in full vigour. A plentiful supply of fresh meat worked wonders. The usually peaceful island, with the remains of the old fortress, resounded day by day, and sometimes at night, with the most glorious concerts of howling.

These musical performances attracted a number of inquisitive visitors, who were anxious to submit the members of the chorus to a closer examination, and therefore, at certain times, the public were admitted to see the animals. It soon turned out that the majority of the dogs, far from being ferocious or shy, were, on the contrary, very appreciative of these visits. They sometimes came in for an extra tit-bit in the form of a sandwich or something of the sort. Besides which, it was a little diversion in their life of captivity, so uncongenial to an Arctic dog; for every one of them was securely chained up. This was necessary, especially to prevent fighting among themselves.

Sverre Hassel and Adolf Henrik Lindstrøm's receipt for their taxi boat fare to Flekkero – the island of the dogs. Photo: FM

After the Fram's arrival Wisting took over the position of dog-keeper in Hassel's place. He and Lindstrom stayed close to the island where the dogs were. Wisting had a way of his own with his four-footed subjects, and was soon on a confidential footing with them. He also showed himself to be possessed of considerable veterinary skill, an exceedingly useful qualification in this case, where there was often some injury or other to be attended to.

The Fram was anchored off Fredriksholm, and the necessary preparations were immediately made for receiving our four-footed friends. Under the expert direction of Bjaaland and Stubberud, as many as possible of the crew were set to work with axe and saw and in the course of a few hours the Fram had got a new deck. This consisted of loose pieces of decking, which could easily be raised and removed for flushing and cleaning. This false deck rested on three-inch planks nailed to the ship's deck; between the latter and the loose deck there was therefore a considerable space, the object of which was a double one namely, to let the water, which would unavoidably be shipped on such a voyage, run off rapidly, and to allow air to circulate, and thus keep the space below the animals as cool as possible. The arrangement afterwards proved very successful. The bulwarks on the fore-part of the Frams deck consisted of an iron railing covered with wire-netting. In order to provide both shade and shelter from the wind, a lining of boards was now put up along the inside of the railing, and chains were fastened in all possible and impossible places to tie the dogs up to.

There could be no question of letting them go loose to begin with, at any rate; possibly, we might hope to be able to set them free later on, when they knew their masters better and were more familiar with their surroundings generally. Late in the afternoon of August 9 we were ready to receive our new shipmates, and they were conveyed across from the island in a big lighter, twenty at a time.

Wisting and Lindstrom superintended the work of transport, and maintained order capitally. They had succeeded in gaining the dogs' confidence, and at the same time their complete respect just what was wanted, in fact. At the Fram's gangway the dogs came in for an active and determined reception, and before they had recovered from their surprise and fright, they were securely fastened on deck and given to understand with all politeness that the best thing they could do for the time being was to accept the situation with calmness. The whole proceeding went so rapidly that in the course of a couple of hours we had all the ninety-seven dogs on board and had found room for them; but it must be added that the Fram's deck was utilized to the utmost. We had thought we should be able to keep the bridge free, but this could not be done if we were to take them all with us. The last boat-load, fourteen in number, had to be accommodated there. All that was left was a little free space for the man at the wheel. As for the officer of the watch, it looked as if he would be badly off for elbow-room; there was reason to fear that he would be compelled to kill time by standing stock-still in one spot through the whole watch; but just then there was no time for small troubles of this sort. No sooner was the last dog on board than we set about putting all visitors ashore, and then the motor began working the windlass under the forecastle. "The anchor's up!" Full speed ahead, and the voyage towards our goal, 16,000 miles away, was begun.

Before we sailed there was no lack of all kinds of prophecies of the evil that would befall us with our dogs. We heard a number of these predictions; presumably a great many more were whispered about, but did not reach our ears. The unfortunate beasts were to fare terribly badly. The heat of the tropics would make short work of the greater part of them. If any were left, they would have but a miserable respite before being washed overboard or drowned in the seas that would come on deck in the west wind belt. To keep them alive with a few bits of dried fish was an impossibility, etc. As everyone knows, all these predictions were very far from being fulfilled; the exact opposite happened. From the very first I tried in every way to insist upon the paramount importance to our whole enterprise of getting our draught animals successfully conveyed to our destination.

If we had any watchword at this time it was: "Dogs first, and dogs all the time." The result speaks best for the way in which this watchword was followed. The following was the arrangement we made: The dogs, who at first were always tied up on the same spot, were divided into parties of ten; to each party one or two keepers were assigned, with full responsibility for their animals and their treatment. For my own share I took the fourteen that lived on the bridge.

Feeding the animals was a manoeuvre that required the presence of all hands on deck; it therefore took place when the watch was changed. The Arctic dog's greatest enjoyment in life is putting away his food; it may be safely asserted that the way to his heart lies through his dish of meat. We acted on this principle, and the result did not disappoint us.

After the lapse of a few days the different squads were the best of friends with their respective keepers. As may be supposed, it was not altogether to the taste of the dogs to stand chained up all the time; their temperament is far too lively for that. We would gladly have allowed them the pleasure of running about and thus getting healthy exercise, but for the present we dared not run the risk of letting the whole pack loose. A little more education was required first. It was easy enough to win their affection; to provide them with a good education was of course a more difficult matter. It was quite touching to see their joy and gratitude when one gave up a little time to their entertainment. One's first meeting with them in the morning was specially cordial. Their feelings were then apt to find vent in a chorus of joyful howls; this was called forth by the very sight of their masters, but they asked more than that. They were not satisfied until we had gone round, patting and talking to everyone.

If by chance one was so careless as to miss a dog, he at once showed the most unmistakable signs of disappointment. There can hardly be an animal that is capable of expressing its feelings to the same extent as the dog. Joy, sorrow, gratitude, scruples of conscience, are all reflected as plainly as could be desired in his behaviour, and above all in his eyes. We human beings are apt to cherish the conviction that we have a monopoly of what is called a living soul; the eyes, it is said, are the mirror of this soul.

That is all right enough; but now take a look at a dog's eyes, study them attentively. How often do we see something "human" in their expression, the same variations that we meet with in human eyes. This, at all events, is something that strikingly resembles "soul." We will leave the question open for those who are interested in its solution, and will here only mention another point, which seems to show that a dog is something more than a mere machine of flesh and blood; his pronounced individuality. There were about a hundred dogs on board the Fram.

Gradually, as we got to know each one of them by daily intercourse, they each revealed some characteristic trait, some peculiarity. Hardly two of them were alike, either in disposition or in appearance. To an observant eye there was here ample opportunity for the most amusing exercise. If now and then one grew a little tired of one's fellow men which, I must admit, seldom happened, there was, as a rule, diversion to be found in the society of the animals.

I say, as a rule; there were, of course, exceptions. It was not an unmixed pleasure having the whole deck full of dogs for all those months; our patience was severely tested many a time. But in spite of all the trouble and inconvenience to which the transport of the dogs necessarily gave rise, I am certainly right in saying that these months of sea voyage would have seemed far more monotonous and tedious if we had been without our passengers.

Dogs in the sun on the foredeck.

AMUNDSEN LANTERN SLIDE 172: FM/JFO

*Jørgen Stubberud
and his favourite dogs.*

A puppy is fed while the mother is watching.

Lt. Kristian Prestrud and Karenius Olsen feed the puppies.

AMUNDSEN LANTERN SLIDE 167: FM/JFO

Martin Rønne felt more safe when the dogs were wearing a muzzle.

AMUNDSEN LANTERN SLIDE 164: FM/JFO

Isak is having his broken leg mended by the "vets" Oscar Wisting and Hjalmar Fredrik Gjertsen.

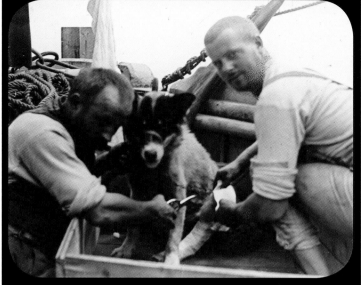

AMUNDSEN LANTERN SLIDE 175: FM/JFO

Fram's deck in the trade wind region.

AMUNDSEN LANTERN SLIDE 169: FM/JFO

Editor's note:

From Roald Amundsen's The South Pole:

We had expected to reach the Equator by October 1, but the unfavourable conditions of wind that we met with to the north of it caused us to be a little behind our reckoning, though not much. On the afternoon of October 4 the Fram crossed the line. Thus an important stage of the voyage was concluded: the feeling that we had now reached southern latitudes was enough to put us all in holiday humour, and we felt we must get up a modest entertainment. According to ancient custom, crossing the line should be celebrated by a visit from Father Neptune himself, whose part is taken for the occasion by someone chosen from among the ship's company. If in the course of his inspection this august personage comes upon anyone who is unable to prove that he has already crossed the famous circle, he is handed over at once to the attendants, to be "shaved and baptized." This process, which is not always carried out with exaggerated gentleness, causes much amusement, and forms a welcome variety in the monotonous life of a long sea voyage, and probably many on board the Fram looked forward with eagerness to Neptune's visit, but he did not come. There simply was no room for him on our already well-occupied deck. We contented ourselves with a special dinner, followed by coffee, liqueurs, and cigars. Coffee was served on

October 4, 1910: The crew is celebrating the crossing of the equator.

AMUNDSEN LANTERN SLIDE 171: FM/JFO

the fore-deck, where by moving a number of the dogs we had contrived to get a few square yards of space. There was no lack of entertainment. A violin and mandolin orchestra, composed of Prestrud, SundBeck, and Beck contributed several pieces, and our excellent gramophone was heard for the first time. Just as it started the waltz from "The Count of Luxembourg," there appeared in the companion-way a real ballet-girl, masked, and in very short skirts. This unexpected apparition from a better world was greeted with warm applause, which was no less vigorous when the fair one had given proof of her skill in the art of dancing. Behind the mask could be detected Gjertsen's face, but both costume and dance were in the highest degree feminine.

Rønne was not satisfied until he had the lady on his knees hurrah for illusion. The gramophone now changed to a swinging American v/cake-walk, and at the same moment there opportunely appeared on the scene a negro in a tail-coat, a silk hat, and a pair of wooden shoes. Black as he was, we saw at once that it was the second in command who had thus disguised himself. The mere sight of him was enough to set us all shrieking with laughter, but he made his great success when he began to dance. He was intensely amusing. It did us a great deal of good to have a little amusement just then, for this part of the voyage was a trial of patience more than anything else.

Through the big waves in the "Roaring Forties".

AMUNDSEN LANTERN SLIDE 159: FM/JFO

AMUNDSEN LANTERN SLIDE 158: FM/JFO

*The Fram sailed well,
in spite of her rounded hull.*

*Top right:
Fredrik Hjalmar Gjertsen, Thorvald Nilsen
and Kristian Prestrud taking an observation.*

*Bottom right:
Martin Rønne and Andreas Beck
after a successful albatross hunt.*

The saloon of the Fram decorated for Christmas Eve.

AMUNDSEN LANTERN SLIDE 178: FM/JFO

AMUNDSEN LANTERN SLIDE 178: FM/JFO

AMUNDSEN LANTERN SLIDE 176: FM/JFO

Editor's note:

From Roald Amundsen's The South Pole:

At nine in the morning of the next day we had our first opportunity of seal-hunting; a big Weddell seal was observed on a floe right ahead. It took our approach with the utmost calmness, not thinking it worth while to budge an inch until a couple of rifle-bullets had convinced it of the seriousness of the situation. It then made an attempt to reach the water, but it was too late. Two men were already on the floe, and the valuable spoil was secured. In the course of a quarter of an hour the beast lay on our deck, flayed and cut up by practised hands; this gave us at one stroke at least four hundredweight of dog food, as well as a good many rations for men. We made the same coup three times more in the course of the day, and thus had over a ton of fresh meat and blubber. The dogs did their utmost to avail themselves of the opportunity; they simply ate till their legs would no longer carry them, and we could grant them this gratification with a good conscience. As to ourselves, it may doubtless be taken for granted that we observed some degree of moderation, but dinner was polished off very quickly. Seal steak had many ardent adherents already, and it very soon gained more. Seal soup, in which our excellent vegetables showed to advantage, was perhaps even more favourably received.

Hunting for seal.

AMUNDSEN LANTERN SLIDE 189: FM/JFO

*Hunting for seal
in the Ross Sea.*

AMUNDSEN LANTERN SLIDE 188: FM/JFO

The Fram in drift ice.

AMUNDSEN LANTERN SLIDE 177: FM/JFO

The ice in the Bay of Whales had just broken up, and to such an extent that we succeeded in sailing quite a distance further south than any of our predecessors, and found a little cozy corner behind a projecting icecap, from which we, in comparative safety, could bring our outfit on to the barrier. Another great advantage was that the barrier here sloped very gently down to the sea ice, and this gave us the best ground for sledging. The first thing we did on our arrival was to climb the barrier to examine the nearest surroundings and find a convenient place for the house we had brought from home. The supposition that this part of the barrier rested on subjacent land the surroundings at once seemed to confirm. Instead of the plain, smooth surface that the outer barrier wall shows, we found the surface here greatly disturbed.

Steep hills and crests, with intervening dales, filled with huge hummocks and pressure ridges, were seen everywhere. And these formations were not of recent date. It was easy to notice that they dated from a time far beyond the days of old father Ross. Our original plan was to build our station several miles from the barrier edge in order to guard us against unwished-for sea-trip, in case the part of the barrier, on which our house was built, should break off. But that was not necessary. The formations we met on our first examination were warrant enough for the barrier's stability in this region. In a little valley 2 nautical miles (3 ½ kiloms.) from the spot where we had made fast the ship, we sheltered against all winds, we selected the place for our winter quarters.

The Fram arrived at the Bay of Whales on January 14, 1911. They called the harbour "Cape Man's Head".

AMUNDSEN LANTERN SLIDE 183: FM/JFO

Editor's note:

From Roald Amundsen's The South Pole:

We had thus arrived on January 14 a day earlier than we had reckoned at this vast, mysterious, natural phenomenon, the Barrier. One of the most difficult problems of the expedition was solved, that of conveying our draught animals in sound condition to the field of operations. We had taken 97 dogs on board at Christiansand; the number had now increased to 116, and practically all of these would be fit to serve in the final march to the South.

AMUNDSEN LANTERN SLIDE 190: FM/JFO

"Cape Man's Head."

"Cape Man's Head" seen from the north.

AMUNDSEN LANTERN SLIDE 185: FM/JFO

A group of Adele penguins.

AMUNDSEN LANTERN SLIDE 186: FM/JFO

Flensing a seal.

AMUNDSEN LANTERN SLIDE 184: FM/JFO

The first camp on the barrier.

AMUNDSEN LANTERN SLIDE 203: FM/JFO

The first camp from another angle.
Amundsen's film camera on the left side of the tent.

AMUNDSEN LANTERN SLIDE 210: FM/JFO

On the following day we commenced to discharge the ship: - materials for house building, outfit and provisions for nine men for several years. We were divided into two parties, the ship and the shore party. The first consisted of the master of the ship, Captain Nilsen, and the nine men, who would stay on board to navigate the Fram out of the ice and up to Buenos Aires.

The other party consisted of those of us who would go into winter quarters and march towards the south. It was the duty of the ship's party to unload everything from the ship on to the ice. There the shore party took it and drove it to the spot we had selected for our house. In the beginning we were a little unaccustomed to this work, untrained as we were after a long voyage. But it didn't take long before all of us were well trained, and then everything went along at a dizzy speed between the ship and our future home,

Unloading the Fram.

AMUNDSEN LANTERN SLIDE 195: FM/JFO

Framheim, which daily increased in size. As soon as all the materials for the hut had been driven up, our experienced carpenters, Olav Bjaaland and Jörgen Stubberud, commenced to erect the house. It was a ready-built house, and now there was nothing to do but to put together the different parts, all of which were marked. That the house might be able to withstand all the storms we expected, the site was excavated to a depth of 4 feet below the barrier surface.

On January 28, fourteen days after our arrival, the home was ready and provisions ashore. A giant work had been done and everything promised well for the future. But time was precious, and it was our duty to make the best of it. The shore party was again divided into two. One would go on driving up from the ship the rest of the stores, outfit, and the like, while the other would prepare for a trip southward for the purpose of exploring our immediate surroundings and establish a depôt.

The Fram in the Bay of Whales. A carcass of seal in the foreground.

AMUNDSEN LANTERN SLIDE 200: FM/JFO

Editor's note:

From Roald Amundsen's The South Pole:

On Monday, January 23, we began to carry up the provisions. In order to save time, we had decided not to bring the provisions right up to the hut, but to store them for the time being on an elevation that lay on the other side, to the south of Mount Nelson. This spot was not more than 600 yards from the hut, but as the surface was rather rough here, we should save a good deal in the long-run. Sledging up to this point offered some difficulties at first. The dogs, who were accustomed to take the road to the lower camp between Nelson and Ronniken could not understand why they might not do the same now. The journey with empty sledges down to the ship was often particularly troublesome. From this point the dogs could hear their companions on the other side of Nelson in the lower camp, and then it happened more than once that the dogs took command. If they once got in the humour for playing tricks of that sort, it was by no means easy to get them under control. As the provisions came up each driver took them off his sledge, and laid the cases in the order in which they should lie. This plan had the advantage that everything would be easy to find. The load was usually 660 pounds, or 6 cases to each sledge. We had about 900 cases to bring up, and reckoned that we should have them all in place in the course of a week. Everything went remarkably well according

Ready to move into Framheim.

AMUNDSEN LANTERN SLIDE 211: FM/JFO

to our reckoning. By noon on Saturday, January 28, the hut was ready, and all the 900 cases were in place. Great rows of cases stood in the snow, all with their numbers outward, so that we could find what we wanted at once. And there was the house, all finished, exactly as it had stood in its native place on the Bundefjord. But it would be difficult to imagine more different surroundings: there, green pinewoods and splashing water; here, ice, nothing but ice. But both scenes were beautiful; I stood thinking which I preferred. My thoughts travelled far thousands of miles in a second. It was the forest that gained the day. As I have already mentioned, we had everything with us for fastening the hut down to the Barrier, but the calm weather we had had all the time led us to suppose that the conditions would not be so bad as we had expected. We were therefore satisfied with the foundation dug in the Barrier. The outside of the hut was tarred, and the roof covered with tarred paper, so that it was very visible against the white surroundings. That afternoon we broke up both camps, and moved into our home, "Framheim." What a snug, cosy, and cleanly impression it gave us when we entered the door! Bright, new linoleum everywhere in the kitchen as well as in our living-room. Another important point had been got over, and in much shorter time than I had ever hoped. Our path to the goal was opening up; we began to have a glimpse of the castle in the distance.

Constructing the living quarters at Framheim.

AMUNDSEN LANTERN SLIDE 197: FM/JFO

Editor's note:

From Roald Amundsen's The South Pole:

The Terra Nova had come in at midnight. Our watchman had just gone below for a cup of coffee. There was no harm in that and when he came up again, there was another ship lying off the foot of the Barrier. He rubbed his eyes, pinched his leg, and tried other means of convincing himself that he was asleep, but it was no good. The pinch especially, he told us afterwards, was horribly painful, and all this led him to the conclusion that there really was a second vessel there. Lieutenant Campbell, the leader of the eastern party, which was to explore King Edward VII. Land, came on board first, and paid Nilsen a visit. He brought the news that they had not been able to reach land, and were now on their way back to McMurdo Sound. From thence it was their intention to go to Cape North and explore the land there. Immediately after my arrival Lieutenant Campbell came on board again and gave me the news himself. We then loaded our sledges and drove home. At nine o'clock we had the great pleasure of receiving Lieutenant Pennell, the commander of the Terra Nova, Lieutenant Campbell, and the surgeon of the expedition, as the first guests in our new home. We spent a couple of very agreeable hours together.

The Fram and Robert Falcon Scott's expedition ship the Terra Nova in the Bay of Whales on February 4, 1911.

AMUNDSEN LANTERN SLIDE 182: FM/JFO

Later in the day three of us paid a visit to the Terra Nova, and stayed on board to lunch. Our hosts were extremely kind, and offered to take our mail to New Zealand. If I had had time, I should have been glad to avail myself of this friendly offer, but every hour was precious. It was no use to think of writing now. At two o'clock in the afternoon the Terra Nova cast off again, and left the Bay of Whales. We made a strange discovery after this visit. Nearly all of us had caught cold. It did not last long only a few hours and then it was over. The form it took was sneezing and cold in the head.

Adolf H. Lindstrøm on his way from the Fram to take command of the kitchen in Framheim. Lindstrøm was the first man to have sailed round the continent of America, participated in Otto Sverdrup's expedition on the Fram (1898-1902) and in Amundsen's expedition through the Northwest Passage (1903-06).

AMUNDSEN LANTERN SLIDE 237: FM/JFO

On February 10, the last named party was off. We were four men, eighteen dogs and three sledges, fully laden with provisions. How well I remember that morning, when we for the first time made our way towards the south! It was calm and slightly overcast. Ahead of us the vast, endless snowplain; behind us the Bay of Whales with the great prominent icecapes, and the further end of the bay our dear Fram. The flag was hoisted, a last farewell from our comrades on board. Nobody knew when we should see them again. Most likely they would be gone when we returned, and then a year would elapse before we should see them. Another look behind, another farewell, and then southward.

This first trip of ours on the barrier was an exciting one. What would the region be like? How about the sledging? Did we have the proper outfit? Did we have the right traction power? If our task should be solved, everything had to be the best. Our equipment was essentially different from that of our English competitors. We pinned all of our faith to our dogs and skis. We travelled fast on the smooth, flat snow-plain. On the 14th we reached 80° S, having travelled a distance of 85 nautical miles (160 kiloms.) and established a depôt, consisting chiefly of provisions to be used on our main march towards the south, when spring came. The weight of the provisions was 1200lbs. The return trip was made in two days.

The Fram just before their departure on February 10.

AMUNDSEN LANTERN SLIDE 182: FM/JFO

The first day we travelled 46 nautical miles (75 kiloms.), and the second day 50 nautical miles (93 kiloms.). On our arrival at the station, the Fram had sailed. The bay looked dreary and desolate. Seals and penguins had taken possession of the place. Our first trip southward, however short, was of great importance. We now knew to a certainty that our equipment and traction power was of the very best. No errors had been made in the selection of same. Now it was for us to use them in the best manner possible.

We did not stay long at home. On the 22nd we were once more ready to carry our depôt towards the south. The intention was to take them as far south as possible.

We were eight men, seven sledges, and forty-two dogs. The cook alone stayed at home. On the 27th we passed the depôt at 80° S, where everything was in first-class order. On March 4, we made 81° S, and deposited there 1050 lbs. of provisions. From here three men returned, while five men continued their way southward and on March 8 reached 82° S, where 1250 lbs. of provisions were left. We then returned, and were at home again on the 22nd. Once more before the winter set in we were in the field, and carried 2200 lbs. of fresh sealmeat and 400 lbs. completed, and all the depôt work had come to an end. Up to this time we had carried 7500 lbs. of provisions, distributing them at three depôts.

Some of the expedition members on the barrier. From the left: Alexander Kutchin, Thorvald Nilsen, Martin Rønne, Ludvig Hansen, Halvardus Kristensen, Adolf H. Lindstrøm, Fredrik Hjalmar Gjertsen, Karl Sundbeck, Karenius Olsen & Jacob Nødtvedt.

AMUNDSEN LANTERN SLIDE 180: FM/JFO

The part of the barrier over which we had travelled had an average height of about 150 feet, and looked like a smooth plain, rising in the great waves or undulations without characteristic marks of any kind. It has been the common opinion that depôts might not be laid out on such an endless plateau without an imminent probability of losing them. But if there should be any chance for us to reach our goal, we had to lay out depôts, and that even on a large scale. We talked much over the question, and arrived at the conclusion that we must use signals athwart our course instead of along it as commonly the case. Consequently, we put down a line of flags at right angles to our goal, that is, in an east-west direction, with the depôt as central point. Each of the three depôts was marked in this manner, 5 nautical miles (9 kiloms.) on each side of the depôt, and half a mile (1 kilom.) between each flag.

Besides, all of the flags were marked, so that we, wherever we met them, were able to know in which direction lay the depôt and how far we were from it. This plan proved to be absolutely reliable, and even in the densest fog we succeeded in finding our depôts. Our compasses and distance meters were examined at the station, and we knew that we could depend upon them.

We had gained much on our depôt trips. Not only had we succeeded in carrying plenty of provisions southward, but we had acquired a lot of experience, which was possibly more important and came in handy on our final dash for the pole. The lowest temperature observed on these depôt trips was – 50 ° Fahr. Considering that it was still summer when this temperature was observed, it was a serious warning to us that we must have our equipment in good order.

Sketch of the depôts and the signal flags placed on each side of the depôt.

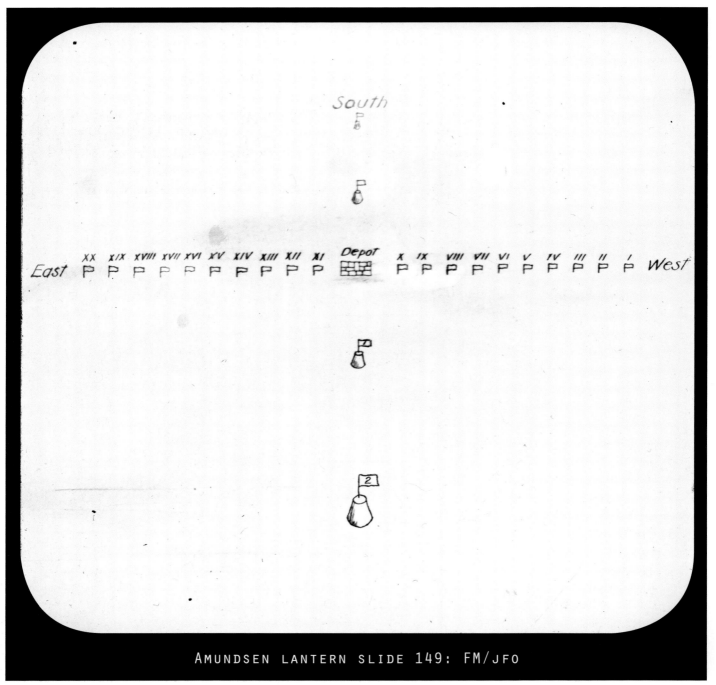

AMUNDSEN LANTERN SLIDE 149: FM/JFO

We had also seen that our solid, heavy sledges were too clumsy, and that without risk they could be lightened considerably. The same could be done with the greater part of our other outfit.

Some days more were spent on seal hunt, before the sun disappeared. The total weight of seals killed amounted to 120,000 Ibs. Thus we had provisions in plenty for ourselves as well as for our 115 dogs. The first thing we did was to give our dogs a shelter. We had brought with us ten very big tents, large enough to accommodate sixteen men. They were pitched on the barrier, after which the snow under each tent was dug out, 6 feet down, so the ultimate height of these dog houses became 18 feet. The diameter of the floor was 15 feet. Our intention in building these houses so large was to make them as airy as possible, in order to avoid the hoar frost so annoying to the dogs. We achieved our object. Even during the most severe period of the winter no frost could be noticed. The tents were always cozy and warm. Each tent had room for twelve dogs, and every man had its own team to look after.

Having thus cared for our dogs, the turn came to ourselves. Mother nature had stretched out a helping hand, and we were not slow in catching it. In April the house was completely covered with snow. In this newly drifted snow were made excavations in direct communication with the hut. Thus we got large and spacious rooms without buying or fetching materials. There were workshops, forge, sewing room, packing room, a space for coal, wood and oil, ordinary bath and steam bath. However cold and stormy the winter might be, it would not annoy us at all.

Research on the ice-formation near Framheim.

AMUNDSEN LANTERN SLIDE 113: FM/JFO

AMUNDSEN LANTERN SLIDE 187: FM/JFO

The village of Framheim.

AMUNDSEN LANTERN SLIDE 215: FM/JFO

AMUNDSEN LANTERN SLIDE 201: FM/JFO

The "city plan" for Framheim.

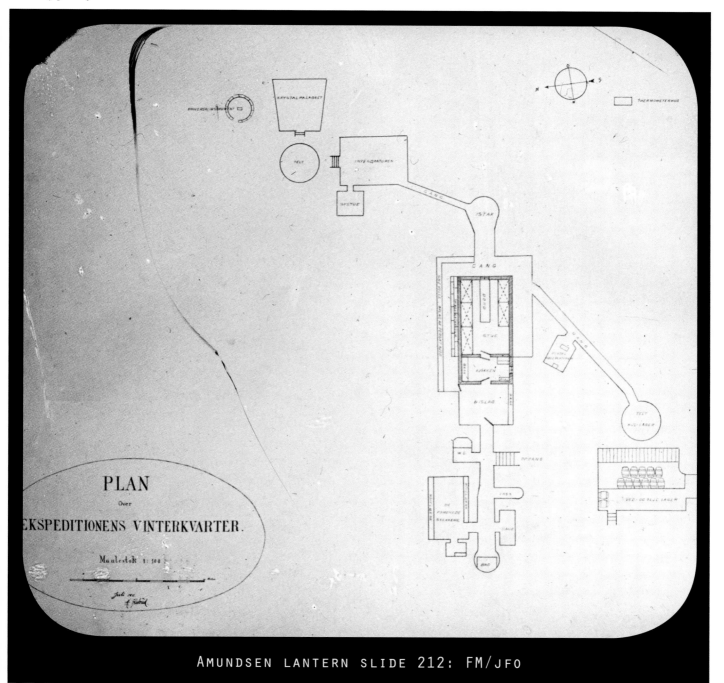

AMUNDSEN LANTERN SLIDE 212: FM/JFO

AMUNDSEN LANTERN SLIDE 217: FM/JFO

AMUNDSEN LANTERN SLIDE 216: FM/JFO

The passageway between the house and the coal tent.

AMUNDSEN LANTERN SLIDE 175: FM/JFO

The entrance to the house.

AMUNDSEN LANTERN SLIDE 222: FM/JFO

On April 21 the sun disappeared, and then began the longest night ever experienced by men in the Antarctic. We had no fear of meeting it. We had provisions enough for years, a cozy house well ventilated, well lighted, and well heated, with an excellent bath – a complete sanatorium, indeed. As soon as all these buildings were finished we began to make preparations for the final journey in the spring. Our business was to improve our equipment and reduce its weight. Thus we condemned all our sledges. They were too heavy and clumsy for the smooth surface of the barrier. The weight of such a sledge was 150 lbs. Our ski and sledgemaker, Bjaaland, took care of the sledges and did all the necessary work concerning them, and when the spring came, a completely new sledge outfit was ready from his hand.

These sledges weighed only one-third of the original ones. In a like proportion we succeeded in reducing the weight of everything. Of the utmost importance was the packing of the provisions selected for the trip. It was the work of Captain Johansen during the winter. It had to be done with care and attention. Of the 42,000 biscuits that were packed, each and every one was turned in the hand, before the right place for it was found. In this manner the winter passed quickly and comfortably. Everyone had his hands full all the time; our house was warm and dry, light and airy; consequently, the health of everybody was excellent. We had no physician, and we didn't need one.

The kitchen in Framheim.

AMUNDSEN LANTERN SLIDE 119: FM/JFO

The storage tent for meat. Photo FM

The polar chef,
Adolf H. Lindstrøm,
serving his speciality,
hot cakes.
Photo: FM

Amundsen lantern slide 199: FM/JFO

The crew testing their designer googles.

Framheim covered in snow.

AMUNDSEN LANTERN SLIDE 218: FM/JFO

Waiting for Lindstrøm's latest culinary creation? Photo FM

Sverre Hassel in the oil storage.

AMUNDSEN LANTERN SLIDE 224: FM/JFO

Kristian Prestrud and Helmer Hanssen packing sledges in the "crystal palace".

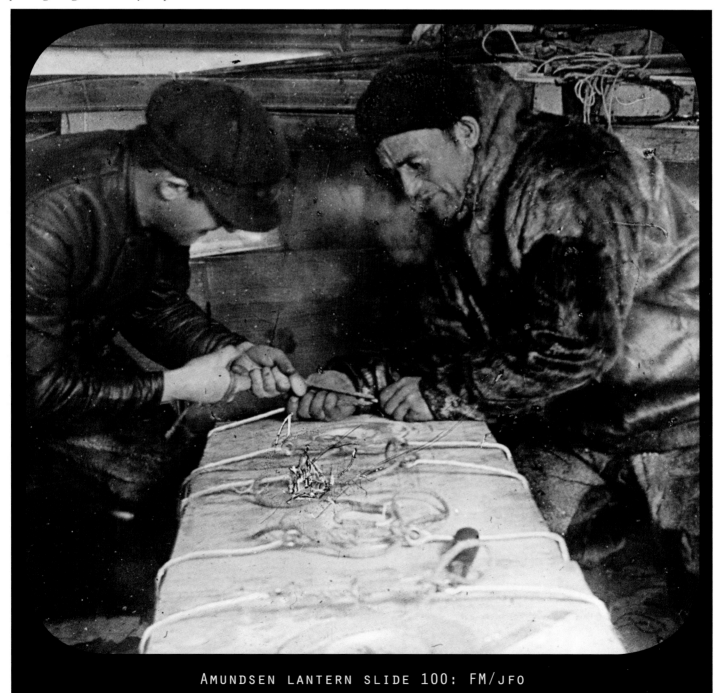

AMUNDSEN LANTERN SLIDE 100: FM/JFO

*Olav Bjaaland, Kristian Prestrud
and Oscar Wisting strapping boxes
to the sledges.
Photo: FM*

Oscar Wisting at the sewing-machine.

AMUNDSEN LANTERN SLIDE 241: FM/JFO

Hjalmar Johansen boxes the biscuits and updates the inventory.
Photo: FM

Hjalmar Johansen packing provisions in the "crystal palace".

AMUNDSEN LANTERN SLIDE 225: FM/JFO

Sverre Hassel assembles the steam bath.
Photo: FM

Boots and bindings were altered several times before the final sledging expedition.

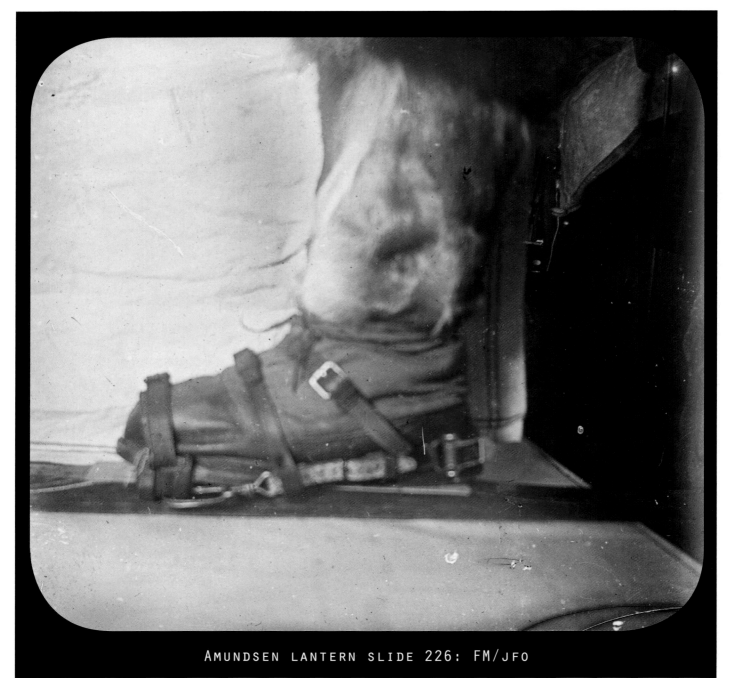

AMUNDSEN LANTERN SLIDE 226: FM/JFO

Kristian Prestrud with the pendulum in his observatory. Photo: FM

Olav Bjaaland shaving off weight from the South Pole sledges.

AMUNDSEN LANTERN SLIDE 223: FM/JFO

AMUNDSEN LANTERN SLIDE 121: FM/JFO

Olav Bjaaland .

Meteorological observations were taken all the time; the results were surprising. We believed that we should encounter unpleasant, stormy weather, but it proved to be contrary to expectations. During the whole year we stayed there we didn't have more than two moderate storms; for the rest calm and light breezes – mostly easterly. The atmospherical pressure was mostly very low, but steady.

The meteorological screen.

AMUNDSEN LANTERN SLIDE 120: FM/JFO

The temperature became very low, and it is probable that the mean temperature for the year, - 14° Fahr. (-26° C), which we observed, is the lowest mean temperature on record. In five months of the year we had temperatures below – 58° Fahr. (-50° C). On August 13, we had the lowest temperature observed, - 74° Fahr. (-59° C). The aurora australis was very frequent in all directions and shapes; it was extremely lively, but not very intense. There were, however, a few exceptions.

Inside one of the dog tents. Photo: FM

Adolf H. Lindstrøm, the meteorologist.

AMUNDSEN LANTERN SLIDE 101: FM/JFO

On August 24 the sun returned; the winter was over. Some days before we had all our things in full order, and when the sun peeped over the barrier everything was ready for a start. The dogs were in excellent condition, some of them too much so. From now we watched the temperatures daily. As long as the glass remained as low as -58° Fahr. (- 50 ° C), there could be no question of starting. In the first day of September there was every sign that it would rise, and we therefore resolved to push off as soon as possible.

On September 8 we had a temperature of – 31° Fahr., and off we were. But this trip could not be one of long duration. On the following day the temperature began to go down rapidly, and within days we had – 72° Fahr. (- 58° C). We human beings might have kept going for some time in this temperature, well clothed as we were, but our dogs could not stand it very long. We were therefore satisfied to reach 80° south, and arriving there we laid all our provisions and outfit in the old depôt and returned to Framheim.

Now came a period of doubtful weather, the change from winter into spring, and we never knew what the next day would bring forth.

Some frost-bittens heels from the last trip forced us to wait until we knew for certain that the spring had come in earnest. On September 24 the first obvious signs of spring appeared – the seals began to go up on the ice. This sign was welcomed with rejoicing and not least the fresh seal meat, which Bjaaland brought in every day. The dogs also appreciated the sign of the spring. They were especially fond of fresh blubber. On the 29th appeared another and more obvious sign – a flight of Antarctic petrels; they were flying round the house, to the delight of the men as well as of the dogs.

The dogs were wild with joy and excitement, ran after the birds and stupidly counted on a delicate bird for dinner; the hunt resulted in a wild fight. At last at October 20 the weather had settled so much that we were able to start. The original plan, that all of us should march southward, had to be changed during the interval. We understood that without risk we could divide into two parties, and in this manner do considerably more work. We had arrived at the decision, that three men should go east to King Edward VII. Land and examine it, while the other five should carry out the main plan – the dash for the pole.

Ready for the start of the polar journey.

AMUNDSEN LANTERN SLIDE 221: FM/JFO

*Hunting for seal close to
the edge of the barrier.*

Amundsen lantern slide 116: FM/JFO

Lifting the packed sledges up to the surface.

Amundsen lantern slide 220: FM/JFO

Editor's note:

From Roald Amundsen's The South Pole:

Hanssen's sledge stands first, bow to the south; behind it come Wisting's, Bjaaland's and Hassel's. They all look pretty much alike, and as regards provisions their loads are precisely similar.

Case No. 1 contains about 5,300 biscuits, and weighs 111 pounds. Case No. 2: 112 rations of dogs' pemmican; 11 bags of dried milk, choc-olate, and biscuits. Total gross weight, 177 pounds. Case No. 3: 124 rations of dogs' pemmi-can; 10 bags of dried milk and biscuits. Gross weight, 161 pounds. Case No. 4: 39 rations of dogs' pemmican; 86 rations of men's pemmican, 9 bags of dried milk and biscuits. Gross weight, 165 pounds.

Case No. 5: 96 rations of dogs' pemmican. Weight, 122 pounds. Total net weight of provisions per sledge, 668 pounds. With the outfit and the weight of the sledge itself, the total came to pretty nearly 880 pounds.

Hanssen's sledge differed from the others, in that it had aluminum fittings instead of steel and no sledgemeter, as it had to be free from iron on account of the steering-compass he carried. Each of the other three sledges had a sledge-meter and compass.

The depôt at 80° S on October 23.

AMUNDSEN LANTERN SLIDE 135: FM/JFO

We were thus equipped with three sledge-meters and four compasses. The instruments we carried were two sextants and three artificial horizons, two glass and one mercury, a hypsometer for measuring heights, and one aneroid. For meteorological observations, four thermometers.

Also two pairs of binoculars. We took a little travelling case of medicines from Burroughs Wellcome and Co. Our surgical instruments were not many: a dental forceps and a beard-clipper. Our sewing outfit was extensive. We carried a small, very light tent in reserve; it would have to be used if any of us were obliged to turn back. We also carried two primus lamps.

Of paraffin we had a good supply: twenty-two and a half gallons divided among three sledges. We kept it in the usual cans, but they proved too weak; not that we lost any paraffin, but Bjaaland had to be constantly soldering to keep them tight. We had a good soldering outfit. Every man carried his own personal bag, in which he kept reserve clothing, diaries and observation books. We took a quantity of loose straps for spare ski-bindings. We had double sleeping-bags for the first part of the time; that is to say, an inner and an outer one. There were five watches among us, of which three were chronometer watches.

Olav Bjaaland soldering a tank of paraffin.

AMUNDSEN LANTERN SLIDE 131: FM/JFO

October 20 was a fine day. Clear and mild; -1° Fahr. We were five men, fifty-two dogs, and four sledges. Our sledges were light, and the going was lively. It was not necessary to cheer the dogs, they were willing enough without. With our depôts in 80°, 81° and 82°, we had provisions enough for 120 days. Two days after our departure a series of accidents happened, Bjaaland's sledge falling down one of the many crevasses we had to pass over that day. He got assistance at the last moment, but it was in the nick of time, or his sledge with the thirteen dogs would have disappeared in the apparently bottomless pit.

On the fourth day we arrived at our depôt in 80° S. Here we rested two days and gave our dogs as much fresh seal meat as they could eat. Between 80° and 81° in the direction we went, the barrier is smooth and fine with the exception of a few low undulations, and there are no hidden dangers.

Quite different is it between 81° and 82°. On the first 15 miles we were in a perfect labyrinth of crevasses and pressure ridges, rendering the passage extremely dangerous. Big pieces of the surface have been broken off, and grinning abysses are met with everywhere. From these gulfs cracks are to be found in all directions, and the surface consequently is very unsafe.

We passed this bit of road four times. The three first times it was such a dense fog, that we could not see many yards ahead of us. Only the fourth time did we get clear weather, and we saw then what difficulties we had escaped. On November 5th we reached the depôts in 82°, and found everything all right. For the last time our dogs could get a good rest and plenty of food. And they got it thoroughly during a two-days' stay. In the 80° we commenced to build snow mounds, intended to serve as track marks on

The depôt at 81° S on October 30.

AMUNDSEN LANTERN SLIDE 137: FM/JFO

the homeward trip. The mounds proved to answer expectations, as by them we followed precisely the same route we had gone.

The barrier south of 82° was, if possible, still more smooth than the north of that latitude, and we were marching along at good speed. We agreed in laying down a depôt at each whole degree of latitude, on our way south. Undeniably we ran a risk in doing it, as there was no time for putting down cross-marks. But we had to be satisfied with the snow mounds and pin our faith to them. But, on the other hand, our sledges became so much lighter that they were never too heavy for our dogs. In 83° S, we sighted land in the south-westerly direction. It could be nothing else but South Victoria land, and probably a continuation of the mountain range, running in a south-easterly direction, as drawn by Shackleton in his chart. From day to day the land became more distinct, one peak more magnificent than the next one – being from 10,000 to 15,000 feet in height, sharp cones and sharp needle-like spurs. I have never seen a landscape more beautiful, more wild, and more imposing. Here a weathered summit – dark and cold – there snow and ice glaciers in a terrible chaos.

On November 11 we sighted land due south, and pretty soon ascertained that South Victoria Land in about 86° S and 163° W is met by a range trending east and north-east. This mountain range is considerably lower than South Victoria Land's mighty mountains. Summits from 2000 to 4000 feet were highest. We were able to see the range to 84° S, where it disappeared on the horizon. On the 17th we arrived at the spot where the ice barrier and the land are joined. We had all the time been steering due south from our winter quarters.

The depôt at 82° S on November 4.

Amundsen lantern slide 122: FM/JFO

The latitude was 85°, and the longitude was 165° W. The junction between barrier and land was not followed by any great disturbances. A few large undulations broken off at intervals by crevasses. Nothing there could impede our progress. Our plan was to go due south from Framheim to the pole, and not go out of the way unless natural obstacles should force us to do so. If we succeeded, we would be able to explore an absolutely unknown land, and to do good geographical work.

The nearest ascent due south was between the mighty peaks of South Victoria land. Obviously there were no serious difficulties in store for us. We might probably have found a less steep ascent if we had crossed over to the newly discovered range. But we had once taken the notion, that due south was the shortest way to the goal, and then we had to take the chances. On this spot we established our main depôt and left provisions here for thirty days. On our four sledges we carried provisions for sixty days. And up we went to the plateau. The first part of the ascent went over sloping, snow-covered mountain sides, in places rather steep, although not bad enough to prevent each team managing to haul up their own sledges. Further up we met with some short, but very steep glaciers, in fact, they were so steep that we had to harness twenty dogs to each sledge. But now they went lively enough in spite of precipices which were so steep that we had the greatest difficulty in climbing them on our skies. The first night we pitched camp at a height of 2000 feet. The second day we climbed mostly up some small glaciers, and camped at a height of 4000 feet. The third day we unfortunately had to swallow the pill and descend about 2000 feet, being surprised by a large glacier running east-west, which divided the mountains we had climbed from the higher peaks further south.

AMUNDSEN LANTERN SLIDE 114: FM/JFO

Downhill the exhibition went again at a dizzy speed, and in a very little time we were down on the before-mentioned mighty glacier, Axel Heiberg glacier. That night our camp was about 3000 feet above sea-level. The following day began the longest part of our climb, we being obliged to follow Heiberg glacier. This glacier was in places filled with hummocky ice, the surface rising into hillocks and splitting into chasms, and we had to make detours in order to escape the broad chasms which open into great gullies.

The latter were of course mostly filled, the glacier apparently having stopped every movement long ago. But we had to be very careful, not knowing how thick was the layer that covered. Our camp that night lay in very picturesque surroundings, the altitude was 5000 feet above sea-level. The glacier here was in between the two 15,000-feet high mountains – Fridtjof Nansen and Don Pedro Chris-

tophersen mountains. To the west in the further end of the glacier rose mount Ole Engelstad to a height of 13,000 feet. The glacier was in this comparatively narrow passage very hummocky and broken by huge crevasses, so that our progress very often seemed to be impeded. On the following day we reached a light sloping plateau, what was supposed to be the plateau described by Shackleton. Our dogs performed that day a work so well that their superiority once for all must be admitted.

Added to the toil of the preceding weary days, they travelled this day 17 nautical miles (33 kiloms.), ascending 5600 feet. We camped that night in an altitude of 10,600 feet. Now the time had come when, unfortunately, we were obliged to kill some of our dogs. Twenty-four of our brave companions had to lay down their lives. We had to remain here for four days on account of bad weather.

AMUNDSEN LANTERN SLIDE 115: FM/JFO

When we at last broke up on November 26, we had only ten carcasses left, and these we laid in depôt. Some fresh provisions on our return trip would not do any harm. During the following days the weather was stormy and the snowdrift dense, so we were not able to see any of the surroundings. That much did we notice, that we were going downhill very fast. Once in a while when the drift lifted we saw high mountains due east.

In the dense snowdrift on November 28 we were close under two peculiar-looking crests of mountains, running north-south, the two only peaks we observed on our right side. Helland Hansen mountains were wholly snowclad and had a height of 9000 feet. They became later an excellent landmark. The gale slackened the next day and the sun shone through. Then it appeared to us as if we were transported to an absolutely new country.

In the direction of our course trended a huge glacier. On its eastern boundary was a range running south-east-north-west. To the west the fog was dense over the glacier and hid even the nearest surroundings. The hypsometer gave 8000 feet above sea-level at the foot of "The Devil's Glacier," which means that we had descended 2600 feet from the Butchery. It was no pleasant discovery. Without doubt we would have the same climb again and probably more.

Ruth Gade's Mountain.

AMUNDSEN LANTERN SLIDE 229: FM/JFO

AMUNDSEN LANTERN SLIDE 123: FM/JFO

The Devil's Glacier.

The dogs Lussi, Karenius and Sauen (the Sheep).

AMUNDSEN LANTERN SLIDE 103: FM/JFO

We established a six-day depôt and continued our march. From our camp that night we had a splendid view of the eastern mountain range. There was the most peculiar-looking peak I have seen. It was 12,000 feet high. The top of it was round in shape and was covered by a torn glacier. It looked as if nature in a fit of anger had showered sharp ice-blocks on it. It was called Helmer Hansen Mountain, and became our best landmark. And there were Oscar Wisting, Olav Bjaaland, Sverre Hassel mountains, glittering dark and red, glaring white and blue in the rays of the midnight sun. In the distance appeared the romantic mountain - enormous to behold through the heavy masses of clouds and fog, which from time to time drifted over, now and then exposing to our view their mighty peaks and broken glaciers.

On December 1 we had left behind us this crevassed glacier, so full of hulls and bottomless chasms. Our altitude was 9100 feet. Ahead of us, and looking as a frozen sea in the fog and snowdrift, was a sloping ice-plateau studded with hummocks. The march over "The Devil's Ballroom" was not entirely pleasant. Gales from south-east, followed by snowdrift, were of daily occurrence.

We saw nothing, absolutely nothing. The ground below us was hollow, and it sounded as if we were walking on the bottom of empty barrels. We crossed this unpleasant and ugly place as quick and as light of foot as possible, all the time with the unpleasant possibility of being engulfed.

On December 6 we reached the greatest height – 10,750 feet above sea-level, according to hypsometer and aneroid. From here the main inland plateau didn't rise anymore, but ran into an absolutely flat plain. The height was constant as far as 88° 25′, from where it began to slope down to the other side. In 88° 23` we had reached Shackleton's furthest south, and camped at 88° 25′. Here we established our last depôt - depôt No.10, and deposited 200 lbs. of provisions. Then it began to go very slow down-hill. The state of the ground was excellent, absolutely flat without undulation, hills and sastrugi. The sledging was ideal and the weather beautiful. We covered daily 15 nautical miles (30 kiloms.). There was nothing to prevent us from a good deal longer marches, but we had time and food enough, and considered it more prudent to save the dogs and not to overwork them. Without adventures of any kind we had latitude 89° on December 11.

Hoisting the Norwegian flag on Ernest H. Shackleton's furthest south.

AMUNDSEN LANTERN SLIDE 124: FM/JFO

It seemed that we were in a region with perpetually fine weather. The most obvious sign of constant, calm weather was the absolutely plain surface. We were able to thrust a tent-pole 6 feet down into the snow without being met with any resistance. It is a proof, clear enough, that the snow has fallen in the same kind of weather – calm or very light breeze. Varying weather conditions – calm and gale – would have formed layers of different compactness, which soon have been felt, when one stuck the pole through the snow.

Dead reckoning and observations had always given like results. The last eight days of our outward march had sunshine all the time. Every day we stopped at noon to take a meridian latitude, and every day we took an azimuth observation. On December 13 the latitude gave 89° 37′; dead reckoning 89° 38′. In 88° 25′ we got the last good azimuth observations. Later on they were of no use. As the last observation gave pretty near the same result, the variation being almost constant, we used the observation taken in 88° 25′.

We made out, that we would reach the goal December 14. The 14th arrived. I have a feeling that we slept less, breakfasted at a greater speed and started earlier this morning than the previous days.

The day was fine as usual. Brilliant sunshine with a very gentle breeze. We made good headway. We didn't talk much. Everybody was occupied with his own thoughts, I think. Or had probably all of us the same thought? Which brought all of us to look and stare towards the south over the endless plateau. Were we the first or?

–Halt! It sounded like a sound of exultation. The distance was covered. The goal reached. Calm, so calm stretched the mighty plateau before us, unseen and untrod by the foot of man. No sign or mark in any direction. It was undeniably a moment of solemnity when all of us with our hand on the flag-staff planted the colours of our country on the geographical south pole, on King Haakon the 7th plateau.

The critical moment in "The Devil's Ballroom".

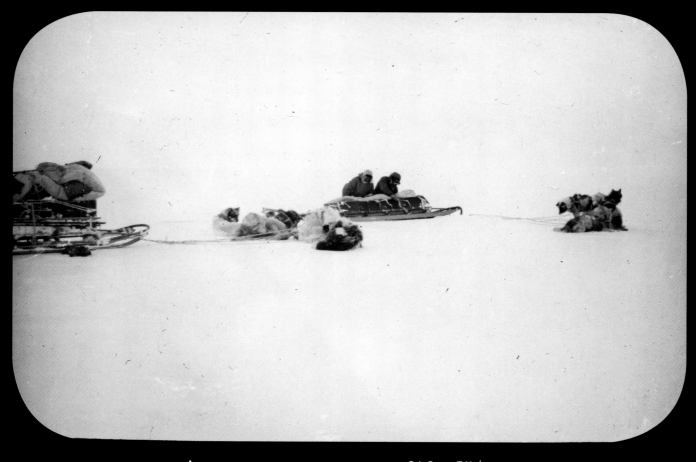

AMUNDSEN LANTERN SLIDE 242: FM/JFO

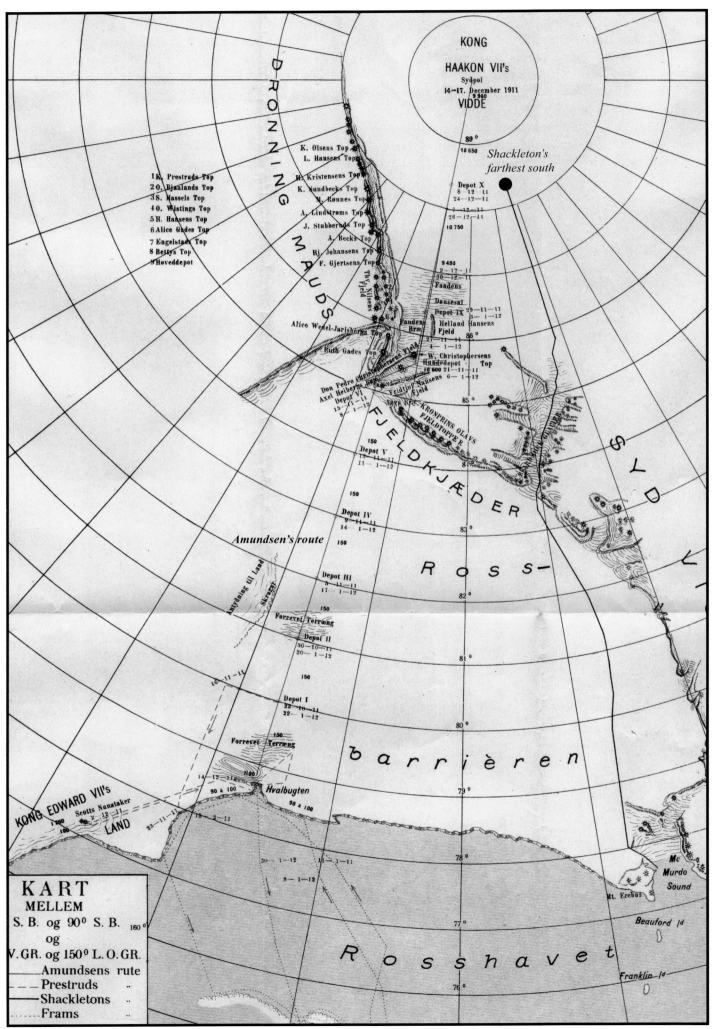

KONG
HAAKON VII's
Sydpol
14–17. December 1911
9 960
VIDDE

89°
10 650

*Shackleton's
farthest south*

K. Olsens Top
L. Hansens Top
H. Kristensens Top
K. Sundbecks Top
M. Rønnes Top
A. Lindstrøms Top
J. Stubberuds Top
A. Becks Top
Hj. Johansens Top
F. Gjertsens Top

1 K. Prestruds Top
2 O. Bjaalands Top
3 S. Hassels Top
4 O. Wistings Top
5 H. Hansens Top
6 Alice Gades Top
7 Engelstad Top
8 Bettys Top
9 Hoveddepot

Depot X
8 –12 –11
24 –12 –11
 –12 –11
26 –12 –11
10 750

9 450
9 –12 –11
30 –12 –11
Fandens
Dansesal
Depot IX 29 –11 –11
3 – 1 –12
Helland Hansens
Fjeld
86°

Thv. Nilsens Fjeld

Fandens
Bræ

Alice Wedel-Jarlsbergs Top

Ruth Gades Top

W. Christophersens
Hundedepot   Top
10 600 21 –11 –11
6 – 1 –12

Don Pedro Christophersens Fjeld

Axel Heibergs
Depot VI
15 –11 –12
8 – 1 –12

Fridtjof Nansens Fjeld

85°

KRONPRINS OLAVS
FJELDTOPPER

FJELDKJÆDER

Depot V
11 – 1 –12

150

150

Depot IV
9 –11 –11
14 – 1 –12

ROSS-

83°

Amundsen's route

150

150

Anryding til Land
Skrugel

Depot III
8 –11 –11
17 – 1 –12

82°

150

Forrevet Terræng

Depot II
30 –10 –11
20 – 1 –12

81°

150

16 –11 –11

Depot I
23 –10 –11
22 – 1 –12

80°

150

barrièren

Forrevet Terræng

150

14 –12 –11 1100

79°

90 á 100
Hvalbugten

90 á 100

KONG EDWARD VII's
Scotts Nunataker
1 260   2 –12 –11
100   28 –11 –11   10 2 –11
LAND

78°

30 – 1 –12   11 – 1 –11

8 – 1 –12

Mc
Murdo
Sound

77°

Mt. Erebus

Beauford Id

76°

Rosshavet

SYD VI

Franklin Id

KART
MELLEM
S. B. og 90° S. B.
og
V. GR. og 150° L. O. GR.
160°
——— Amundsens rute
– – – Prestruds   "
—·— Shackletons   "
········ Frams   "

DRONNING MAUDS

During the night – according to our time – three men encircled our camp, the length of the semidiameter being 10 nautical miles (18 kiloms.), putting down marks, while the two others remained at the tent, taking hourly observations of the sun. These gave 89°55`. We might very well have been satisfied with the results, but we had plenty of time and the weather was so fine so why not try to observe the pole itself? On the 16th we therefore moved our tent the remaining 5 nautical miles (9 kiloms.) further south and camped there. We made everything as comfortable and snug as possible in order to take a series of observations throughout the twenty-four hours of the day. The altitudes were observed every hour by four men with sextant and artificial horizon.

The observations will be worked out at the Norwegian University. With this camp as centre we drew a circle with a radius of 4 ½ nautical miles and marks were put down. From this camp we went out for 4 miles in different directions. A little tent we had carried with us in order to mark the spot was pitched here, and the Norwegian flag with the Fram pendant hoisted on the top of the tent. This Norwegian home got the name "Polheim." Judging from the weather conditions, this tent may stay there for many years to come. In the tent we left a letter addressed to H.M. King Haakon the 7th, with information of what we had done. The next man will bring it home. Besides we left some clothing, a sextant, an artificial horizon and a hypsometer.

Roald Amundsen and Helmer Hanssen checking their position, using a sextant and an artificial horizon.

AMUNDSEN LANTERN SLIDE 126: FM/JFO

Editor's note:

Your Majesty, 15th December, 1911

Allow me to inform you that yesterday, on the 14th December, after a successful sledge journey from our winter quarters at Framheim, five men from the Fram expedition - myself included - arrived at the South Pole area. According to observations, the position was 89°57′30′′ S. We left for the pole on 20th October with four sledges, 52 dogs and provisions for four months. We have ascertained the southernmost point of the Great Ross Ice Barrier [86°S], as well as the point where Victoria Land and King Edward VII Land meet. Victoria Land ends here, while King Edward VII Land continues southwards to 87°S, where we found an impressive chain of mountains with peaks up to 22,000 feet. I have taken the liberty - with your permission, I hope - of naming them the Queen Maud Range.

We have found that the great inland plateau begins to slope gently downwards from 89° S, with an altitude of approximately 10,750 feet.

Today we marked the geographical South Pole with a radius of 8 km and raised the Norwegian flag. We have called this gently sloping plain, on which we have succeeded in establishing the position of the geographic South Pole, King Haakon VII's Plateau, with, I hope, Your Majesty's permission.

We will start the journey back home tomorrow with two sledges and 16 dogs. We are well provided for with provisions.

Yours sincerely,

Roald Amundsen

Fram-Expeditionen

15 decbr 1911.

Deres Majestæt.

Hermed tillater jeg mig at meddele, at 5 mand av Framexpeditionen – mig selv iberegnet – ankom her til sydpolområdet – ifölge obs. 89°57′30″ S.Br. – igår den 14 decbr. – efter en vellykket sledetur fra vort vinterkvarter "Framheim". Vi forlot dette den 20 oktbr. med 4 sleder, 52 hunde og proviant for 4 måneder. Vi har på vor vei bestemt den store "Ross barrierens" utstrækning mot syd – ca 86° S.Br. – samt Kong Edward VII's Land's og Victoria Lands sammenslutning på samme sted. Victoria Land ophörer her, mens Kong Edwards Land fortsætter i SØ'lig retning indtil ca 87° S.Br. med en mektig fjeldkjede med topper indtil 22000 f.o.h. Disse sammenslutende fjeldkjeder har jeg tillatt mig at kalde – som jeg håper med tilladelse – "Dronning Maud's kjeder". – Det store inlandsplatau fandt vi – på ca 88° S.Br. – at gå over i en helt flat höislette, som atter ved 89° S.Br. ganske svakt begyndte at skråne ned mot den anden side. Slettens höide o.h. er ca. 10750 f. –

Vi har idag med en radius av 8 km omkredset den geografiske sydpol, heist det norske flag og kaldt den svakt skrånende slette, hvorpå det har lykkes os at bestemme den geografiske sydpols beliggenhet for "Kong Håkon VII's Vidde" med – som jeg håper – Deres Majestæts tilladelse.

Vi begynder tilbakereisen imorgen med 2 sleder, 16 hunder og vel utstyrt med proviant.

Ærbödigst

Roald Amundsen

Halvorsen & Larsen Ld, Kristiania

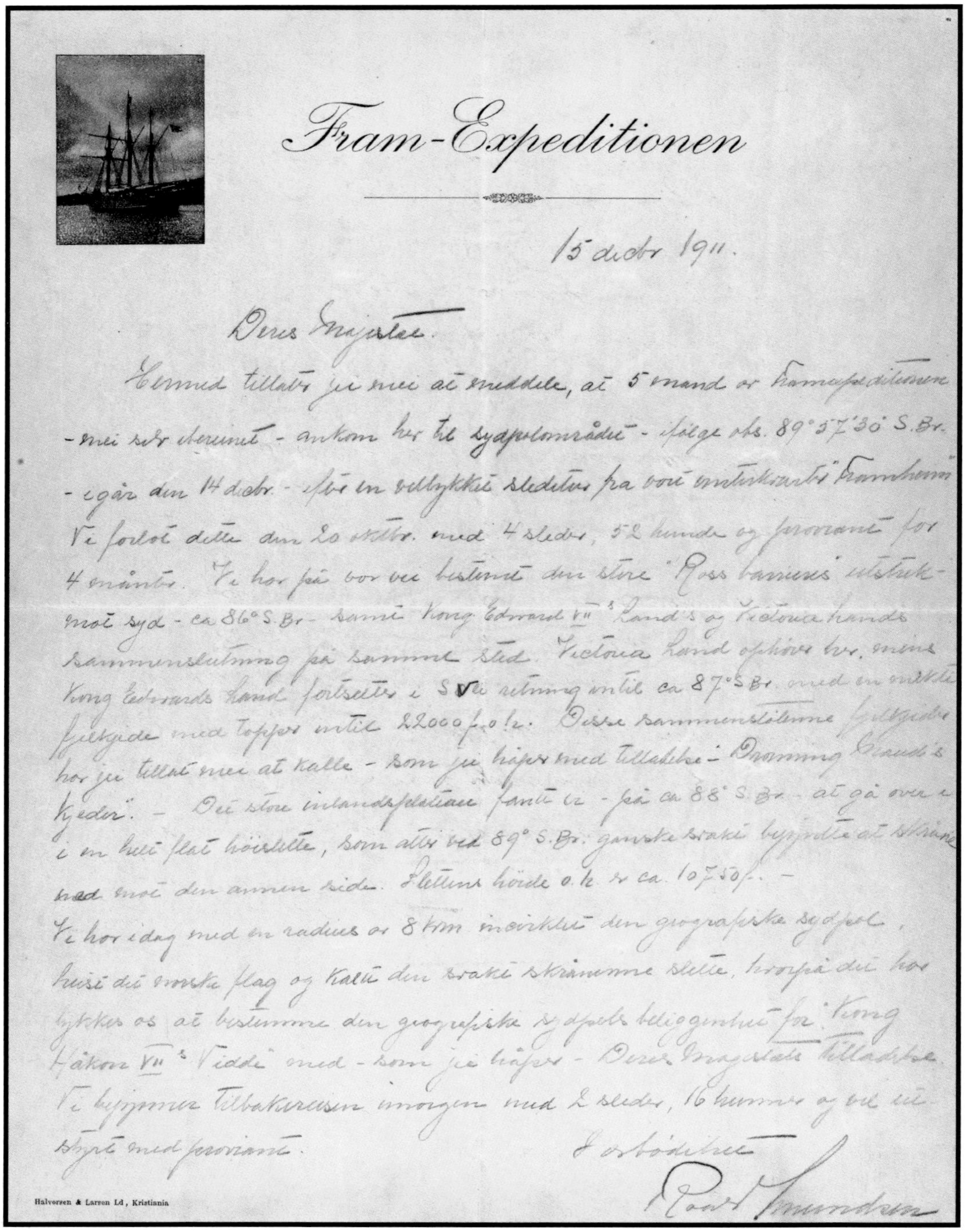

Photo: NB

On December 17 we were ready to start on the return journey. The outward journey had according to distance-meters a distance of 750 nautical miles (1400 kiloms.). The daily average speed had been 13 nautical miles (25 kiloms.). When we left the pole we had two sledges and seventeen dogs. Now we enjoyed the great triumph of being able to increase our daily rations, unlike earlier expeditions, all of which were obliged to go on short commons – already at a much earlier moment of time. The rations were also increased for the dogs, getting from time to time one of their comrades as an extra. The fresh meat had a recreating effect on the dogs and contributed, no doubt, to the good result.

A last look and farewell to Polheim and then off. We see the flag yet. It was still waving at us. It is gradually diminishing. Then it disappears; a last good-bye from the little Norway on the South Pole. We left King Haakon's Plateau as we had found it, bathed in sunlight. The main temperature during our stay here was – 13 Fahr. (-25° C). It felt much milder.

Oscar Wisting and his dogs.

AMUNDSEN LANTERN SLIDE 134: FM/JFO

Helmer Hanssen and his dogs at the South Pole.

AMUNDSEN LANTERN SLIDE 132: FM/JFO

AMUNDSEN LANTERN SLIDE 231: FM/JFO

Roald Amundsen, Helmer Hanssen, Sverre Hassel and Oscar Wisting are ready to return to Framheim on December 17.
Olav Bjaaland is taking the photo.

A chart showing the observations made at the South Pole.

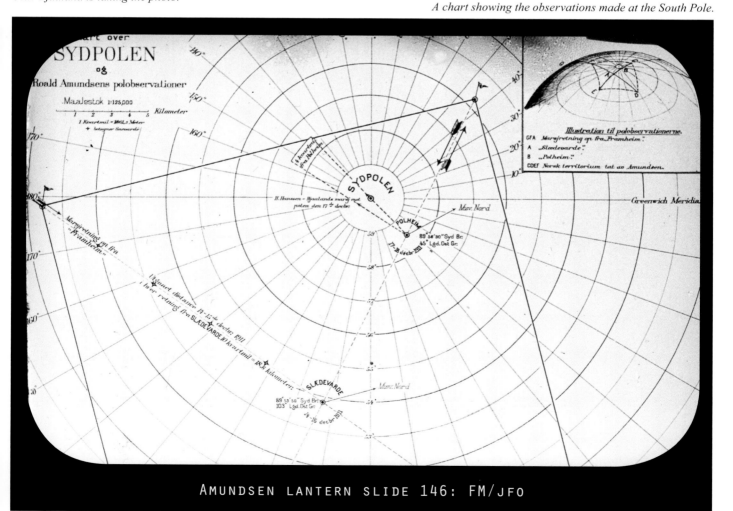

AMUNDSEN LANTERN SLIDE 146: FM/JFO

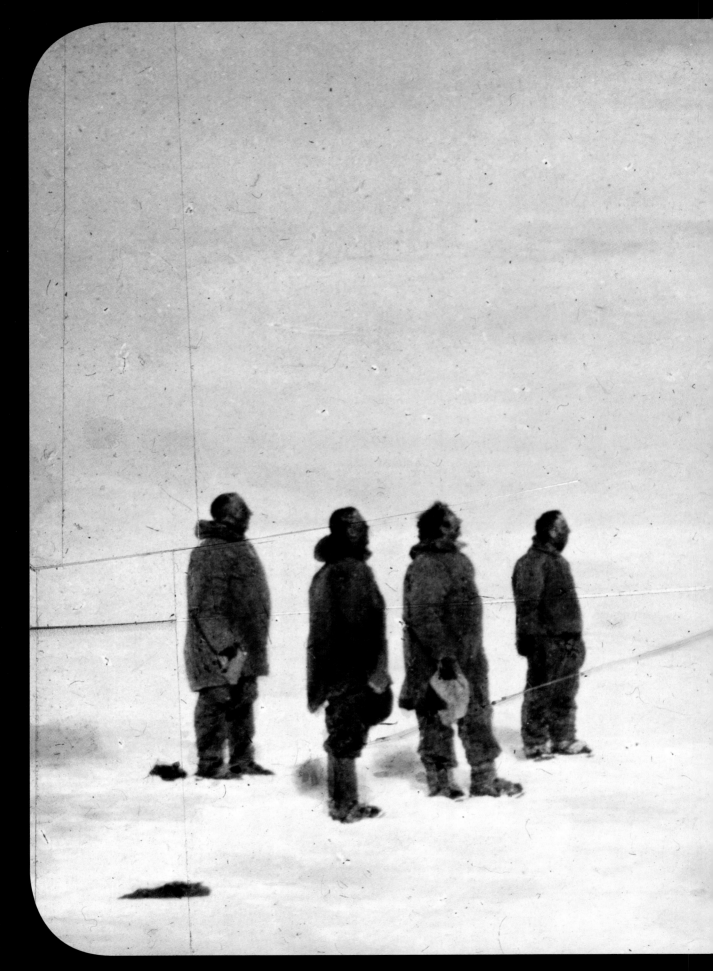

AMUNDSEN LANTERN SLIDE 233: FM/JFO

Editor's note:

From Roald Amundsen's The South Pole:

Of course, there was a festivity in the tent that evening not that champagne corks were popping and wine flowing no, we contented ourselves with a little piece of seal meat each, and it tasted well and did us good. There was no other sign of festival indoors. Outside we heard the flag flapping in the breeze.

Conversation was lively in the tent that evening, and we talked of many things. Perhaps, too, our thoughts sent messages home of what we had done. Everything we had with us had now to be marked with the words "South Pole" and the date, to serve as souvenirs. Wisting proved to be a first class engraver, and many were the articles he had to mark. Tobacco in the form of smoke had hitherto never made its appearance in the tent. From time to time I had seen one or two of the others take a quid, but now these things were to be altered. I had brought with me an old briar pipe, which bore inscriptions from many places in the Arctic regions, and now I wanted it marked "South Pole." When I produced my pipe and was about to mark it, I received an unexpected gift: Wisting offered me tobacco for the rest of the journey. He had some cakes of plug in his kit-bag, which he would prefer to see me smoke. Can anyone grasp what such an offer meant at such a spot, made to a man who, to tell the truth, is very fond of a smoke after meals? There are not many who can understand it fully. I accepted the offer, jumping with joy, and on the way home I had a pipe of fresh, fine-cut plug every evening. Ah! that Wisting, he spoiled me entirely. Not only did he give me tobacco, but every evening and I must confess I yielded to the temptation after a while, and had a morning smoke as well he undertook the disagreeable work of cutting the plug and filling my pipe in all kinds of weather. The weather had brightened again, and it looked as if midnight would be a good time for the observation. We therefore crept into our bags to get a little nap in the intervening hours. In good time soon after 11 p.m. we were out again, and ready to catch the sun; the weather was of the best, and the opportunity excellent. We four navigators all had a share in it, as usual, and stood watching the course of the sun. This was a labour of patience, as the difference of altitude was now very slight. The result at which we finally arrived was of great interest, as it clearly shows how unreliable and valueless a single observation like this is in these regions. The arrangement now was that we should encircle this camp with a radius of about twelve and a half miles. By encircling I do not, of course, mean that we should go round in a circle with this radius; that would have taken us days, and was not to be thought of. The encircling was accomplished in this way: Three men went out in three different directions, two at right angles to the course we had been steering, and one in continuation of that course. To carry out this work I had chosen Wisting, Hassel, and Bjaaland. Having concluded our observations, we put the kettle on to give ourselves a drop of chocolate; the pleasure of standing out there in rather light attire had not exactly put warmth into our bodies. On December 17 at noon we had completed our observations, and it is certain that we had done all that could be done. In order if possible to come a few inches nearer to the actual Pole, Hanssen and Bjaaland went out four geographical miles (seven kilometres) in the direction of the newly found meridian.

Bjaaland astonished me at dinner that day. Speeches had not hitherto been a feature of this journey, but now Bjaaland evidently thought the time had come, and surprised us all with a really fine oration. My amazement reached its culmination when, at the conclusion of his speech, he produced a cigar-case full of cigars and offered it round. A cigar at the Pole! What do you say to that? But it did not end there. When the cigars had gone round, there were still four left. I was quite touched when he handed the case and cigars to me with the words: "Keep this to remind you of the Pole." I have taken good care of the case, and shall preserve it as one of the many happy signs of my comrades' devotion on this journey. The cigars I shared out afterwards, on Christmas Eve, and they gave us a visible mark of that occasion. When this festival dinner at the Pole was ended, we began our preparations for departure. First we set up the little tent we had brought with us in case we should be compelled to divide into two parties. It had been made by our able sailmaker Rønne, and was of very thin windproof gabardine. Its drab colour made it easily visible against the white surface. Another pole was lashed to the tent-pole, making its total height about 13 feet. On the top of this a little Norwegian flag was lashed fast, and underneath it a pennant, on which "Fram" was painted.

Inside the tent, in a little bag, I left a letter, addressed to H.M. the King, giving information of what we had accomplished. The way home was a long one, and so many things might happen to make it impossible for us to give an account of our expedition. Besides this letter, I wrote a short epistle to Captain Scott, who, I assumed, would be the first to find the tent. Other things we left there were a sextant with a glass horizon, a hypsometer case, three reindeerskin foot-bags, some kamiks and mits. When everything had been laid inside, we went into the tent, one by one, to write our names on a tablet we had fastened to the tent-pole. On this occasion we received the congratulations of our companions on the successful result, for the following messages were written on a couple of strips of leather, sewed to the tent "Good luck," and "Welcome to 90." These good wishes, which we suddenly discovered, put us in very good spirits. They were signed by Beck and Rønne. They had good faith in us. When we had finished this we came out, and the tent-door was securely laced together, so that there was no danger of the wind getting a hold on that side. And so goodbye to Polheim. It was a solemn moment when we bared our heads and bade farewell to our home and our flag. And then the travelling tent was taken down and the sledges packed. Now the journey was to begin homeward, step by step, mile after mile, until the whole distance was accomplished. We drove at once into our old tracks and followed them. Many were the times we turned to send a last look to Polheim. The vaporous, white air set in again, and it was not long before the last of Polheim, our little flag, disappeared from view.

Kristian Prestrud ready for King Edward VII. Land.

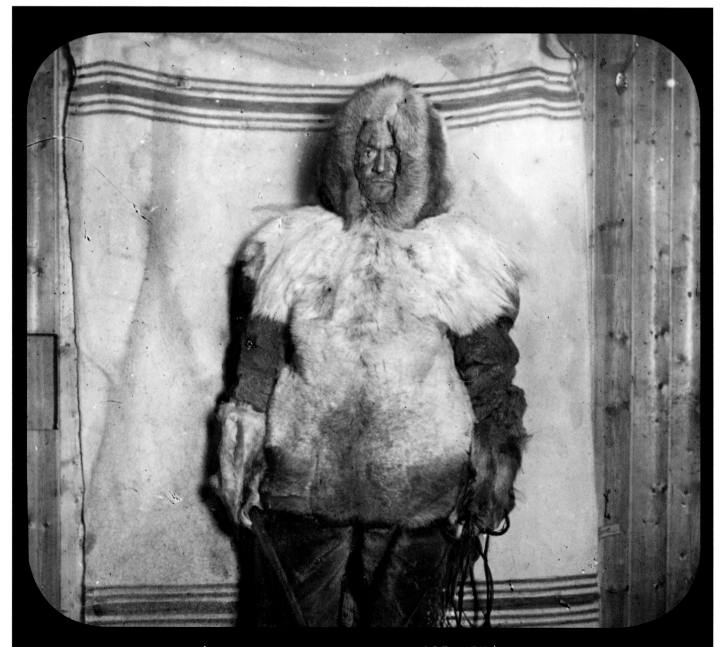

AMUNDSEN LANTERN SLIDE 105: FM/JFO

I am not going to weary the audience with detailed account of the return of the journey. I shall only mention a few incidents of interest. The beautiful weather we got on our homeward run exposed to our view the whole of the mighty mountain range, that is, the continuation of the two ranges joined in 86° S. The newly discovered range, trending in south easterly direction, was everywhere studded with peaks of height of from 10,000 to 15,000 feet. In 88° S the range disappears on the horizon. The whole of the newly discovered mountain ranges – about 460 nautical miles (850 kiloms.) - has got the name "Queen Maud's range."

All the depôts – ten in all – were found, and then abundant provisions, of which we at last had plenty, was taken along down to 80°, where they were deposited. From 86° we didn't go on rations, but everybody could eat as much as he liked. On January 25, we arrived at our winter quarters after an absence of ninety-nine days. The distance home, 750 nautical miles (1400 kiloms.) was thus covered in thirty-nine days without a single day of rest.

The daily average speed was 19,2 nautical miles (36 kiloms.). On our arrival we had two sledges and eleven dogs safe and sound. Not even a moment had we helped the dogs to pull the sledges. Our provision consisted of pemmican, biscuits, milk in powder and chocolate. Not much of a variation, but a healthy, nutritious food which invigorated the body, just what it needed. The best proof was, that we always felt well and were never raving about food, which has been so common in all longer sledge journeys and an infallible sign of deficient nourishment.

Prestrud, Stubberud and Johansen's camp on the barrier.

AMUNDSEN LANTERN SLIDE 204: FM/JFO

In the meantime Lieutenant Prestrud and his two companions had succeeded in doing excellent work to the east and in the neighbourhood of the Bay of Whales. They succeeded in reaching King Edward VII. Land – discovered by Scott – and confirm what we had seen. Alexandra Mountains appeared to be a holly snow-covered crest – 1200 feet high – stretching in a south-easterly direction as far as the eye could see, the northern boundary being two bare peaks - Scott's Nunataks - 1700 feet high. This expedition's exploration of Framheim's surroundings is of great interest. It appears from their observation, that the Bay of Whales is formed by underlying land still snow-covered.

Johansen and Stubberud on the top of Scott's Nunatak in King Edward VII. Land.

AMUNDSEN LANTERN SLIDE 127: FM/JFO

Stubberud and Johansen sounding through a crack in the ice using a hammer and a thin rope.

AMUNDSEN LANTERN SLIDE 128: FM/JFO

AMUNDSEN LANTERN SLIDE 219: FM/JFO

Framheim on the return of the South Pole party.

On January 16, 1912, the crew of the Fram met the Japanese expedition ship the Kainan Maru. It anchored near the Norwegian base.

AMUNDSEN LANTERN SLIDE 193: FM/JFO

AMUNDSEN LANTERN SLIDE 104: FM/JFO

Editor's note:

Nobu Shirase, the expedition leader of the Kainan Maru had originally intended to reach the South Pole but it was clear to him that he was now too far behind the other expeditions led by Roald Amundsen and Robert Scott. The second attempt at landfall on the Antarctic mainland began from Sydney Harbour on November 19, 1911. Now that the quest for the Pole was out of the question, attention was turned towards completion of scientific work and exploration at King Edward VII Land. They reached the Ross Ice Shelf on January 16, 1912. A party was sent ashore at a spot they named Kainan Bay but the ice was filled with so many crevasses that the safety of the men would be in constant jeopardy. Before long the men were startled to see another ship dead ahead.

At first they thought it might be a pirate but were subsequently reassured to learn that it was Amundsen's FRAM, which was waiting for Amundsen's return from the Pole. Visits were exchanged but language difficulties prevented any serious discussion.

A small party was sent ashore to investigate the ice and when they returned with encouraging reports Shirase decided to make it the starting point of his so-called Dash Patrol. On the first day blizzard conditions forced them to make camp after only eight miles. They struggled on, through terrible conditions, until January 28; they had covered 160 miles. The men stuck a Japanese flag, on a bamboo pole, into the ice and saluted the Empire with a threefold Banzai before burying a copper case containing a record of their journey. At this time Shirase made the wise decision to turn back for the ship.

The ship arrived Yokohama on June 20, 1912. The expedition had sailed over 30,000 miles since leaving Japan and despite not reaching the Pole, they had achieved all their other goals after departing from Australia. Their welcome in Yokohama was a tremendous reception. Source: Wikipedia.

Some of the members of the Japanese expedition on the barrier.

AMUNDSEN LANTERN SLIDE 205: FM/JFO

At the same time as our work inshore was going on, Captain Nilsen with his companions on the Fram succeeded in doing work with which, from a scientific point of view, probably will turn out to be the most valuable of the expedition. On an 8000 nautical miles' cruise from Buenos Aires to Africa and back, he took a series of oceanographic stations, sixty in all. Twice they circumnavigated the world, voyages full of dangers and toil. The voyage out of the ice in the autumn 1911 was of a very serious character. They were ten men all told.

Through darkness and fog, cyclones and hurricanes, pack-ice and icebergs, it became their lot to beat their way out. Last but not least let me mention, that the same ten men, on February 15, 1911, hoisted the Norwegian flag further south than a ship has ever sailed before.

A fine record in the century of records:

- Farthest north, farthest south.

The open sea at last.

AMUNDSEN LANTERN SLIDE 128: FM/JFO

AMUNDSEN LANTERN SLIDE 140: FM/JFO

The crew of the Fram on the arrival in Hobart on March 7, 1912. Top row from the left: Sverre Hassel, Ludvik Hansen, Steller (signed on in Buenos Aires), Olav Bjaaland, Halvardus Kristensen, Martin Rønne, Andreas Beck, Oscar Wisting, Halvorsen (signed on in Buenos Aires), Knut Sundbeck. Middle row: Hjalmar Johansen, Kristian Prestrud, Roald Amundsen, Thorvald Nilsen, Hjalmar Fredrik Gjertsen, Helmer Hanssen. Bottom row: Adolf Henrik Lindstrøm, Jørgen Stubberud, Karenius Olsen, A. Olsen (signed on in Buenos Aires).

Before Roald Amundsen's lecture, the President of Royal Geographical Society, made the following introduction:

A year and a half ago, at our annual dinner in London, I said that I hoped it might fall to my lot during my term of office to offer the right hand and welcome to the discoverer of the South Pole; and that, whether he proved to be a Norwegian or an Englishman, or a Japanese – for all three countries had sent out expeditions to the Antarctic Region – it would be a proud day in history of geographical exploration and a happy day for myself. The occasion has arrived, and we are here tonight to welcome, and to receive an account from his journey from, Captain Roald Amundsen, the brave Norwegian who has carried off the prize.

Roald Amundsen is no stranger to us. Five years ago, in 1907, he received the highest honour that is in the power of our society to bestow, viz. our Gold Medal, for his splendid work in the North Polar region. He had just returned from devoting three years of arduous work with a small band of his compatriots to exploration in the neighbourhood of the North Magnetic Pole, which he relocated, and in a tiny vessel of less than fifty tons burden he had been the first to sail through the entire Northwest Passage from Atlantic to Pacific – that passage which an Englishman, Sir John Franklin, had been the first to discover, which another Englishman, sir Robert McClure, had been the first to traverse, partly on the ice, from sea to sea.

The North Polar region has always been the special love of Captain Amundsen's life, and to it, I believe, he is still prepared to devote years of labour, drifting on that broad ocean current that has already carried his countryman and patron, Nansen so far; and thereby resuming the scientific work for which he has received such liberal support from his compatriots. In the interval, fired by the achievements of our countrymen, he diverged from his appointed path, and was suddenly heard of at the other end of the globe, camped on the Great Ice Barrier, with the famous Fram, Nansen's ship, which brought him, lying in the Bay of Whales. It was from this starting point that he had chosen his band of fellow-countrymen, five in number, finally started, on October 20, 1911, for that swift dash to the Pole, the incidents and the issue of which he is here to narrate to-night.

You will gain from his narrative and his slides a picture of that wonderful region; no frozen plain of snow and ice, except on the polar plateau itself – which is 10,000 feet above the level of the sea – but a land of mighty peaks 15,000 feet in height, of riven glaciers, and of formidable danger.

Our guest was attended throughout by a good fortune upon which we congratulate him: fine weather, sound health, a transport that never broke down, a commissariat that never failed. With these invaluable aids, he and his brave companions traversed the 750 miles that separated them from the South Pole and the same distance back with a speed that has never been equalled in the history of polar exploration; and on December 14, 1911, he planted the flag of his country upon the Pole itself. I have seen the results of his scientific observations, which have been carefully worked out by the learned Prof. Alexander, of Christiania, and there can not be a doubt that, though the Pole itself is not a spike or spot in the ground visible to the naked eye, Amundsen and his men crossed and recrossed the actual site.

But pray do not imagine that luck or good fortune is the sole or the main ingredient in such a success. Polar triumphs are not compassed without originality in conception, or without running great human risk; they are not achieved without a courage, a patience, and an endurance that dignify humanity; above all, their main justification lies in addiction that they make the sum total of human knowledge. The whole lifetime of Captain Amundsen has been a scientific preparation for successful accomplishment, in the laboratory, on the sea, and amid polar ice and snow.

He will now himself tell us the tale of his adventures and their results. It is my agreeable task to say that as Englishmen we do not grudge to a Norseman the success which is not inaptly won by the descendant of a race of born explorers and traditional pioneers.

We know no jealousy – though there is abundant emulation – in the field of exploration; and even while we are honouring Amundsen this evening, I am convinced that his thoughts no less than ours, are turning to our brave countryman; Captain Scott, still shrouded in the glimmering half-light of the Antarctica, whose footsteps reached the same Pole, doubtless only a few weeks later than Amundsen, and who with unostentatious persistence, and in the true spirit of scientific devotion, is gathering in, during an absence of three years, a harvest of scientific spoil, which when he returns will be found to render his expedition to the most notable of modern times.

The names of these two men will be perpetually linked, along with that of a third, Sir Ernest Shackleton, in the history of Antarctic exploration, and two of the three we shall have the pleasure of hearing tonight.

I will now call upon Captain Amundsen to read his paper.

After the lecture, there was a list of speakers:

Ernest H. Shackleton (1874-1922). Photo: FM

Sir Ernest Shacleton:

I will be very brief over this, because time is getting late. It is very easy to move a vote of thanks after hearing a lecture such as this, and all I can say is that I congratulate Captain Amundsen most heartily on the way he has told the story and on the way he has done the work. Lord Curzon, at the beginning of the lecture, said that a great point about it was organization and efficiency of equipment, at that seems to have been the keynote of the whole expedition, and it is by efficiency, not only by good luck, that such an expedition can come to a successful conclusion.

Of course, I say quite frankly that we all here no doubt wish it had been a British expedition that got there first, but none the less we are proud of Amundsen having got there, and we can all recognize that not only has he done the work well, but was supported by loyal comrades.

There is one thing – throughout the lecture tonight I never heard the word "I" mentioned; it was always "we". I think that that is the way which Amundsen got his men to work along him, and it brought the successful conclusion.

I have nothing more to add but to give a vote of thanks to Captain Amundsen for the splendid lecture and the work he has done so well, and which everyone in the world must be proud of.

The President:

I am going to ask Dr. W. S. Bruce, one of our most successful scientific explorers, who himself has been three times to the Antarctic Regions, besides being one of our Gold Medallists, to second the vote of thanks.

William Speirs Bruce (1867-1921). Photo: FM

Dr. W. S. Bruce:

It gives me very great pleasure indeed to second the vote of thanks which Sir Ernest Shackleton has so ably proposed. We have listed to Captain Amundsen's account of his work in the South Polar regions with intense interest, though one feels that he has really told us very little in proportions to all he has done. Thinking of the fine record from the athletic point of view, one and all of us agree in giving all praise to Captain Amundsen for his successful efforts in that direction. But this Society must do something more than that, and it has done so this evening in recognizing the valuable scientific work Captain Amundsen has done in the South Pole regions. He has twice traversed a course of more than 900 miles over land and ice, which no human being has ever traversed before; and has consequently brought back entirely new geographical information of an extensive unknown portion of the Earth's surface, thus adding to the sum of human knowledge in a most important manner.

The map he showed us and the pictures of the lands in those regions were of the greater interest. It is of special importance that I have heard from him to-day that he has succeeded in bringing back rock-specimens, not only from south of 85° S, but from King Edward VII. Land, which may give us the clue to the whole geology of the Antarctic continent on that side of the pole. The most important is that he has found the mountain range that Shackleton discovered extending to the south-east as far as 80° S, and also that from a point in 86° S, he has found a range stretching to the north-east.

He also saw an "appearance of land" between that range and King Edward VII. Land to the east of his track in 83° S. That solves a very important problem; for there are two theories of the Antarctic continent which have advocated in recent years. The one is that there is one land-mass, and the other that there are two land-masses divided by a barrier running from the Ross Sea to the Weddell Sea. To my mind the researches of the Scotia condemned the idea that there could be such a barrier running across. Later Shackleton's discoveries condemned that suggestion, which was not founded on scientific fact, and now Amundsen has thoroughly cleared up the matter, for he found the great mountain range bounding the inland plateau to the north continuing north-east to King Edward VII. Land, thus shutting the Ross Barrier into a bight.

That is a scientific result of the greatest possible importance. Amundsen had also done much more which one cannot refer to this evening, in meteorological, oceanographical, and other lines of scientific research.

Great as have been my pleasure in listening to Captain Amundsen tonight, still more am I glad to have been allowed to the privilege of seconding the vote of thanks to him.

The President:

I will now put the vote of thanks for one of the most absorbing and, as Sir Ernest Shackleton truly said, one of the most modest lectures to which we have ever listened, and almost I wish that in our tribute of admiration we could include those wonderful good-tempered, fascinating dogs, the true friends of man, without whom Captain Amundsen would never have got to the Pole. I ask you to signify your assent by your applause.

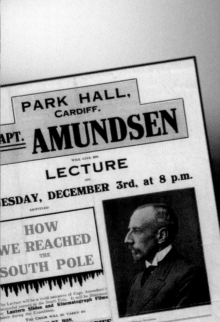

Paper read by Hon. HENRY LUND, Consul of Sweden and Norway before the GEOGRAPHICAL SOCIETY OF THE PACIFIC in San Francisco, California, on 28th February, 1905

Subject:

To the Magnetic North Pole

The Norwegian "GJÖA" Expedition

Under the Command of ROALD AMUNDSEN

THE GEOGRAPHICAL SOCIETY OF THE PACIFIC

SAN FRANCISCO, April, 1905.

At a special meeting of the Council held April 11th, 1905, Mr. Lund's paper upon the Amundsen expedition to the North Magnetic Pole was ordered printed, with chart and illustrations.

PUT TO PRESS, APRIL, 1905

THE NORWEGIAN "GJÖA" EXPEDITION TO THE MAGNETIC NORTH POLE.

IN THE Summer of 1903 Captain Roald Amundsen and seven men left Norway in the little sloop "Gjöa" for Greenland, whence to go into the Arctic north of this Continent for the purpose of ascertaining the exact present location of the magnetic north pole and afterwards to endeavor to find their way through the northwest passage and then via the Bering Strait to the port of San Francisco.

In February last year I received a letter for Capt. Amundsen from his brother Mr. Leon Amundsen in Christiania with a request to have same sent, if possible, up to the mouth of the Mackenzie River there to await him, and also asking me, if I could arrange for further communications for the vessel to be transmitted there. To this I replied, that Mr. H. J. Knowles of this City very kindly offered to carry all such letters by his whaling ships, leaving this port every spring, to Herschel Island, and that he furthermore promised, that his captains would render the expedition all the assistance in their power, should they meet with the "Gjöa". In October last Mr. Leon Amundsen thanked me very much for this and begged me to draw the attention of the public here to this expedition through our local press, and which I again wrote him, that I should be most happy to do, provided the matter could come to me in some official or semi-official way, and as to which I suggested him seeing Professor Nansen or Consul Heiberg of Christiania. Some few weeks since I received his reply to this with a letter to me from Professor Nansen, of which the following is a translation.

LYSAKER PER CHRISTIANIA, 10 Decbr. 1904.

Dear CONSUL LUND,
San Francisco.

By Mr. Leon Amundsen here, a brother of Capt. Roald Amundsen, I am told that you desire some direct communication from me regarding the Amundsen expedition, I will therefor inform you, that I myself have had considerable to do with this affair, and that I am personally well acquainted with Capt. Amundsen. He has made a very favorable impression upon me, and he possesses all the qualities necessary for a first class leader of an expedition. Besides he has thoroughly studied and made himself conversant with the matter, viz: the solving of the question of the magnetic pole. Adding to this, that the expedition is exceedingly well prepared for several years and is well fitted out in every way, I believe, that there is every reason to hope that it will bring results of much value. I for my part should also consider it very probable, that it will be able to find the much sought after northwest passage. From the article I wrote and which Mr. Leon Amundsen will send you herewith together with the article written by Capt. Amundsen himself, you will no doubt get a good impression, together with all the particulars of the object of the expedition. It would unquestionably be well, if something could be done beforehand to make the expedition known to the American public, and I believe particularly, that it would be desirable, if the authorities in Alaska could be made acquainted with the expedition and its object, so that they there would be prepared to extend assistance to its members, should such be needed. To me it appears possible, that the "Gjöa" may already next fall show up on the coast of Alaska, though I consider it more probable, that it will not happen before 1906 or 1907.

With friendly greetings,
Yours Respectfully,
(signed)   FRIDTJOF NANSEN.

On receipt of this letter I consulted with my much esteemed friend here Professor George Davidson, how something about this matter could best be made known, and I suggested, that I might get up a paper on the subject to be read before the Geographical Society of the Pacific, of which he is the President, and I am one of the Directors. Of this he approved, and I have him to thank for this excellent chart of the regions Capt. Amundsen is exploring, and for other particulars regarding distances, locations, etc.

In the early part of the nineteenth century geographers were much occupied with the question of a passage north of this continent from the Atlantic to the Pacific; this lead to the first Sir John Franklin and the Lieutenant Parry expeditions. A few years later Professor Hansteen of the University of Christiania published researches made by him on terrestrial magnetism, and in 1828 his Government with the co-operation of that of Russia sent him on a mission to Western Siberia, where, erroneously, a pole of magnetism was then believed to exist. This attracted much the notice of all the students of physics of Europe, and particularly of England, where the search for a formula, by which the variation of the needle might be found at any given time

and place, was then being actively pursued, which brought about the expedition of Sir James Ross to the waters north of this continent resulting finally in his locating on the 1st June 1831 the Magnetic North Pole on the Boothia peninsula at 70° 05' N. Lat. and 96° 46' W. Long. The next expedition into these waters was with a view of finding the Northwest passage, and which was the tragic second one of Sir John Franklin, that left England on the 19th May 1845 in the ships "Erebus" and "Terror" with 138 officers and men. In order finally to ascertain the fate of this expedition several subsequent ones were sent out, the last of which was the one by Lady Franklin in the steam yacht "Fox" in 1857 in command of Sir Leopold McClintock, who eventually brought back the sad news, that Sir John Franklin died on 11th June 1847, and the survivors deserted their ships on 22nd April 1848, but perished afterwards from hunger, cold and privations. Numerous expeditions have since gone into the Arctic Ocean amongst others the one of Baron Nordenskjöld in the "Vega" in 1878, who succeeded in finding the north-east passage, viz: north of Europe and Asia from the Atlantic to the Pacific. Then came the ill fated expedition of Capt. De Long, who left this port in 1879 in the "Jeannette" via Bering Strait to endeavor to reach the Geographical North Pole, the still unaccomplished aim of so many others since, amongst them Lieutenant Peary, Dr. Fridtjof Nansen in the "Fram" and Prince Luigi of Savoy, not to mention the deplorable one of Professor Andrée in his balloon.

The subject of this paper however, the expedition of Capt. Roald Amundsen in the little Norwegian sloop "Gjöa" is the first one since that of Sir James Ross having for its main object the exact locating of the Magnetic North Pole, and must therefor from a scientific standpoint be considered the most important one, but it is also the intention of Capt. Amundsen subsequently to endeavor to find his way through to the Bering Strait, whence to come to this port possibly this fall, but more probable not before next year or even 1907.

I shall now with your permission give you a translation of what Capt. Amundsen had to say about his expedition before starting, and then follow that up with Professor Nansen's comments at the time on the undertaking.

CHRISTIANIA, 2nd Novr. 1902.

TO THE MAGNETIC NORTH POLE.

THE "GJÖA" EXPEDITION BY ROALD AMUNDSEN.

Since the finding of the position of the Magnetic North Pole by

THE NORWEGIAN "GJÖA" EXPEDITION

Sir James Ross in 1831, this part of the earth, where the magnetic needle points straight towards the center of the earth, and where the ordinary compass becomes useless, has not been further explored. As most of you will know it is supposed that the magnetic poles are not fixed points, but move slowly in the course of years. Different opinions have been entertained by the Scientists regarding this change of the poles as well as the position of the pole and the direction of the possible move. No certainty can be arrived at, before a series of exact investigations have been carried out at the very spot.

The expedition, which I now intend to undertake, will have for its main object the location of the magnetic pole and in the whole surrounding locality to carry out a number of continuous observations through an extended period in order, if possible, to determine these open questions. It is certainly superfluous to mention, that the solution of these questions is of great importance for the understanding of the earth's magnetism and physics.

The plans of my expedition have therefor also met with much interest in the scientific world. I shall briefly give the main features of my plans. We will be eight men in all. The vessel of the expedition is the Arctic ocean sloop "Gjöa". This boat, which already on many occasions has proved its staunchness, has now been further strengthened with large cross-beams in the hold, connections between these, the deck beams and the keel, and finally sheathed with 2 inch planks as a protection against the ice. The boat is now also furnished with a petroleum motor, by the aid of which it can make a speed of about 4 miles. As far as I know "Fram" made about 4½ to 5 miles. We will carry with us a supply of petroleum of about 27,000 liter. Of these 10,000 liter are calculated to be consumed for lighting, heating and cooking. The remaining 17,000 liter will be sufficient for the use of the motor for 100 days at full speed, which will correspond with a distance of 2400 Norwegian sea miles. The distance between the island of Disco on the west coast of Greenland and the Bering Strait, according to the route I intend to follow, is about 700 Norwegian sea miles.

"Gjöa" is of about 47 regr. tons, about 70 feet long from stem to stern and 20 feet broad. This vessel may seem very small, and it is probably one of the smallest, which has ever started on an extended polar expedition; but it is done with full consideration. Many will perhaps say, we cannot force the ice with such a small vessel, and that the room will be too small for both the members and

TO THE MAGNETIC NORTH POLE

stores. To this I will answer, that it has never been my intention to try and force the ice with the "Gjöa". I have concluded to use patience and slip through, when opportunity offers. The passages and straits through which we must seek our way to reach our goal, are all small and narrow and generally filled with drift ice. The many attempts, which have been made in forcing them, have all failed. From experience therefor it is known, that if you want to get through these waters, you must slip through, and just here the small vessel is superior, because it needs less room and consequently is easier to maneuvre. Thus, what has not been attained with large vessels and force, I will try to attain with a small vessel and patience.

The accomodations for the members will not be large, but comfortable and good. There will be sufficient room for provisions and outfit.

We will sail in the beginning of May, 1903, first to Goodhavn on the island of Disco off the west coast of Greenland, where the Danish Government has permitted us to buy Eskimo dogs. (I will here refer you to the map of the Polar region, through which the expedition will pass). From Goodhavn the course is set across Melville Bay to Lancaster Sound—the sound south of Jones' Sound, where the "Fram" was lying during the last expedition. From Lancaster Sound we turn towards the south through the Prince Regent Strait to Bellott Strait, the strait between Boothia Felix to the south and North Somerset Land to the north. Magnetic observations will be taken as often as possible. If the ice conditions are favorable, we will continue through the Bellott Strait southerly along the west coast of Boothia Felix. Should then the magnetic observations so far made signify that we are in the vicinity of the Magnetic Pole, two men will be landed here with provisions for two years and the necessary materials for the building of a magnetic observatory and living house. As materials for the houses it is my plan to use the packing boxes, which therefore are made with this object in view, they being all made of tongue and groove boards and of the same size. By filling these boxes with earth and placing them on top of each other the walls can be quickly raised. The roof will be laid with tongue and groove boards. The inside and outside of all will then be covered with roofing paper and the whole covered with snow, which easily will make a sufficiently warm house. In order to avoid disturbances in the magnetic observations, the boxes will be nailed with copper nails.

8   THE NORWEGIAN "GJÖA" EXPEDITION

The necessary quantities of provisions and material having been brought ashore, these two men will commence the building of the observatory and the installation of the self-recording magnetic instruments, while the vessel continues southward and will seek a harbor for the winter in shelter of King William Island. As soon as the vessel is secure I, with a companion, will start for the two men left on the coast of Boothia in order to give them assistance with the preparations for winter. Everything having been arranged I and my companion will return to the vessel. While the magnetic observations are being attended to by the two men at Boothia Felix, we on board will prepare for the coming spring.

As soon as there is opportunity the sleigh expeditions in different directions will be commenced, and as much scientific work as possible carried out. Myself with a companion will start out for magnetic observations to try to ascertain the position of the pole. In the course of the spring and the fall of 1904 I hope to finish the work.

The spring expedition being over the different sleighing parties will collect at the vessel further west and seek winter quarters on the south side of Victoria Land. The spring of 1905 will be occupied in examining the surrounding lands. In the fall of 1905 I will again seek connection with the magnetic observatory of Boothia Felix to bring instruments, etc., back to the vessel. The direct distance between the south-east point of Victoria Land and the south point of King William Land and Boothia is 40 Norwegian sea miles and between the south point of Victoria Land and Boothia 30 Norwegian sea miles. In the summer of 1906 we will continue further west with the vessel and take magnetic observations as often as there is an opportunity. We will seek winter quarters possibly under the Herschel Island. The winter and spring will be used for different observations.

With the breaking of the ice in the summer of 1907 we will seek around the northwest point of America and down the Behring Strait.

(Signed)   ROALD AMUNDSEN.

As for distances I may mention, that from Erebus Bay, Beechey Island (which is in latitude 74-¾°) to the Magnetic Pole is about 320 English nautical miles. From the Magnetic Pole to anchorage under south side of King William Land is about 160. From that anchorage to the southeast point of Victoria Land is about 120 and from the Magnetic Pole to the southeast point of Victoria Land is about 150. The Magnetic pole is just a little west of and about

---

TO THE MAGNETIC NORTH POLE   9

2000 statute miles north of Omaha. The course that Capt. Amundsen will follow after leaving King William Land will be more or less on the 70° north latitude, a little south of the latitude of North Cape, about 600 English miles north of the latitude of the following places, viz. Cape Farewell on the southern point of Greenland, northeast point of Labrador, middle of Hudson Bay, Mount St. Elias, northern neck of peninsula of Kamschatka, Siberia Yakutsk region, St. Petersburg, Stockholm, Christiania, Bergen and Shetland Islands, all of which are in about 60° north latitude.

The distance from Greenland to Bering Strait is 3460 English nautical miles made up thus:

650 miles from Goodhaven to Dalrymple Island
180 miles thence to Cape Horsburg
280 miles thence through Lancaster Sound to Erebus Bay
320 miles thence to Magnetic Pole
160 miles thence to south side of King William Land
740 miles thence to Cape Bathurst on the Arctic Ocean
260 miles thence to Herschell Island
390 miles thence to Point Barrow
480 miles thence to Bering Strait
―――――
3460 miles

Here follows what Professor Nansen says on 7th November, 1902:

THE NEXT POLAR EXPEDITION

THE PLANS OF CAPT. ROALD AMUNDSEN

How many have not, during quiet night watches, in steering their course after the never failing magnetic needle and following the vibrations of the compass needle, with wonder been thinking about the mysterious force, which we do not know, but which is always present, turning the needle towards the North, ready to show the traveler the way both on land and on sea. But still more mysterious is this force, when we reflect, that it steadily from year to year, slowly changes both in direction and strength, without it being as yet possible to find the cause thereof. Already long time ago Arago could say: "Nothing is more mysterious in the physics of the earth than the causes of the ever and everywhere occurring changes in the terrestrial magnetic elements"—and we know no more about it at this day. Are these changes due to changes in the inner mass of the earth? Or are they perhaps due to cosmogenic causes, f. i.: changes on the sun? We do not know! Are these changes followed by transfer of the magnetic poles? We suppose so, but can say nothing thereof with certainty; we must take observations at these very poles through an extended period. Only one thing is certain, that the direct observations at points all over the earth constantly has brought surprises in spite of the most scientific previous calculations. To lift a corner of the veil that covers this riddle, is nothing less than that which Capt. Roald Amundsen has set as his goal, and towards which he has already been working for several years with a patient energy and composure, which is fully in keeping with the importance of the task.

From an article by Amundsen himself of Sunday, 2nd Novbr, the readers of the paper will know the principal features of the plans of the expedition, upon which he will start in the coming spring in his small vessel the "Gjöa" together with seven companions. A venturesome expedition! many will say; too high flying plans with such small means! perhaps others will say: I do not believe either the one or the other. The object is truly nothing less than seeking the magnetic pole itself and there during a period of years make observations,—this pole, that by James Ross only has been incompletely investigated in 1831. Thereupon Amundsen will try to make the northwest passage, that has been tried in vain by so many ships during centuries. Even if the objects may seem big, it is my impression, that the plans are so well considered, and the preparations so carefully made, that the expedition has good prospects of succeeding. Capt. Amundsen is one of those, who have made the important discovery, that the success of a polar expedition principally depends upon the preparations which were made before the expedition started out. It will soon be a year, since on the 25th Novbr, 1901, in the Geographical Society of Christiania he first presented his plans to the public. But already in the previous year he had quietly commenced the preparations for his expedition, the cost of which he intended entirely to defray from his own means. Already as a boy the polar regions attracted him, and he has continued to educate himself in the thought thereof. In 1890 he took his student examinations; in 1894 he made his first trip to the Arctic ocean in the sealer "Magdalena;" in 1895 he passed his examinations for mate; in 1896 we find him again in the Arctic ocean, this time in the sealer "Jason;" in 1897 to 1899 he took part in the Belgian South Pole Expedition with the "Belgica"

as first mate. Shortly afterwards in the fall of 1900 he was asked from the United States of America, if he would be willing to take a vessel up to Peary, who was then on his expedition to Smiths Sound. This offer he declined, because the plans for his own polar expedition had now taken definite shape, and he went systematically ahead with the preparations for it. It is characteristic for Amundsen, that first of all he thought of his scientific observations and sought the famous Magnetician Dr. Neumayer of Hamburg, under whose guidance he studied the use of the magnetic instruments. Upon his consultations with him he also ordered the number of instruments, which are necessary for a satisfactory accomplishment of his great task.

The next step was to secure the vessel with which to undertake the voyage. First he thought of making a trial trip in one of the sloops from Tromsö to the Arctic Ocean in order simultaneously to carry on oceanographic investigations, particularly of the east Greenland polar-current, which were considered very important to complete the observations made during the first "Fram" expedition across the polar sea. But Amundsen, finding that he could not arrange satisfactorily for any vessel, bought just as well at once in Jany., 1901, his vessel the Arctic Ocean sloop "Gjöa". With this he then made a five months trip, from April to Septbr., 1901, to the Barentz Sea and to the Arctic Ocean between Spitzbergen and the east coast of Greenland. During this voyage he collected valuable material of oceanographic investigations. It is of particular importance, that he penetrated far into the east Greenland polar-current, with which the "Fram" drifted across the polar sea, and there made a series of highly important observations. The revision of this material, which rests with the present author, is not yet completed, but will contribute in throwing a new light over the circulation of these seas, they being more complete and taken with far greater accuracy, than the very deficient material we previously had.

Since that time Amundsen has been constantly occupied with the preparations for his expedition, and these he has completed with the thoroughness, which is particularly his. The vessel has been furnished with a petroleum motor and strengthened with large inside beams, etc., instruments have been tried and new ones procured, the question of provisions discussed most carefully with Professor Torup, and the experiments carried out, etc. In short, there is nothing thoughtless about it.

What prospect has the expedition of success? I believe good.

The magnetic North Pole differs from that of the earth's (let us call it mathematical North Pole, because it is only a mathematical point) in two particular respects: 1. The magnetic North Pole is comparatively easy to reach, whereas the mathematical North Pole has proved itself as presenting some difficulties. 2. Investigations of the magnetic pole is of much scientific interest, whereas the mathematical pole is of small or no scientific interest, to reach it is to be compared with the ascension of a high mountain.

Admitting that Amundsen's vessel is small, and smaller than that of most of the polar expeditions, still I see no reason, that he should not with that and with sleighs be able to push forward to the magnetic pole, wherever it may be—either on land or sea. It is true, that with the small power of his engines he cannot expect to force his way, where the ice prevents, but when it comes to the point, it would not be any far distance, that any vessel could force itself through ice on an expedition of that kind, it would cost too much fuel. In a pinch, when a narrow strip of ice obstructs, it is well to have power, but against this counts strongly, that a small vessel like "Gjöa" is much easier to handle in the ice, to find a secure harbor on the Coast, when the ice is pressing, and especially that it draws so little water, that it can slip through into the open water, which usually is found between the drift ice and the land along most of the coast lines; there the small vessel will have advantages over the large one, as it can steal along the shallow coast, where the ice bergs, going so much deeper, perhaps lie grounded outside, and if the vessel itself should ground, it is easier to get her off than a larger and heavier vessel. I therefore think, that as for the main goal, Amundsen has reasonable prospects of reaching it, if not opposed by obstacles entirely unforeseen. The most pleasing in his plans however is perhaps, that he will not be satisfied by getting there and setting a record, but has planned his expedition so, that he should undertake a systematic investigation of the whole field around the magnetic north pole, and will in a way commence, where James Ross ended, and so to say make a magnetic chart of all this region and determine, whether this pole is one point or an extended area, or perhaps even several points. The investigations of James Ross were made with the incomplete instruments of that time, and in several respects may be doubtful; to have this region researched with a magnetic outfit so completely modern as Amundsen's is, as the prominent magnetician Professor

A. Schmidt has stated, at present the most important matter at issue in the domain of terrestrial magnetism. To find a man who has so many qualifications in the different respects, to solve the question, would be difficult.

When Amundsen has also thought of trying for the northwest passage, he does not himself seem to lay much stress thereon, but he evidently thinks, it will be an achievement, which he may take in, when anyway he has arrived so far west; and certainly many will agree with him herein. Scientifically considered this part of his plan is not so much of interest as the first; but it fits so beautifully into all of it, that it would be almost a sin to exclude it, especially as this continuation of the voyage will not fail to give important scientific results, when the time is made use of. Nor do I see any reason, that it should not succeed. That the vessel is small may as we have seen, be a defect, but has also its great advantages, and it is possible to carry fuel for the engine for many times the distance to be covered, if the vessel should find open water the whole way. The most difficult piece perhaps will be to penetrate from Bellott Strait along the west coast of Boothia Felix, the peninsula, where Ross found the magnetic pole. In the straits of this region the conditions of the ice may possibly be difficult, we know little thereof, but there is hardly any reason to suppose that they should be impossible. There is a strong, tearing current, which would seem to be strong enough to break up the ice in the summer; it only depends upon finding the favorable moment, and Amundsen is a man who seems to have time to wait; does he not get through one summer, he may succeed the next. It is also fortunate for him that this is just the locality where, for the sake of his principal object, it is especially important to make a long stay. When he first has got through this portion and reaches south to the coast of the American continent, there seems hardly to be any greater difficulties to reach the Bering Strait, and thus for the first time complete the northwest passage. Along the American north coast there is certainly every summer sufficient open water for the "Gjöa" to steam through with its little petroleum motor.

I have heard the objection, that it would be venturesome to start out on such a long voyage with so few companions; but this objection seems little considered.

The few companions, in my opinion, is rather an advantage, especially for long voyages.

has threatened such is the scurvy; but the best remedy against this is, besides a supply of good provisions from home, to be able to procure for the members sufficient fresh food; it is therefore plain that the fewer the members, the better will the game hold out that can be found in the locality. And another point: if an accident should happen, and the vessel had to be abandoned, then it is better the less members. If it becomes necessary to procure food with the rifle, it is important not to have too many mouths to feed, and even eight men may then be too many; it would be of advantage to divide in still smaller bodies, in order to have less difficulty in finding the necessary game. If the unfortunate Franklin expedition had consisted of 8 men and not of 138, we might have seen them all back to Europe in good health; instead of that, they all perished. Another advantage of Amundsen's plan is, that the whole time he will be passing through a region comparatively rich in game, where there are good prospects of keeping alive by hunting, if the vessel and outfit should get lost. It will thus be understood, that even if the expedition at the first glance may appear venturesome, it is, when more closely examined into, solidly planned and not any bolder than compares with the importance of the task.

I mentioned before, that from the beginning it was the intention of Amundsen to carry on the expedition with his own means. His plans were then to allow himself to be landed on the Hudson Bay, and then send the vessel out for a catch, in order thus to cover part of the expenses. He has certainly in a high degree improved upon the prospects of a rich scientific result, when he now will seek directly to the field of his labors with the vessel itself. But this has increased the expenses, and his own means do not any longer suffice. He has already from two private persons received substantial aid; but he needs more, and here is an opportunity for those who take an interest in this part of the research.

When Capt. Amundsen next year with his little vessel starts out on his well prepared expedition, he will be sure to have the best wishes of the whole Norwegian people, and with great expectation, we will after some years, wait for the first tidings from the brave little band, that the Norwegian flag has been carried to a new victory in the service of science.

LYSAKER PER CHRISTIANIA, 7 Novbr. 1902.
(Signed)   FRIDTJOF NANSEN.

The "Gjöa" Capt. Roald Amundsen finally left Christiania, Norway, at midnight 17th June 1903 with his crew of seven men, and in due course arrived safely in Greenland. Before leaving there he presumably made known certain places on his contemplated voyage, where reports of his voyage might be looked for by whalers. The first, and only one so far, reached Norway 29th Novbr. last, having been found cached at the foot of the Franklin Monument on Beechey Island by the Captain of a Danish whaling ship and brought by him to Copenhagen. This was published, reading translated as follows:

"Gjöa". EREBUS BAY, BEECHEY ISLAND, 24 Aug. 1903.

The expedition left Dalrymple Island on Sunday the 16th August 1903 at 8 p. m., after having taken onboard the deposits left there, the weather being quite favorable. The members of the Danish Literary Greenland expedition were landed on Saunders Island (Agpar) and the course was then set true west. Wostenholme Sound was almost entirely free from ice, though there was considerable grounded ice bergs at the entrance. From the latitude of Cary Island the course was set straight for Cape Horsburgh, and which the expedition reached on Thursday the 20th August. The weather was clear and calm, the waters free from drift ice and but very few ice bergs were to be seen. Sailing through Lancaster Sound the weather was thick and foggy, and the wind was fresh easterly. Around Philpot Island there was a small stretch of drift ice with some stranded ice bergs in between. Outside of that no ice was met with in the Sound. Erebus Bay was reached on Saturday the 22nd, the bay completely free of ice. Yesterday from the highest point on Beechey Island it was observed, that the sea westward was free of ice. There was fog in the Wellington Channel and southward.

The Depots of the British Government were found completely destroyed. The Franklin Monument and the graves are in order. Some coals were taken onboard from the depots.

Both declination and inclination observations were taken on shore.

Declination (or variation of the compass) is about 135° west. Inclination about 88½°.

Some geological material has been obtained. The expedition leaves this P. M. for Peel Sound.   (Signed)

ROALD AMUNDSEN.
GODFRED HANSEN.
(")   K. D. F.
All well on board.

P. S.—This document will be enclosed in a tin box, which after being soldered will be deposited at the foot of the Franklin monument.

In conclusion, I can only add, that this report giving the deviation as 135° west goes to show that the magnetic pole must be to the southwest from where the observation was taken, and, what is of more importance, the inclination being 88½° is conclusive proof that Capt. Amundsen was then not far from the spot where the pole is situated, for the nearer you get to it, the greater the angle until at the pole it is 90°.

The expedition was certainly extraordinarily fortunate the first year. The wind and the ice conditions were so unusually favorable, that it was not found necessary to seek the first winter quarters at North Devon Island, but the voyage was continued the first summer westward and southward towards the intended field of observations to Peel Sound and Franklin Strait along the west coast of North Somerset Island and the Boothia peninsula, where the magnetic pole is supposed to be. Under these favorable conditions the expedition will in all probability have saved one year.

We will now hope that Capt. Amundsen's expectations may be fully realized, so that he will be able to give to the world all that valuable information he is now seeking, and that we may have the pleasure of welcoming him and his seven other brave companions here healthy and well, if not this year, then next year.

Subsequent to the above paper being read, I may now add that I directed a letter to the Honble. F. S. Stratton, Collector of Customs at this port, asking the favor of having the information about this expedition conveyed to the Captain of any U. S. Revenue Vessel that might go into Alaska waters, and in case they should fall in with the expedition, to kindly render it such assistance as it might require, In reply to this, which the Honble. Mr. Stratton sent on to the Government at Washington, he kindly sent me a copy of letter received from the Treasury Department informing him that my request would be complied with, and that the Captains would be directed to obtain information, if possible, of the expedition. The Honble. Governor of Alaska I also wrote, in case inhabitants of that Territory should fall in with the expedition, to render it what assistance it should require.

No. 57 MAYFAIR.
TELEPHONE:

1, Savile Row,
Burlington Gardens,
London, W.

October 12th, 1906.

Capt. Amundsen,
  C/o The Norwegian Consul.,
  San. Francisco.,
     United States.

Dear Capt. Amundsen,

Let me send you on behalf of the Society, and on my own behalf, our warmest congratulations on the success of your Expedition. You have accomplished a great feat in getting your ship right through the North West Passage, and I am quite sure from what Dr Nansen tells me that your two years observations around the North Magnetic Pole must be of the greatest scientific value. I am sure that you have made many observations in other directions which will be of much Geographical interest.

I had a long talk with Dr Nansen about you, in which he told me a good deal about your affairs. I think that if matters are properly managed you ought to make a considerable sum out of the results of your Expedition. I am sure that you will be careful not to give away any information about your work, and about your adventures to Newspaper Interviewers for nothing.

If things are properly managed you ought to make a considerable sum out of Articles for the Newspapers, out of Lectures, and also out of the book which I have no doubt you will publish as soon as possible. But you must not be in too great a hurry to make definite arrangements with American Newspapers and American Publishers, or even with English Newspapers and Publishers. It is possible that you might receive a handsome offer for Articles, or for your book before you return to England, but you must be careful to see that whatever arrangement is made, is made in writing.

Personally, I think that your best plan would be to wait until you come to England, when I think that Dr Nansen and I might be of real service to you in enabling you to make the best of the results of your three years work. Dr Nansen and I discussed whether it would be better for you to come home in your ship, or to leave the ship and come home direct, and arrive here as soon as possible. Dr Nansen says that if you can get a handsome sum for your ship, he thinks you might sell it, if not, there is no

LETTERS REGARDING THE NORTHWEST PASSAGE LECTURES

TELEPHONE:
No. 57 MAYFAIR.

1, Savile Row,
Burlington Gardens,
London, W.

ROYAL GEOGRAPHICAL SOCIETY · 1830

2.

doubt that if you came home round Cape Horn with your ship, and so practically circumnavigated America and then came straight across the Atlantic and came up the River Thames to London, it would produce a very great effect upon the British Public, and thereby you would probably be able to get more money out of the Newspapers and out of the Publishers. At any rate we both agreed that you should come to London first and give your first account of the Expedition to our Society. Without going into details you will see the importance of doing so.

In order to please the Americans you may have to give a Lecture to one of the Societies in America and Dr Nansen thinks that if you do so, you may be able to make arrangements to return to America and give a series of Lectures in different cities, for which you will be well paid. However, I have no doubt that you will use your own judgement in the matter and do what you consider best in your own interests, and in the interests of the Expedition and of Science. I need not say how anxious we are all

here to learn the detailed results of your long and continued work. You have managed the whole of the Expedition wonderfully well, and deserve every credit. Of course, we should like to publish in our Journal a summary account of the results of your work as soon as possible, with a good map, which I have no doubt you have made, and also with some of your photographs. I should be glad to hear from you as soon as you arrive in San Francisco.

Hoping to see you soon.

Yours very truly,

J. Scott Keltie

TELEPHONE:
No. 67 MAYFAIR.

1, Savile Row,
Burlington Gardens,
London, W.

November 22nd, 1906.

Capt. R. Amundsen,
    Christiana,
Norway.

Dear Capt. Amundsen,

Let me congratulate you on your safe and successful return to your home; I am glad to see that you have met with a reception which you thoroughly well deserve. I hope that we shall see you here very soon. No doubt Dr Nansen will arrange with you as to the date. I should like of course, that Dr Nansen himself should be here when you come over, and as he will be in Norway during the whole of January, we had better make your Meeting in February; I think February 11th. Please let me know if that will suit you. I suppose December would be too soon for you. Our two dates for that month are already engaged, but of course if December would suit you better than any other month, we could manage to arrange a date. Of course we should pay your expenses, and should probably be able to put you up at the Royal Societies Club. I should like to hear

from you on this subject as soon as possible. If I can be of any service to you with regard to the English Edition of your book, or for Articles in English Papers, I should be very glad.

Yours very truly,

[signature]

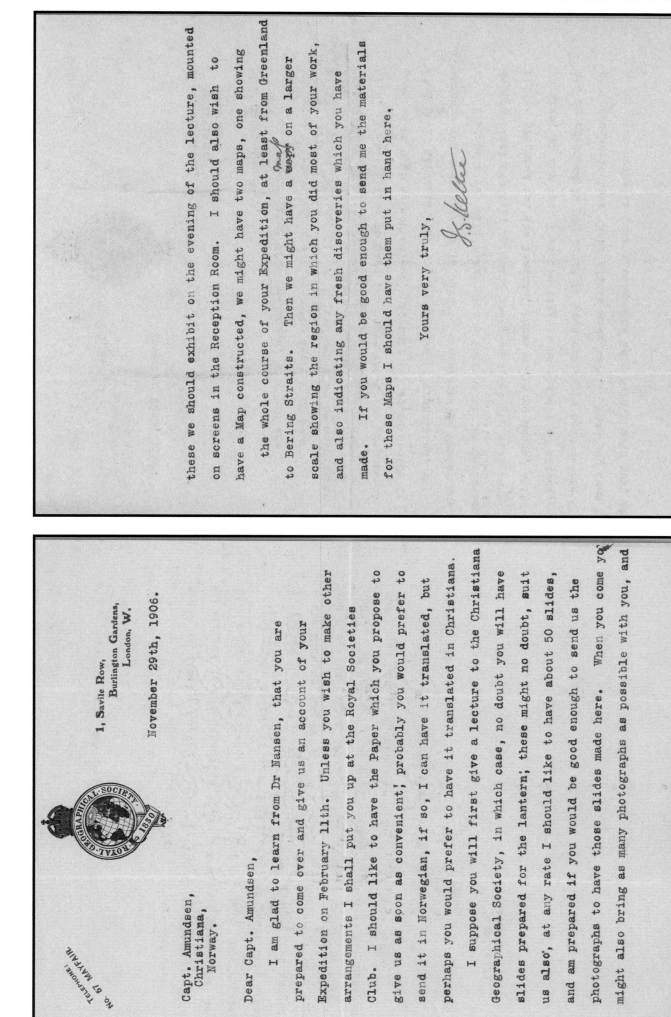

these we should exhibit on the evening of the lecture, mounted on screens in the Reception Room. I should also wish to have a Map constructed, we might have two maps, one showing the whole course of your Expedition, at least from Greenland to Bering Straits. Then we might have a copy on a larger scale showing the region in which you did most of your work, and also indicating any fresh discoveries which you have made. If you would be good enough to send me the materials for these Maps I should have them put in hand here.

Yours very truly,

TELEPHONE.
No. 67 MAYFAIR.

1, Savile Row,
Burlington Gardens,
London, W.

November 29th, 1906.

Capt. Amundsen,
Christiana,
Norway.

Dear Capt. Amundsen,

I am glad to learn from Dr Nansen, that you are prepared to come over and give us an account of your Expedition on February 11th. Unless you wish to make other arrangements I shall put you up at the Royal Societies Club. I should like to have the Paper which you propose to give us as soon as convenient; probably you would prefer to send it in Norwegian, if so, I can have it translated, but perhaps you would prefer to have it translated in Christiana.

I suppose you will first give a lecture to the Christiana Geographical Society, in which case, no doubt you will have slides prepared for the lantern; these might no doubt, suit us also, at any rate I should like to have about 50 slides, and am prepared if you would be good enough to send us the photographs to have those slides made here. When you come you might also bring as many photographs as possible with you, and

your work better known in England, and thus you will have a better chance of getting a good price both for your book and your lectures. Mr Randall will explain things fully to you when he returns to Norway; I have told him also about your lecture. The paper which you ought to write should be a Paper for publication in the Journal giving an adequate account of your scientific work, including your Geographical work and of your voyage through the North Western Passage. Extracts from that might do for the Lecture; but you might prefer to prepare a somewhat popular lecture dealing with what you consider would be the incidents and results of your Expedition likely to interest an intelligent audience, who do not profess to be specialists. This, with a good series of lantern slides, would I feel sure prove quite interesting, and probably lead to satisfactory arrangements being made for a course of Lectures elsewhere.

I shall be glad to get the materials from which to make a Map, not only of your route, but of the work which you did all round the region of the North Magnetic Pole. I would like to

---

TELEPHONE No. 67 MAYFAIR

ROYAL GEOGRAPHICAL SOCIETY. 1830

1, Savile Row,
Burlington Gardens,
London, W.

December 13th, 1906.

Capt. Roald Amundsen,
Missions Hotellet,
Christiania, Norway.

Dear Capt Amundsen,

I have had a long talk with Mr Randall about your affairs. He is doing his best here to get your Article accepted for some English Magazine; I have tried to put him in the way of getting this done. I impressed upon him as I wish to do upon you, that you should not hurry to make any bargain about the publication of your book in England until you have given your lecture to this Society; also you should not make any arrangement with Mr Christie about giving Lectures in England until after that. You ought to get a good price for your Lectures here. Mr Chrisite might offer you £10 a lecture, but you should not lecture for that, I think you ought to get at least £25 a Lecture, but as I say do not be in any hurry to make any arrangements.

I have no doubt that when you give us your Lecture here it will attract a good deal of attention and make your name and

1, Savile Row,
Burlington Gardens,
London, W.

January 16th, 1907.

Capt. Roald Amundsen,
Christiania,
Norway.

Dear Capt. Amundsen,

I have yours of the 8th, in which you state that you are sending me some Maps of your expedition, and also 100 photographs for exhibition. We shall take care that they are not copied. I presume that you will bring with you your own slides for showing by means of the lantern during the time that you give your lecture. Please to let me know this, as otherwise we must make the slides ourselves. Also let me know what are the dimensions of your slides so that we may see whether or not they fit our lantern. It is very important also that I should have the MS. of your lecture within the next few days, especially if it is written in Norwegian, as I must then have it translated. But even if it is in English I ought to have it without delay.

You say that you will bring with you a Secretary, perhaps

1, Savile Row,
Burlington Gardens,
London, W.

2.

get this put in hand as soon asppossible in order to be ready for the Meeting.

Yours very truly,

TELEPHONE:
No. 67 MAYFAIR.

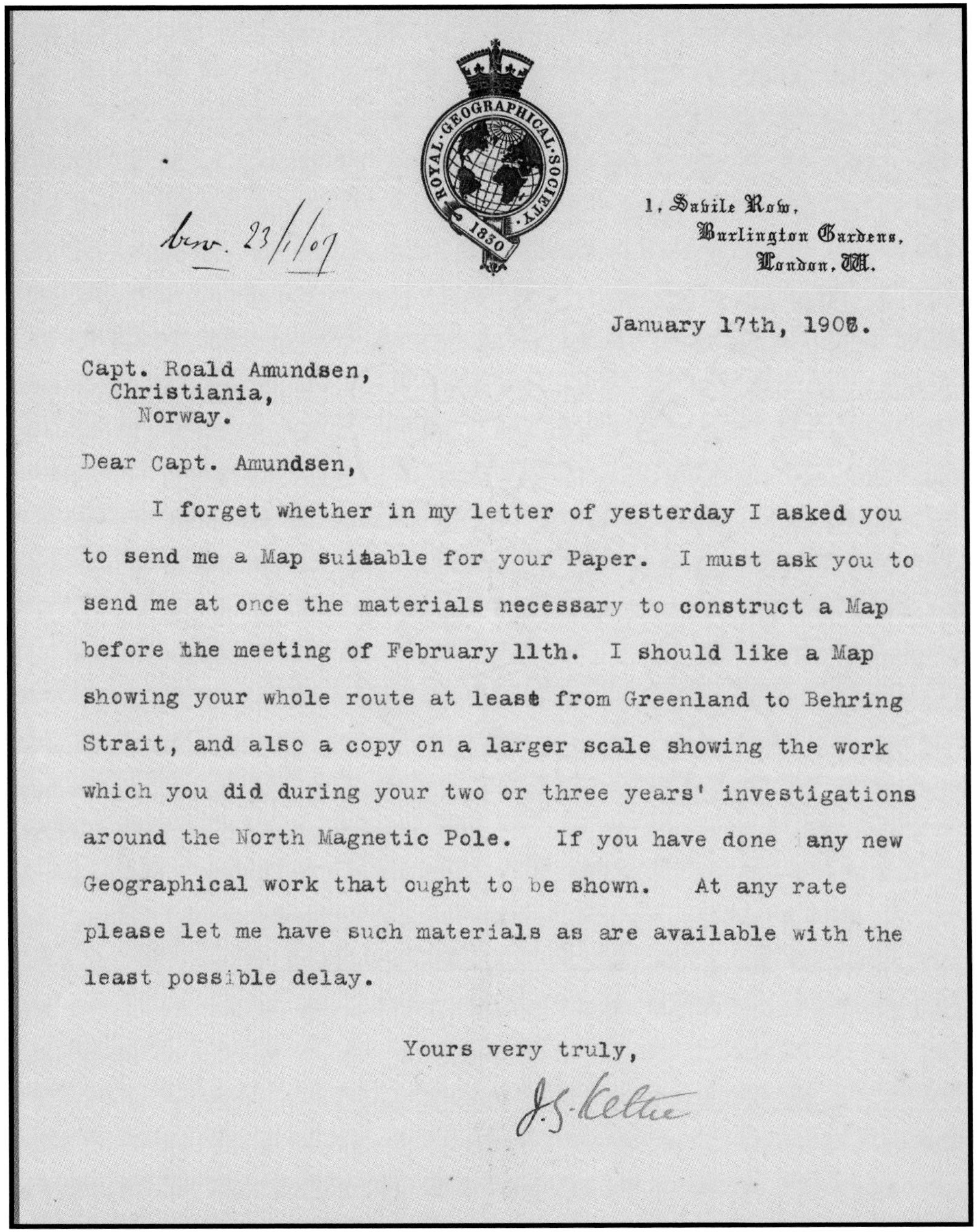

1, Savile Row,
Burlington Gardens,
London, W.

January 17th, 1908.

Nov. 23/1/01

Capt. Roald Amundsen,
Christiania,
Norway.

Dear Capt. Amundsen,

I forget whether in my letter of yesterday I asked you to send me a Map suitable for your Paper. I must ask you to send me at once the materials necessary to construct a Map before the meeting of February 11th. I should like a Map showing your whole route at least from Greenland to Behring Strait, and also a copy on a larger scale showing the work which you did during your two or three years' investigations around the North Magnetic Pole. If you have done any new Geographical work that ought to be shown. At any rate please let me have such materials as are available with the least possible delay.

Yours very truly,

J.S. Keltie

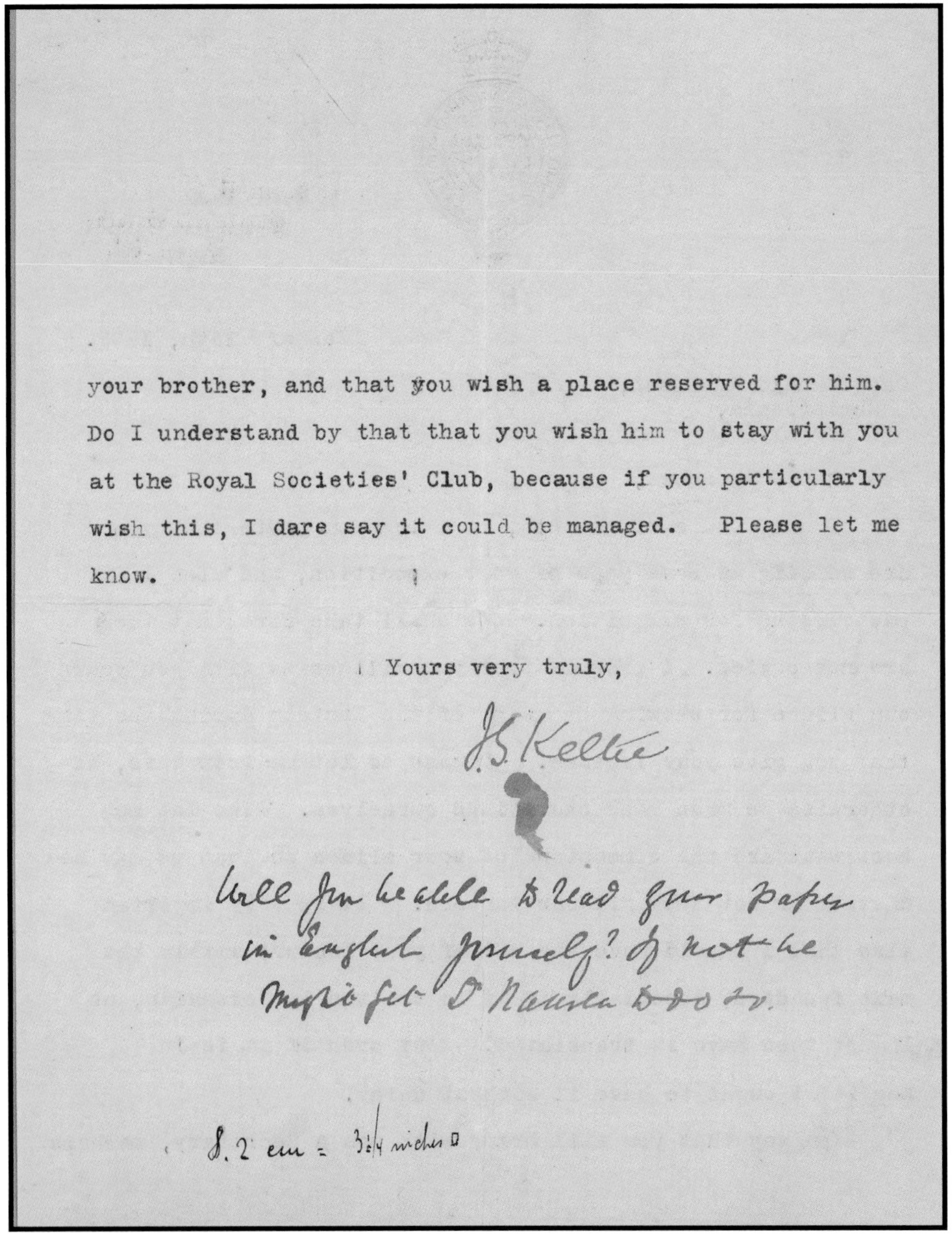

your brother, and that you wish a place reserved for him.

Do I understand by that that you wish him to stay with you at the Royal Societies' Club, because if you particularly wish this, I dare say it could be managed. Please let me know.

Yours very truly,

J.S. Keltie

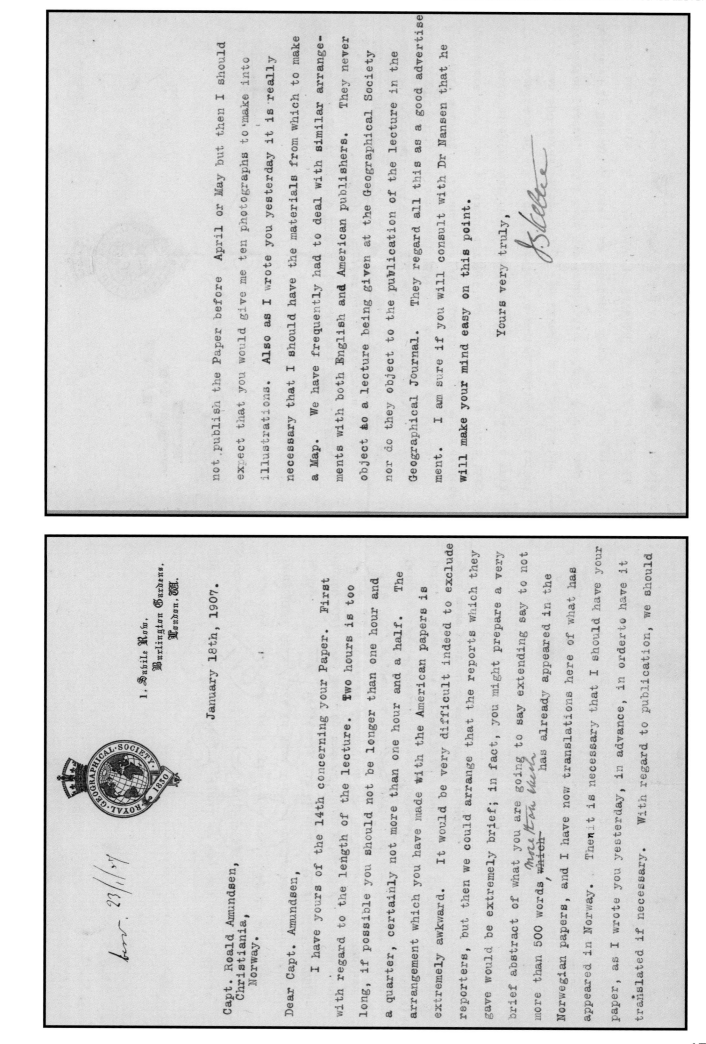

1, Savile Row,
Burlington Gardens,
London, W.

January 18th, 1907.

Capt. Roald Amundsen,
Christiania,
Norway.

Dear Capt. Amundsen,

I have yours of the 14th concerning your Paper. First with regard to the length of the lecture. Two hours is too long, if possible you should not be longer than one hour and a quarter, certainly not more than one hour and a half. The arrangement which you have made with the American papers is extremely awkward. It would be very difficult indeed to exclude the reporters, but then we could arrange that the reports which they gave would be extremely brief; in fact, you might prepare a very brief abstract of what you are going to say extending say to not more than 500 words which has already appeared in the Norwegian papers, and I have now translations here of what has appeared in Norway. Then it is necessary that I should have your paper, as I wrote you yesterday, in advance, in order to have it translated if necessary. With regard to publication, we should

not publish the Paper before April or May but then I should expect that you would give me ten photographs to make into illustrations. Also as I wrote you yesterday it is really necessary that I should have the materials from which to make a Map. We have frequently had to deal with similar arrangements with both English and American publishers. They never object to a lecture being given at the Geographical Society nor do they object to the publication of the lecture in the Geographical Journal. They regard all this as a good advertisement. I am sure if you will consult with Dr Nansen that he will make your mind easy on this point.

Yours very truly,

for him there, so that you may always have him when you want

him. Please let me know the exact date, and if possible the

hour when you will arrive in London.

Yours very truly,

1, Sabile Row,
Burlington Gardens,
London, W.

ROYAL GEOGRAPHICAL SOCIETY. 1830

January 22nd, 1907.

Capt. Roald Amundsen,
Christiania,
Norway.

Dear Capt. Amundsen,

I am glad to have yours of the 19th, and to find that

you are sending me your Maps and Paper in English. I have

no doubt you speak English very well, but the best plan will

be when you arrive in England to get you to read a portion of

the Paper in the Hall where the lecture will take place. If

you find that you could not make yourself quite intelligible,

perhaps you might read a portion of the Paper at the meeting,

and allow Dr Nansen if he is willing, to read the remainder.

However, we shall see about this when you come over, and also

decide as to how many slides it will be possible to show in

an hour and a quarter.

If you would prefer to have your Secretary to stay in

the Club with you, - and I have no doubt he would be quite a

suitable person for the Club, - I shall be glad to engage a room

1, Savile Row,
Burlington Gardens,
London, W.

January 30th, 1907.

Capt. Roald Amundsen,
Christiania,
Norway.

Dear Capt. Amundsen,

I am sending you two proofs of your Lecture. Each of the pages will take 6 minutes at least to read and if you read the whole of it it would take you nearly two hours. I am sorry to say that this would be much too long and you should not take much more than one hour or one hour and 10 minutes. I must ask you therefore to be good enough to take out what is equivalent to about 7 pages, in order that when you really read it at the Meeting you may not exceed the limit of time. Of course we shall publish the whole of the lecture in the Journal. I have marked some passages which might be omitted in reading but of course you will use your own judgement as to what shall be left out. Perhaps some of the more scientific passages might be omitted. I think I have already stated that it would not be possible to show 150 slides. I think that you

should try and reduce them to about 80 or 90 and what I particularly wish to do is to arrange so that each may be thrown on the screen exactly at the place where it is required in your paper. In this way there will be no difficulty in using 80 or 90 slides during the lecture as each would refer to a particular statement in your lecture, it would probably not be necessary for you to stop except occasionally in order to explain the slides. This I may say is what was done at the Duke of the Abruzzi's meeting and it was most successful. We also did it at Dr Nansen's meeting in the Albert Hall and also at Capt. Scott's. You could simply number the slides 1,2,3,4, etc., and put the corresponding number on the margin of your Paper. I send you the second Paper in order that you may put the numbers of the slides upon the margin of that, This second copy would be in the hands of the man who worked the lantern, so that he would be always ready without any signal from you to throw the slide upon the screen at the proper moment. I hope I have succeeded in making this quite plain to you. Please let me

1, Savile Row,
Burlington Gardens,
London. W.

February 2nd, 1907.

Capt. Roald Amundsen,
Christiania,
Norway.

Dear Capt. Amundsen,

I have read through your paper very carefully and find it quite interesting. I have already indicated what parts of it I thing you might either omit or cut down. I do not wish you to leave out all about the magnetic results as that is very important but I wish you could give a more definite statement as to the conslusions which you draw from your observations. And in the end you might also sum up the results as a whole with regard to the magnetic work, with regard to your Geographical discoveries, of which you made some, and also with regard to the Eskimo. You might also be able to state whether you think the ice in the Arctic is advancing or receding.

Yours very truly,

J. Scottletu

1, Savile Row,
Burlington Gardens,
London. W.

know if you have any doubt about what I mean. I hope you will let me know, if possible on the morning of Saturday February 9th, when you expect to arrive in London. When you do arrive take a cab and go direct to the Royal Societies' Club, 63, St. James's Street, where I hope to be able to meet you on your arrival.

Will you please when you are marking the passages of your paper to be omitted in reading at the lecture, to mark them on both copies so that I may have one to give to the man who works the lantern.

Yours very truly,

J. Nelce

A PROPOSED NORTH POLAR EXPEDITION BY ROALD AMUNDSEN.

READ AT THE ROYAL GEOGRAPHICAL SOCIETY, JANUARY 25, 1909

"By far the most important task left for geographical research to perform in the Arctic Regions is the exploration of the extent, depth, and character of the polar basin. A great part of this work could be accomplished by drifting through the unknown part of the polar basin – as the Fram Expedition in 1893-96 – north of the Fram's route."

These words were spoken by Prof. Nansen in his lecture before the Royal Geographic Society in London on April 29, 1907. There can scarcely be any difference of opinion on this question. The great polar basin is still lying there with its many unsolved problems, and seems to challenge us; and in our own minds we know perfectly well that we shall not give up until all these problems are solved. Nansen's drift in the Fram was an epoch-making event in the history of North Polar research. It showed us clearly and distinctly the only way in which the exploration of the polar basin could be accomplished – so clearly and distinctly that I have often and often been astonished that not one of the many who have since endeavoured to penetrate the mystery has profited by its teaching. But that is not all. It raised the veil that covered the Great Unknown, and showed us how much there was to be done. Side by side with the important results of this great expedition – perhaps, in front of the results – is the experience gained by the leader of the expedition. It was while drifting across the Polar Sea that prof. Nansen's eyes were opened to the numerous great defects that attached to the old methods of observation in use in the field of oceanic research. Since his return in 1896, he has contributed greatly to the creation of precise methods that have raised this branch of science from a more or less close approximation to a very high degree of accuracy.

If you take a map of the world and glance at it, you will at once be stuck by the proportion of land to water. While the mass of known land only amounts to one quarter of the Earth's surface, the remaining three quarters consist of sea. In order to put this in a still clearer light, I will mention a few figures.

The entire surface of the Earth measures 196,740,000 square miles in area, of which 141,011,000 square miles is sea, and 55,729,000 square miles land. The unknown region round the North Pole amounts to 1,930,000 square miles. The extent of the Polar Sea is about 5,790,000 square miles; that is to say, seven times larger than Greenland and twenty times larger than the Scandinavian Peninsula. The North Sea has an area of 193,000 square miles, or thirty times less than the Arctic Ocean. The

highest measured mountain, Mount Everest, is 29,002 feet in height, while the greatest observed deep, Nero deep, near the island of Guam in the Pacific Ocean, is 51,615 feet (5269 fathoms or about 6 miles).

It will be clearly apparent from these figures how small the amount of land is in comparison to the sea. It is, therefore, astonishing that men have not given more attention to oceanic exploration than has been the case. If you look at the list of the various exploring expeditions that have been undertaken in past years, you will soon see that only a very small number of them have had oceanic research as their object. It is a significant fact, too, that when "discoveries" were mentioned, it was always land that was meant, never sea; and an expedition that returned without knowledge of new lands, but only reported new seas, was considered to have yielded only negative results. That this was the case with the earlier expeditions is quite understandable. The hope of gain and power was the main force, and this could naturally only be gratified on dry land. No one saw the importance of the great ocean. It thus happened that most of the land was discovered and made known in a comparatively short time. But with the growth of culture, the exploration of the ocean came to be looked upon as quite as great a necessity as that of the land. The interest in the unknown depths of ocean increased greatly when the Atlantic cable came to be laid. And since the middle of last century, several large expeditions of this kind have gone out. Among the most important of these may be mentioned the Challenger expedition, 1872-76, under Sir Wyville Thomson and Sir John Murray, and the Norwegian North Atlantic Expedition in the Vöringen, under Profs. Mohn and Sars, 1876-78.

The Fram Expedition, as I have already said, was of very great importance in many respects. The fact, however, that Nansen did not wholly succeed in solving all the problems that the polar basin presents was due to the defective oceanographic methods of that day. It will be another matter now, after the progress that the science of method has lately made. An expedition with a modern equipment will be able to make its way into the polar basin with every prospect of being able to clear up much that is still incomprehensible to us.

I will now endeavour to set forth the problems that such an expedition will encounter, their significance and their manner in which they are to be solved.

valuable aid in the clearing up of the questions.

During the last few years, apparatus have been constructed, by Nansen and others, that can take samples from the bottom of the sea in such a way that not only the upper-most layer of ooze or mud can be examined, but also layers below that, to the depth of a couple of metres. The various layers of deposit can thus be seen, sometimes animal and vegetable remains, sometimes fine sand or other organic material. In most places, several such layers are found one above another, and they can then tell the history of long ages, in the same way that geological stratification of the deposited matter has been found in many places, such as the deeper parts of the North Sea, the Skagerak, the Atlantic and the Pacific. It tells of great changes that have taken place in the ocean basins, and of great variations in the temperature of the sea-water, and much more be-sides. It is just in a sea like the Polar Sea that such investigations will be of great inter-est. One naturally thinks of what geologists have found regarding the varying climatic conditions in Siberia, Greenland, on the Scandinavian Peninsula, and in many other places. The earlier expeditions have not had the necessary apparatus for such investi-gations; but now we have them, and all that is needed is that they shall be used.

I have endeavoured to put before you briefly some of the problems that it would be in-teresting to have investigated as far as the bottom of the polar basin itself is concerned; but it would be still more important to have the enormous volumes of water that fill this basin examined by means of the aids now at our disposal.

With the reversing thermometers of the latest construction, the temperature can be determined anywhere in the sea and in all depths with an accuracy of 1/100° C. The latest investigations in the Norwegian Sea, for instance, have been made with this degree of accuracy, and among other things it has been found that in the stratum, at a depth of between 546 and 820 fathoms, the temperature is between -1° and -1,3°. In the deepest strata it is uniform and quite constant. At the bottom of the Polar Sea, Nansen found somewhat higher temperatures, about -0,9°. This was one of the things that made him put forward his hypothesis of a ridge between Greenland and Spitsbergen. Further, his observations seem to indicate that the temperatures at the greatest depths rose somewhat towards the bottom. If there were no such ridge between Spitsbergen and Greenland, as Nansen assumes, the difference between the bottom-water of the Norwegian Sea and that of the polar basin might be explained as an effect of the tem-perature of the earth; but as the salinities, according to the determinations, are higher in the polar basin than in the Norwegian Sea, it does not appear to be the same kind of bottom-water; and this indicates the existence of a ridge.

When Nansen went out in 1893, he supposed, as he himself says, that he would find a relatively shallow Polar Sea, and had not, therefore, provided himself with sound-ing apparatus for great depths. It proved, however, that this assumption did not hold good. Instead of the shallow Polar Sea, he found a sea with depths of as much as 2187 fathoms. Sounding under these circumstances was a very difficult matter. We probably all remember the exertions of the Fram men to procure sounding lines for these great unsuspected depths; but they managed it, and made a number of very important soundings, which showed us that there was work enough to do here. They could not, however, with their primitive implements, satisfy the requirements of modern oceanic research. Nor was the one line in which the Fram drifted sufficient to determine the appearance of the entire sea; and we therefore still know nothing with certainty concerning the size, the form, and the greatest depths of this deep ba-sin. The methods of deep-sea sounding are now very good. By the aid of piano-wire and a winch with gearing, soundings of very great depths may be made in quite a short time, where the Fram's men would have toiled and slaved for days.

We have here (p. 443) a chart of the bottom of the Polar Sea and adjoining waters. The land here is white, and the various tints indicate the depths. Depths of more than 2000 metres (1093 fathoms) are black. As regards the Polar Sea itself, the only certain parts are those that lie along the line taken by the Fram, all the rest is guess-work. The deep part of the basin is bounded with relatively steep edges, just as in the Norwegian Sea; and between the edge and the shore there are flat banks of various widths. We notice the great continental shelf to the north of Siberia, where these shallow places are of much greater extent than in most other parts of the world. The continental shelf to the north of America we are still unacquainted with.

Nansen, after his investigations with the Fram, has assumed that there is a ridge running from the north-east of Greenland to Spitsbergen, which separates the deep parts of the Norwegian Sea and the Polar Sea from one another. The beginning of this ridge on the Spitsbergen side has been proved by soundings; and the discovery, by the Denmark Expedition, of a peninsula that stretches eastwards in 81° N. lat. seems to strengthen this assumption.

These different topographical questions – the appearance of the continental shelf, the extent, form and depths of the basin itself, and its transition into the surrounding deep seas – are questions of special interest. The complete charting of this immense basin will not, of course, be effected in a single expedition similar to the first Fram Expedition, even if the course of the drift were quite different to that taken by the Fram; but the material that might be procured by such an expedition would be a

These questions still remain unsettled, but might be settled now that the instruments have attained such a high degree of exactness. Measurements of temperature, together with determinations of salinity, are the most important means for determination of the extent and origin of the various strata of water. The salinity of water from any depth can now be determined with very great accuracy.

Here (p. 446) we see a couple of the more modern water-bottles that have been constructed within the last few years. They take absolutely reliable samples of water from every possible depth, and work with certainty and ease. Determinations of the salinity of water-samples can now be made with an accuracy of 1/1000 per mille; whereas formerly one had to be content with an accuracy of 1/10 per mille, and often even less than that. The variations in the salinities of the Polar Sea, from 100 fathoms or so below the surface to the bottom, are very slight, less than they are inaccuracies in the determinations with the older methods; but though slight, they are still of decided importance for a comprehension of the different origin of the various water-strata.

We here (p. 447) see a section from the New Siberian Islands, through the Polar Sea towards Spitsbergen and into the Norwegian Sea, drawn after Nansen's investigations. To the right are the flat, shallow banks, which end at the edge of the Polar Sea. On the left is the deep polar basin. On the surface there is water with low salinity and temperature between 0° and -1,9° C. It forms the real polar current, the current with which the Fram drifted. It is due in a great degree to the precipitated water from Asia. This stratum of water is nearly 110 fathoms thick. Beneath it comes another, warmer layer. The maximum temperature of this layer decreases regularly from Spitsbergen towards the New Siberian Islands. The layer extends from 110 fathoms down to about 440 fathoms. Then finally, lowest of all, comes the deep stratum of cold bottom-water. These three different strata of water forms at least as many different current-systems; but for a full comprehension of these, minute investigations will be required with our newest instruments.

Before going any farther, I will say a few words on the subject of some remarkable observations that were made during the Fram Expedition in the Polar Sea, and the cruises of the Michael Sars in the Norwegian Sea. It appears that the salinity and temperature at a certain depth may vary in the course of quite a short time. The salinity and temperature that might be found, for instance, at a depth of 11 fathoms, were soon after found at a depth of 8 fathoms. In the Norwegian Sea it has further been proved that exactly the same conditions may be found at one station at a certain depth that are found at neighbouring stations – on either side – at quite different

depths. The difference in depth may be 30 fathoms, or it may be 110. There are two possible explanations of these phenomena. To some extent these apparent irregularities or changes in the depths of the strata are due to submarine or intermediate waves, which occur at the boundary between the two strata of water, and may often attain greater dimensions than the waves with which we are acquainted on the surface of the sea, at the boundary between the water and the air; and to some extent they may be due to vortex motion on the borders of two volumes of water, moving with unequal velocities or in different directions. The latter explanation will probably be the correct one of the great irregularities. Movements of this kind must continually occur in the sea, and have a very important part to play. They will more easily be studied from the ice on the Polar Sea than anywhere else, both because there a steady point of observation can be obtained – that is, the ice – and because the marked stratification of the volumes of water makes it easy to follow all variations at the transition from one stratum to another.

The currents in the deep seas have never been investigated by direct determinations. The reason of this has partly been that hitherto we have not had good and sufficiently accurate current-gauges, but more especially that on the sea it is not generally possible to obtain a steady point from which to make observations. A vessel on the open sea will, as a rule, make many chance movements that will greatly affect a current-gauge, and prevent it from giving only the movements of the water. In the Polar Sea the difficulties will be much smaller. The ice is, of course, not liable to any wave-motion, and its slow drifting is even, through long periods, and may therefore easily be determined more or less exactly, for instance, by the aid of current-gauges that are lowered deep enough to reach the comparatively quiet stratum of bottom-water. In this way the current-gauges may be employed as logs. From an ice-floe, whose rate of drifting is determined, the currents at the various depths may be measured, and the actual motions of the water-strata be determined. Among the current-gauges that have been constructed during the last four or five years, I will only mention Nansen's pendulum current-gauge and Ekman's propeller current-gauge (p. 449), both of which were constructed at the International Central Laboratory for Oceanic Research in Christiania. The first of these is exceedingly well adapted for determining the velocity and direction of the bottom currents, even when they are very slight. The second has been much used lately to measure intermediate currents and those in the upper layers of water, in places where the entire depth has been from 250 to 350 fathoms. No reliable current-measurements have yet been made in deeper places, just on account of the difficulties in obtaining a reliable point of observation on the open sea.

These current-measurements of the last few years have yielded a series of very interesting results. I will mention some of them, chiefly as instances of the problems that present themselves for solution when the movements in the sea are in question. We see here (p. 450) a curve which represents the velocities that were measured during some investigations in one of the fjords near Bergen last summer. At a depth of 3 feet below the surface, current-measurements were made uninterruptedly for many hours; there were only a few minutes between the observations. The velocities that were then found are represented in the figure in such a way that they can be found by the vertical scale; while the horizontal scale gives the time of the observations. One is struck by the irregularity of the curve. It goes unceasingly up and down with wide oscillations. At one moment, for instance, the velocity was 11,8 inches per second, a few seconds later 17,7 inches, and again a few minutes later 9,8 inches. The current thus varies incessantly at quite short intervals. What the cause of this may be has still to be discovered; but it is evidently of the greatest importance to have this matter cleared up, if we are to understand what the sea is. And this kind of question might be thoroughly studied on the drift-ice in the Polar Sea, and the ordinary movements in the various depths of that sea be determined by a multitude of current-measurements.

There are two or three other problems, which also merit a more detailed mention. The first of these is the phenomenon of tides, which are so well known in their visible effects, by the rising and falling of the sea, but which are still, as regards many important particulars, unexplained. High tide is due, as we know, to the attraction of the moon and the sun upon the masses of water. In the form of a great wave the high tide spreads over the sea, and this tidal wave will occasion tidal currents. The tidal currents have been studied in littoral waters, but nothing is yet known of them in the deep sea, where they have not been observed with sufficient certainty. It has been doubted whether, in a deep sea, there are tidal currents strong enough to be observed even with finely registering instruments; but the experience of the Fram, that the tide regularly occasioned screwing, indicates that such is the case. The observations that we have, however, are too few to allow of any conclusion being drawn as to the advance of the tidal wave. During the drift of the Fram, Nansen found that the screwing of the ice occurred at regular intervals, sometimes twice in the twenty-four hours, sometimes only once. It looks as if this screwing were connected with the tide, and that there are thus tidal currents in the Polar Sea. A closer investigation of this matter would be particularly interesting in the first place in order to discover whether there are tidal currents in the deep sea – a discovery that might be of practical importance to navigation – and in the second place because, according to

Helland-Hansen's investigations, there may be some hope of determining the advance of the tidal wave by the aid of current-measurements. We see here (p. 451) the advance of the tidal wave along the shores of the Pacific, the Indian Ocean, and the Atlantic. In the so-called "Southern Ocean", the wave follows the moon; it is not hindered by land there, because the ocean is circumpolar. As the wave passes the southern opening of the Atlantic it slips in there, and spreads northwards right to the shores of northern Europe. In the Atlantic itself, the moon and the sun will produce a corresponding wave from east to west; but Europe and Africa on the one side, and America on the other, will prevent the wave from attaining the size and development that it can have in a circumpolar sea. It is therefore thought that a large proportion of the changes in water-level in northern Europe are due to the wave that is developed in the "Southern Ocean", while a smaller proportion are due to the action of the moon and the sun upon the waters of the Atlantic and the Norwegian Sea. But how does this matter stand with regard to the Polar Sea? If it is quite circumpolar, without being interrupted by unknown land-masses, towards the pole, a tidal wave will probably be developed there, similar to that which we assume to be in the South Pacific. This wave will occasion rising and falling of the water-line, and probably cause currents. It is natural to suppose that these questions can be elucidated by the aid of current-measurements. Much would therefore be gained towards a knowledge of tides in general.

The second problem, which I will specially emphasize, is the question as to how the wind affects the currents in the sea. On the open sea the wind will easily produce waves, thereby raising a surface of attack, against which it beats, and often causes a strong surface-current. The effect is propagated downwards, but the strength and species of this effect of the wind is a much-contested question in oceanography. While some scientists think that the great ordinary ocean currents, even at great depths, are due to the average wind blowing along the surface of the sea, others believe that as a rule the wind has little or nothing to do with such great currents, but that it only produces a more or less temporary displacement of the uppermost layer of water. It is extremely difficult, not to say impossible, to observe the currents produced by the wind on the open sea; for the wind will give the vessel so much independent motion, that it will be more difficult than usual to procure the fixed point of observation that is requisite for all current-measurements. But in this respect the Polar Sea offers particularly favourable conditions. In no condition of the wind do waves arise. The ice lies as a protection to the water, but is itself driven by the wind with more or less velocity. This drifting can be measured by the modern method, and the relation between the strength of the wind and the movement of the ice can be studied. One particularly interesting result from the first Fram Expedition was that Nansen found that the ice was driven off at an angle of from 30° to 35° to the right of the average direction of the wind. This deflection he ascribed to the rotation of the Earth, and further concluded that if the ice were so deflected as compared with the atmospheric currents, it must in its turn produce a current in the underlying strata of water, that would be still more deflected on account of the same rotation of the Earth. And in this way, Nansen thinks, it must continue downwards in the open sea; in some depth or other the current caused by the wind has become so much deflected, that it moves in exactly the opposite direction to the wind that produced it. Dr. Ekman has investigated the question theoretically, and has confirmed Nansen's conclusions. On the other hand, theoretical objections have been made quite recently by Profs. Mohn and Schiötz. We have no direct observations, however, of the magnitude of the currents caused by the wind, and of their propagation from stratum to stratum of the water. Nansen had no opportunity of measuring these currents, because the methods at that time were not sufficiently developed. But now it can be done, and it will be possible to study the effect of the wind upon the sea from the ice of the polar basin better than from any other place.

Before concluding this mention of the problems that present themselves in the Polar Sea for solution by an expedition that is equipped with the best scientific aids of the present day, I will mention yet a few more important points. You all know that the sea contains various quantities of gases in solution. There is much to be done in a study of these gases in solution in the sea-water; but I will touch upon one thing only. It is well known that all animals require oxygen in order to live; in breathing, oxygen is consumed and carbonic acid is given off. This is also the case with plants in the dark. In the light, on the other hand, it is the opposite; plants then consume carbonic acid and produce oxygen. With regard to the sea, a number of interesting observations have been made of the reciprocal action of animals and plants, of light and darkness. The Polar Sea offers very favourable conditions for the study of these questions, with its summer one long light day, and its winter one equally long dark night. It would be exceedingly interesting to study this reciprocal action under such characteristic conditions. As aids in these studies we now have apparatus that can measure the strength of the light at the various depths of the water, both under ice and in open water. And the quantity of the little plants and animals that are found in the sea can be measured. One of the most important questions in the physiology of the ocean and the circulation of its organisms can thus be minutely studied.

In addition to the oceanographic problems here mentioned, which it will be the chief aim of my proposed expedition to solve, there are a number of other questions of almost equal importance. Closely connected with the oceanographic observations

are the meteorological. It is true that the meteorological phenomena were carefully studied during the drifting of the Fram; but this would not prevent a new series of being of great importance. I do not expect to meet with any new remarkable phenomena, hitherto unknown – the meteorological conditions of the polar basin are probably too uniform for that; but merely as a check and for comparison with those previously made, they will be of great interest. I therefore intend to take with me a complete meteorological outfit of the most modern instruments. The investigation of the terrestrial magnetic conditions will be of less importance, but still interesting; of less importance because the unstable drift-ice affords only a bad basis for observations that demand such a high degree of accuracy as the magnetic, but still interesting as a supplement to the magnetic observations taken by Captain Scott Hansen on the first Fram Expedition.

In connection with the magnetic observations, the observations of aurora will be of great interest. We all know the magnificent auroras up there in the deep, gloomy polar night, from Nansen's excellent description – we know them all, those strange, flaming, shooting movements across the sky on calm winter nights – we know them all so well, and have so often admired the mysterious spectacle. No one can doubt that a remarkable force is the back of this, a force that we human beings are determined to find, bind, and utilize.

And the polar regions are just the place for the study of these phenomena, which occur there more frequently and with greater splendour than anywhere else. Profs. Birkeland and Störmer have, as we know, made exceedingly important investigations in this field, which seem to promise a solution of these difficult problems; but by investigations continued for so long a time, valuable contributions to their study will certainly be obtained.

I have now attempted to put before you some of the problems in which the polar regions are so rich. I have, however, only made a selection, having, in particular, the polar basin in view. It is the exploration of this basin, the nucleus of the polar regions, to which we must turn all our attention. Many people think that a polar expedition is connected in their minds with that of a record, of reaching the pole or farther north than any of its predecessors; and if that is the case, I agree with them. But I must emphatically assert that this storming of the pole will not be the object of this expedition. Its chief aim will be a scientific study of the Polar Sea itself, or rather an investigation of the bottom and oceanographic conditions of this great basin. In my opinion, work with this object in view might be of very great scientific importance, for several reasons. In the first place, it will be very interesting geographically to become better

It has been said that after the number of years that have passed since then, the Fram would be rotten and unfit for further work in the Polar Sea; but I can personally testify that this is not the case, for I subjected the vessel to a very careful inspection last year, at Horten. Colin Archer, the builder of the Fram, who was so kind as to assist me in this inspection, sent me, shortly after, the following letter: -

"In compliance with your request, I beg to impart to you my opinion concerning the condition of the polar vessel Fram, with regard to a further employment of the vessel, after having yesterday, together with you, inspected her in the harbour at Horten.

"During the inspection it transpired that the head-carpenter at the yard, Johannesen, who was present all the time, had already subjected the vessel to a thorough examination, both outside and in, and could point out the defects. Some of the fittings were removed in order to facilitate the examination; the masts were taken out, and in some places the ceiling was removed, where signs of rottenness appeared. The defects pointed out were examined and inspected; and further, some borings were made in other places in beams, ceiling, and frame, both between-decks and on the topsides, without bringing to light any further damage.

"In my opinion, the ship shows no sign of strain at the joints or bindings; in this respect there is no change to be discovered since the ship was built and her strength and capability of withstanding strains may thus practically be said to be unimpaired.

"The defects that exist are for the most part local and of a kind that readily appears in any ship built of wood, after years have passed, especially when she has been laid up, like the Fram, during a great part of the time. Owing to her peculiar construction for a special purpose, the same consideration could not be paid in the building of this ship to the abundant supply and circulation of fresh air as in an ordinary wooden ship; and it was therefore only to be expected that certain covered-in parts would suffer on account of imperfect ventilation. The damage is not, however, of such a nature that, when repaired, the vessel can be said to have suffered any essential diminution of solidity. I can thus express as my firm opinion that after undergoing repairs in accordance with the plan suggested by Horten Dockyard, the Fram will be in a perfectly fit condition to start on an expedition to Arctic waters.

"Yours faithfully,

"COLIN ARCHER."

acquainted with the conditions in those unknown regions in the vicinity of one of the poles of the Earth; and, in the second place, it will be an important matter to know those northern waters in their relation to the surrounding seas – for instance, the reciprocal action between the Atlantic or the Norwegian Sea and the Polar Sea. There is a constant interaction between these ocean regions, which cannot be fully understood until each of them has been explored.

Finally – and this is the point that will weigh more heavily in the scale in favour of an expedition through those regions – the Polar Sea, in most respects, affords a far more favourable practical opportunity of studying the ordinary conditions in the sea than any other place. This is due to the peculiar conditions there – a sea 2200 fathoms deep, or even more, upon the surface of which one can move about almost as on dry land. One can live and build upon the ice, and from it lower all one's instruments into the sea, and reach down to the greatest depths, without all the difficulties with which one has to contend in storm and rough water on the open sea. There is no more ideal place to be found for oceanic investigation.

I sincerely hope that I have succeeded in so putting my views before my audience, that I shall not be the only person present who considers that a new expedition across then Polar Sea is desirable. I will now briefly put before you the manner in which I have thought of exploring the polar basin. The manner is not original: we are all acquainted with it already. I have thought of employing the same mode of procedure as Prof. Nansen with his Fram, but, it should be observed, with the benefit of all his experience, which he has placed at my disposal. I will not weary you with a repetition of all the evidence upon which Nansen's theory of the polar current was based. We know it all so well. We now have evidence that is far more certain and better than all these little, apparently insignificant things that Nansen had taken with great difficulty and labour from the various regions of the Polar Sea, and form which he evolved his ingenious theory of the polar current, and upon it performed his splendid achievement; we have, I repeat, far more certain evidence, and that is Nansen himself. Relying upon his experience, I have determined to choose my point of departure at a considerable distance from the spot where Nansen found himself obliged to let the Fram begin to drift.

I intend to ask the Norwegian State for the loan of the Fram for my contemplated voyage of discovery. The Fram was built in the years 1891 to 1893, at Colin Archer's shipbuilding yard at Larvik, and was so constructed that she not only withstood the tremendous pressure of the ice to which she was subjected, but even came home without a single scratch from her long severe combat with the huge masses of ice.

mayer at Hamburg, in order to thoroughly learn all that were necessary for that line of investigation. He then purchased a small ship called Gjoa, and he took with him only six men, all of whom were more or less experts. He first went to the ocean between Spitsbergen and Greenland, and his researches there were of considerable value, and were afterwards worked out by Dr. Nansen. In the year 1903 he went from thence to the region round the magnetic north pole, and he devoted two years to systematic magnetic work with the best instruments in that region, the result being to largely increase our knowledge of the geographical distribution of those forces. During the stay of the expedition in those regions several expeditions were undertaken in various directions. A considerable section of the coast of North America, hitherto unmapped, was mapped. Careful investigations were made with regard to the Eskimo with whom he lived, and a good deal of scientific work was done. At the conclusion of this magnetic work, this little ship came out through the Behring straits, and thus for the first time in our history completing the north-west passage, which expedition Captain Amundsen has described in his interesting book of that title. It is, I think, clear that Captain Amundsen has already shown that he ought to be classed as belonging to the first rank of scientific explorers. This is Captain Amundsen's record as regards the past. He has, during recent years, moreover, been studying arctic problems with extreme care, not only the problems themselves, but the best method of solving them. His record shows that he is not a man to take up any project hastily or without the most mature consideration. Undoubtedly his expedition which he proposes is a hazardous one, but I think when you have heard him speak you will agree that the objects he has in view are ones of great scientific interest, including as they do the sounding and dredging of the ocean, measurements of temperature and salinity of the sea and of the movements of the ice, and many other phenomena, all of which will help us to solve various arctic problems. As to the means of effecting this work, he has the encouragement and the great example of Nansen before him. It is not for me, however, to express an opinion, either in my own capacity, or my capacity as President of this Society, on the methods he proposes for this work.

The PRESIDENT (after the paper): Before asking anyone to take part in the discussion, I will ask Colonel Close to kindly read a few important communications we have received concerning this expedition.

The following communications were read:

(1) From Dr. FRIDTJOF NANSEN: I deeply regret that pressing work here prevents me from being present when my compatriot, Captain Roald Amundsen, is going to lay his plan for a North Polar Expedition before the Royal Geographical Society. To give

From this it appears clearly and distinctly enough that the old Fram is not yet so entirely unfit for service as has so often been said latterly. Any vessel, it is unnecessary to say, that is laid up for several years, cannot but suffer from it. Blame has been thrown upon the people to whose care the Fram was entrusted , for not having kept her in good condition; but this criticism seems to me to be uncalled-for. With such means as were at their disposal, they have bestowed such care upon the preservation of the vessel as deserves appreciaton rather than misplaced criticism.

My plan is as follows: With the Fram equipped for seven years, and a capable crew, I shall leave Norway in the beginning of 1910. We shall make for San Francisco round Cape Horn, taking in coal and provisions at the former place. We shall then shape our course for Point Barrow, the most northerly point of North America, which I hope to reach by July or August. From this place the last news will be sent home before the real voyage begins. On leaving Point Barrow, it is my intention to continue the voyage with as small a crew as possible. We shall then make for the drift-ice in a direction north by north-west, where we will then look for the most favourable place for pushing farther north. When this has been found, we shall go as far in as possible, and prepare for a four or five years' drift across the Polar Sea. Throughout the moment the vessel becomes fast in the ice, a series of observations will be begun, our voyage up to this point, I intend to make oceanographic observations; and from with which I hope to solve some of the hitherto unsolved mysteries. What I expect to find in the unknown part of the Polar Sea I will say nothing about at present. Some people have put forward theories of great masses of land, others of small. I ought perhaps also to have put forward my theory, but think it wiser to refrain from doing so until I have investigated matters at closer quarters.

The PRESIDENT (before the paper): Captain Amundsen, whom we cordially welcome here to-night, is going to describe to us his proposals with regard to a polar expedition, both as regards its methods and its objects. Captain Amundsen has had a great deal of experience in arctic work already. His first expedition was undertaken in a whaler, for the sake of learning navigation in the ice. On his return from that journey, he was appointed first-lieutenant on the Belgian vessel, the Belgica, for the exploration of the Antarctic Ocean. After his return from this expedition he conceived the idea of undertaking a magnetic examination of the region close to the magnetic north pole, and for that purpose he placed himself under Dr. von Neuan impartial opinion of Amundsen's plan is, I am afraid, impossible for me, as, on the one hand, I am too much interested in the realization of his planned expedition, and, on the other hand, I have too great an admiration of my friend Amundsen, both as a scientific explorer of the right stuff and also as a leader of men, and my confidence in him makes me believe that he is one of those that carry through successfully, in one way or another, whatever they undertake. The reason why, according to my view, an expedition carried out according to Amundsen's plan will be so very important, is that at the same time as it promises to solve the most important North Polar problems left, which are what I may call of local interest, it will afford the possibilities of solving important problems of very great general interest, especially for geomorphology and oceanography.

I may mention, as an example, the facilities which the slowly drifting ice will afford for taking a unique series of numerous and accurate soundings across the North Polar basin during those long years. On the drifting polar ice more accurate astronomical observations (for determination of latitude and longitude) can be taken than in any other region of the ocean, and also the velocity and direction of the movements of the ice can easily be measured very accurately by current-meters, lowered into the quiet bottomwater of the sea. It may thus be possible at any time to determine the accurate position of the soundings showing in minute detail the relief of the bottom of a deep sea in a section, as we have it, from no other part of the ocean.

I may also mention the unique opportunity which Amundsen's expedition will afford of solving problems of the greatest importance for physical oceanography. We have hitherto studied the water-strata of the deep open ocean chiefly by examining the temperature and salinity (or specific gravity) of the water.

The changes of the movements of the water at different depths can easily be followed by simulta-neously studying the changes of temperature and salinity of the sea, at then different depths, we may attain such an intimate knowledge of the water-strata of the north polar basin and their movements as we cannot, even approximately, obtain in any other part of the ocean. And the knowledge thus acquired cannot fail to give us entirely new views of the dynamics of the ocean, and will carry physical oceanography an important step forward. In this oceanographical laboratory, built of snow on the north polar ice under the polar star, Amundsen may thus be able to find solutions of the many difficult problems which all oceanographers are now waiting for.

I consider it unnecessary for me to say much about the practicability of Amundsen's plan to drift with the ice across the north polar basin. I think that this is fully proved by the first Fram Expedition 1893-1896. And lately it has also been proved by the two American drift-casks placed on the ice, the one north-west of Point Barrow, Alaska, and the other near Cape Bathurst, in North-Western Canada. The former was, six years later, found on the north coast of Iceland, the latter was only a few weeks ago, after eight years, found on the coast of Northern Norway, just where we hope to see Amundsen again after less than eight years, and with his ship loaded with a unique material of scientific observations.

As an example illustrating the steadiness of the drifting polar ice, and how even the most delicate investigations may be carried out there, I may mention that during the Fram expedition 1893-1896 my comrade Captain Scott-Hansen managed to make pendulum observations for determination of the gravity, on board the Fram, frozen fast in the drifting ice. These are the only pendulum observations ever made over a deep ocean. It may thus be understood that from this solid, drifting ice, even the most delicate measurements of the water movements at all depths can easily be carried out, if only the movements of the ice itself can be accurately determined, which is not difficult, as I have already pointed out.

(2) Sir CLEMENTS MARKHAM: I welcome the resolution of my friend Amundsen to follow in the footsteps of Nansen, and continue the exploration of the polar ocean. His plan is well conceived, and its execution, even if only in part, will certainly be productive of very important scientific results. I am satisfied, after a study of the subject during many years, that the chances of success for a well-designed expedition on Amundsen's plan are good.

After the return of the last British naval expedition in 1876, the evidence was completed that there was heavy ice-pressure along the American side of the Arctic regions from Cape Barrow to the north-eastern end of Greenland, and that the only channel of escape for this polar ice was down the east coast of Greenland. It appeared to me that this pointed to a polar ocean of great extent, and to a drift from the Asiatic to the American side. In my paper on the scientific results of the Arctic expedition of 1876, published in our Proceedings in 1877, I held that there was a deep sea to the north of Franz Josef Land, and that most important work would be achieved by pushing northward from the Siberian coast. Many years afterwards Nansen, never having seen my paper, adopted the same view. There were prophets of evil among our experts, as doubtless there will be now. Naturally, I felt confident that his plan was the right one, and never doubted his success. That success threw a flood of light on the Arctic problem.

efforts to carry this important enterprise to a successful conclusion. They go forth in a ship whose efficiency and capabilities have already been well tested, and led by a man who has already made his mark as a brave and energetic arctic explorer.

In order to achieve a drift across the polar ocean, by a route different from that of Nansen, it will be necessary for the Fram to follow the track of the Jeannette for some distance to the eastward, and Amundsen will use his judgment as to the opportunity to be taken for pushing northwards over the continental shelf and into the drifting ice. Whither he will be taken it is impossible to foresee with our limited knowledge. It is sufficient that he will be taken into an unknown region of the deepest interest, and that he will be supplied with all the means of making valuable discoveries and researches. That it will be a very perilous undertaking cannot be disguised. But the guidance of a really capable man very largely reduces the danger. Like the enterprise of Nansen, it is a grand conception, worthy of the first navigator of the north-west passage.

Admiral Sir LEWIS BEAUMONT: The subject has been so entirely scientific, with the exception of the last few remarks of Captain Amundsen, that it hardly comes within my province, which is more the navigator's part and the methods to be employed. I have, therefore, really very few words to say. But when it is remembered that the expedition contemplates being absent for such a very long period of time, possibly seven years, it seems as if it would be of great value, if in some way or other, possibly by wireless telegraphy, it was possible to establish communication with the expedition during the time of its absence. It has always been the custom for those who are responsible for Arctic exploration, to look forward to the time when it would be necessary to search for an expedition that was overdue, but if this expedition actually starts with the idea that it may be away for seven years, it is a very long time to wait before one can feel that it is overdue, and from that point of view it is not too much to expect that some such communication should be established with an absent expedition, in order that fears as to its welfare might be relieved. I make that as a suggestion which seems to me one to be considered in a case of this sort. Except for that, my only remark would be that for such an expedition as this, a ship is absolutely necessary; not only for use as a ship but as a depôt, as a home, and as a starting-point if any accident or danger made it necessary for them to try to reach land; there is no other way in which such work could be done. As regards the actual going for seven years, I entirely sympathize with Captain Amundsen, whose object is to realize the full benefit of his project, and if it was possible to go back forty years, I would be glad to go with him.

(3) Admiral Sir ALBERT MARKHAM: His scheme is, undoubtedly, a daring one, and for the special object which he hopes to achieve, namely an examination of the bottom of the Polar basin, it is, in my opinion, an excellent one, and is bound to produce important and valuable results. I see that he proposes to start in a northerly – or north-westerly – direction from Point Barrow, run his ship into the ice directly he meets it, and trust to the drift to carry his ship whither it will, as it did Nansen on his memorable voyage some fourteen years ago. From all accounts hitherto received of the ice in this neighbourhood, it appears to be of a formidable character, somewhat similar to the heavy impenetrable ice invariably found on the east coast of Greenland, and which we experienced in 1875-6 to the north of Robeson Channel – ice that it would be dangerous – nay madness – to force a ship into with the intention of allowing her to drift with it!

In my opinion it would be better, and lead to more successful results, if he was to follow more closely in the footsteps of Nansen – and he could not follow a better man – and run the Fram into the drifting pack further to the west, but east of the New Siberia islands. In this vicinity the drift of the ice to the north is more likely to be affected by the outflow of the large Siberian rivers, than it would be in the neighbourhood of Point Barrow. A reference to Nansen's track in the Fram shows that the drift of the ice, when he entered it to the north of the New Siberia islands, took him nearly due north for about 150 miles, then away to the N.W. until the latitude of 85° was reached, an thence to the west until the ship was finally liberated from the ice.

Sir JOHN MURRAY: I listened with very great pleasure to this account of the second proposed drift of the Fram across the Polar basin, and I hope that the expedition will be carried out, and if so, I have no doubt it will result in large additions to oceanographical knowledge. It is now just about forty years since I spent a whole season in a Scottish whaler, cruising amongst the ice-floes between the coasts of Greenland and Spitsbergen. From observations made at that time, and from general considerations, I came to the conclusion that in the Polar region there was a deep basin. When in 1887 I published a paper on the heights of the land and the depths of the ocean, I estimated the greatest depth of the Polar basin at about 1500 fathoms, and I estimated that there was an area of about two millions of square miles, with a depth exceeding 1000 fathoms. It may ultimately be found that this estimate is not very far from the truth. Nansen, however, as we have just been told by Captain Amundsen, believed that the Polar ba-

It is to more thoroughly explore this almost unknown basin, to ascertain its depth at various positions, to obtain observations regarding the temperature and salinity of its waters, and the direction of its currents, that the attention of those in the Fram will be especially directed. We wish them good luck and God speed in their brave

sin was a shallow sea, and consequently he did not fit out the Fram with a deep-sea sounding apparatus. Should the Fram on this occasion be fitted out as for a truly oceanic expedition, and the expedition be successfully carried out, most important observations will certainly be made.

The Polar basin must be regarded as a partially enclosed sea, but from the peculiar thermal conditions of the region it should be quite unlike the enclosed seas with which we are acquainted in southern latitudes. The Atlantic water which sinks to the bottom of the Polar seas carries with it an abundance of oxygen, and in this respect should be very favourable for the development of marine organisms in great depths. I therefore hope that this expedition will take with it trained biologists, who (if it be possible, as Captain Amundsen suggests, to dredge from the surface of the ice-floes) will be able not only to give an excellent account of the marine animals in the Polar basin, but to observe the rate of growth, of reproduction, and of assimilation, and generally the metabolism of organisms which live during the whole of their existence at a temperature below the freezing-point of fresh water. These observations could then be compared with similar observations on similar marine organisms, which in the tropics, live all their lives in a temperature between 70° and 80° Fahr. Observations are much needed in this direction, and it would be a pity to lose the opportunity of making them on the proposed expedition.

Dr. MILL: As a student of oceanography I should like to say that, in my opinion, the greatest result of the first voyage of the Fram was that it took out Dr. Nansen as a biologist and brought him back as an oceanographer. He has devoted his life since then to the advancement of oceanography, to the improvement of the methods, and to the study of the results. As one of the representatives on the International Council for the Study of the Sea, it has been my good fortune to be associated very intimately with Dr. Nansen, with Prof. Petterson, and with other continental oceanographers during the last eight years, and I have seen with amazement and delight the enormous advances that have been made in oceanographical apparatus of all kinds. I believe, even though I disagree with trembling from Sir John Murray, that they can read their new thermometers to 1/100°C.

Sir JOHN MURRAY: They can read them, but what is the reading worth?

Dr. MILL: That is very largely a matter to be decided when the results of the various expeditions come home. I believe that very small differences of temperature will be found to be of real physical importance, and that they are capable of being measured with accuracy. The only fear I have for Captain Amundsen is that there may descend

upon him the woe that threatens those of whom all men speak well. When Nansen first proposed his great drift across the Polar basin, the Arctic veterans besought him not to throw his life away on such a wild-goose chase, and those of you who were present then will remember how Nansen replied that he was going all the same, that he took a ticket with the ice, instead of struggling against it. The change of expert opinion now is indeed enormous, and in following Nansen's example I think Captain Amundsen is doing exactly the right thing, and it is surprising to the student of Polar exploration how comparatively seldom the experience of one successful expedition has been made use of by another. It is extraordinary how frequently the old errors have been repeated, and it is remarkable also how much greater has been the success of those expeditions that have gone out on the principle of Nansen when he crossed Greenland, of having no line of retreat, than of those expeditions that went out in the hope of relief expeditions being sent to them in case of need. I rather think more lives have been lost and more money wasted in relief expeditions, than on the expeditions which carried the explorers who set out to do the original work. For all those reasons I wish to express on my own part, and, so far as I may speak for the oceanographers of this country, on their part too, the heartiest wishes for the greatest success to Captain Amundsen, and the hope that he will return triumphant after drifting across the Polar basin in much less time than the generous allowance of seven years which he has provided for his labours.

The PRESIDENT: I do not myself intend to take any part in this discussion, not being an expert on Arctic affairs. But as one who is not an expert, I should like to thank Captain Amundsen sincerely for the extremely clear way in which he has placed these problems before us. It has been one of the most interesting lectures I have ever listened to on Arctic problems. I sincerely trust that the Society, of which I have the honour to be President, may be of some use to Captain Amundsen in his preparations, and I can assure you we shall do our utmost to help him. I have merely now to thank him, as I am certain I may, in your name, for his extremely interesting lecture, and also, though it is somewhat in advance, in the name of everyone here present and in the name of the Society, wish him God-speed and good luck in the venturesome and plucky journey he is about to undertake.

Captain AMUNDSEN: As to the question of Admiral Sir Lewis Beaumont about wireless telegraphy, I must say that I have studied this important question thoroughly. I have come to the conclusion that a wireless in many cases, perhaps, would be of immense value to us, and could render us good services; but nevertheless I have decided not to carry a wireless, and the reason is this. Imagine that we have spent two years in the drifting-pack, and still have three more years to spend – imagine that we suddenly get a dispatch stating that some of our dears are seriously ill or dying, or whatever it may be. What would then be the result? Nobody can tell, but the worst might happen. That is the reason why I do not take any wireless appliances. And then with regard to obtaining an accuracy of 1/100°C I wish to tell you that I think I shall carry home those observations made to that degree of accuracy. As to the apparatus for the search of samples of the bottom, we have it, and I intend using it. I now beg to thank all the gentlemen that have honoured me by taking part in the discussion to-night. The speakers we have listened to; and the gentlemen who have been good enough to address letters to our meeting, represent together the greatest experts and the most profound knowledge of Arctic exploration. I have listened with the greatest interest to everything that has been said with regard to my proposed expedition, and I wish to express my heartfelt thanks for the very kind and valuable advice which has been given me, and for the very kind and sympathetic way in which you have received the plan for my new expedition.

Roald Amundsen's account on expanding the North Polar Expedition

1

Fra Madeira sætter "Fram" kurs mot syd for i de antarktiske egne at delta i kampen om sydpolen.

Dette vil vel ved förste öiekast forekomme mange at være en forandring av den oprindelig lakte plan for den tredie Framfærd. Men saa er imidlertid ikke tilfældet. Det er kun en utvidelse av expeditionens plan ingen forand= ring. Og en nödvendig utvidelse er det for at tilveiebringe de midler, som fremdeles mangler for at utstyre den tredie Framfærd paa en fultt ut be= tryggenne maate for den lange isdrift. Denne beslutning er ikke av ny dato. Den er gammel og vel overveiet. Da amerikanerne Cook og Peary i= fjor i september ventte tilbake og brakte meddelelse om, at de hadde været ved nordpolen, da forstod jeg fultt vel at det ville bli en umulighet for mig at opnaa de nödvendige midler for mit foretagenne. Vistnok var den tredie Framfærd anlakt som en vitenskapelig expedition i alle dele, og jeg sier selv i min plan, fremlakt i det norske geografiske selskap i 1908, at expeditionens maal ikke var rekordjægeri, men en streng vitenskapelig ut= forskning av nordpolarbasinet. Og dette var min mening, og mit haap var det at jeg med dette maal for öie skulle faa den nödvendige assistance. Men dengang, da jeg fremla min plan, var nordpolen ikke naaet, og muligheten for, at Framfærden, tiltrods for dens helt vitenskapelige formaal, allikevel ville naa hen til dette attraaete sted og löse dette problem, som gjennem aarhundreder har været gjenstann for nationers brænnenne kappestrid, visste jeg

2

ville være en spore til assistance for mange vedkommehne. Og mange er og-

saa de,som har optraatt og rukket mig en hjælpenne haang i mit vanskelige

arbeide. Formaaenne mænn har med al sin kraft ydet mig deres stötte,og jeg

tvler ikke paa, at de ville ha rukket maalet og tilveiebrakt de nödvendige

midler,saafremt efterretningen om polproblemets endlige lösning ikke var

kommet dem i veien. Men ved den efterretning forstod jeg,som för nævnt,at

de nödvendige midler ikke kunne opnaaes paa noen almindelig maate. Der maatte

noe til,som kunne tiltrække sig det store publikums opmærksomhet og interesse

for at skaffe den ennu ret betraktelige summ,som manglet. Jeg hadde ikke me-

get at vælge mellem. Var nordpolen rukket gjenstod kun et problem,som med

sikkerhet kunne paaregne at vække publikums interesse, sydpolen. Og saa be-

stemte jeg mig for at utvide expeditionens plan og delta i kampen om denne.

Jeg vet,jeg kommer til at saare mange av dem,som har staaet mig nær i mit ar-

beide og hjulpet mig frem,ved at ta et skritt,som dette uten paa forhaann at

unnerrette dem derom. Men det var en umulighet. Saa mange vanskligheter ville

ha hopet sig op,saafremt planen var blit bekjentt,at jeg kunne ha risikeret

at maatte ha opgit den. Der maatte arbeides i stilhet skulle det lykkes.

Alene har jeg fattet denne beslutning -- alene bærer jeg ansvaret.

Jeg skylder her at meddele,at jeg likeoverfor den komite,som hjalp mig med

innsamling av midler,erklæret,at,saafremt jeg kunne opnaa at faa proviant nok

ombord for to aav og trækken for mine folk dækket,jeg da selv skulle klare

at skaffe de manglenne midler,naar vi engang naaet San Francisco. Jeg skal
gjöre alt for at holle ord.

Fra Madeira sætter,som för nævnt,"Fram" kurs mot syd. Hvorhen kan jeg ennu
ikke med bestemthet si.En del av expeditionens deltagere vil bli landsat.
En del vil gaa ut igjen med fartöiet for at drive havunnersökelser.Disse
vil först anlöpe Punta Arenas i Magellanstrædet,hvorfra den förste efterret=
ning om vort arbeidsfeltt og plan vil sennes ut.Derfra fortsætter de til
Buenos Aires,hvor de antagelig vil inntreffe i juni 1911. Opholet der blir
ca. en maanet. Post vil kunne sennes dertil. Skulle fartöiet mot forvent=
ning ikke la höre fra sig,behöver man ikke derfor at bli ængstelig.Grunnen
er da den,at jeg har funnet det nödvendig at beholle det dernede unner over=
vintringen.

I februar - mars 1912 kan men etter gjöre regning paa at höre fra os. Vi fort=
sætter da til San Francisco,hvor de endlige forberedelser til driften over
polarbasinet gjöres.

"Fram"   september 1910

From Madeira, the Fram sets course southwards for the Antarctic to participate in the battle for the South Pole.

This may at first sight be interpreted as a change of the original plan for the third Fram expedition. But this is not the case. It is only an extension of the original plan for the expedition, not a change. And it is a necessary change to secure the expedition with funds and equipment for the long drift in the polar ice. This decision is not a recent one. It was made one year ago and has been well thought through. When the Americans, Cook and Peary, returned last year and told the world that they had been at the North Pole, I understood that it would be impossible for me to obtain the necessary funds for my enterprise.

The third *Fram* expedition was planned as a scientific expedition in all its parts, as I asserted when I presented my plan at the Norwegian Geographical Society in 1908. The object of the expedition had nothing to do with beating records, but with serious scientific exploration and research of the north polar basin. This was my idea and I hoped that, with this in mind, I would be able to obtain the necessary assistance. But when I presented my plan, the North Pole had not yet been reached. I knew that the possibility that the Fram expedition, in spite of its purely scientific aims, could go to this sought-after place and meet this challenge – for centuries the subject of several nations' burning rivalry – would stimulate support from different individuals and institutions. Many are those that have indeed given me a helping hand in my difficult work. Affluent men have given me their support with all their means, and I do not doubt that they would have found the necessary funds, as long as the information about the final solution to the polar challenge had not come their way. But, with this news I understood, as before mentioned, that the necessary funds could not be obtained in an ordinary way. Something had to be done to attract the attention and interest of the public in order to procure the relatively large amount of money still lacking.

I did not have much to choose between. If the North Pole had been reached, there was only one challenge left that would attract people's interest: the South Pole. I then decided to expand the expedition's plan and participate in the race for this destination. I know that I will offend many of those who have been on my side and helped me forward, by taking a step like this without telling them beforehand. But it was not possible. So many difficulties would have built up if the plan had been revealed, that I might have risked having to abandon the expedition altogether. I had to work in silence if it was to be a success.

I have made this decision alone and I am bearing the responsibility alone.

I must also explain that I have promised the committee that helped me to raise the funds for the expedition, that I will be responsible for raising money for food for two years on board the *Fram*, plus the wages for the crew members once we have reached San Francisco. I will do everything to keep my promise.

From Madeira, the *Fram* sets course southwards, as already mentioned. Exactly where, is still hard to say with certainty. Some of the expedition's participants will be set ashore. The others will carry out oceanographic studies on the *Fram*. Their first port of call will be Punta Arenas in the Magellan Strait, from where the first report of our activities and plans will be broadcast. Then they will carry on to Buenos Aires, where they will probably arrive in June 1911. There, the stop-over will last approximately one month. Mail can be sent to this place. If one should not, contrary to expectations, hear from the ship, there is no need to worry. The reason will be that I have found it necessary to keep the ship during the Winter period.

In February or March 1912 one can count on hearing from us. At that point, we will continue to San Francisco, and do the final preparations for the drift across the polar basin.

The *Fram*, September 1910

197

Letter from Roald Amundsen to Fridtjof Nansen dated August 22, 1910 explaining the change of plans for the North Polar expedition

Fram-Expeditionen

U. B.
Bre
Ms. fol. 1924,
5,3.

"Fram" 22 august 1910

Herr Professor Fridtjof Nansen.

Det er ikke med let hjerte,jeg senner Dem disse linjer,men der finnes
ingen vei utenom,og derfor faar jeg likesaa gott gaa like paa.
Da efterretningen fra Cook og senere fra Peary innlöp ifjor höst om
deres færder til nordpolen,forstod jeg med engang,at dette var döds=
stötet for mit foretagenne. Jeg innsaa straks,at jeg efter dette ikke
ville kunne paaregne den ökonomiske stötte,jeg tiltrænkte. At jeg hadde
ret herti viser stortingets beslutning av mars - april 1910,hvorved det
avslog mit andragenne om en merbevilgning av kr.25000.
At opgi mit foretagenne faltt mig ikke et öieblik inn.Spörsmaalet blev da
for mig,hvad jeg skulle gjöre for at skaffe de nödvendige midler.
At tilveiebringe disse uten at gjöre noe var ikke at tænke paa.Noe,som
kunne vække det store publikums interesse maatte gjöres.Paa den maate
alene ville det bli mig mulig at realisere min plan.Kun et problem staar
igjen at löse innen polaregnene,som kan gjöre regning paa at vække den
store masses interesse, det at naa sydpolen.Kunne jeg utföre dette viss=
te jeg,at midlerne for min planlakte færd ville være sikret.

Halvorsen & Larsen Ld., Kristiania

Fram-Expeditionen

2

Ja,det faller mig tungt,herr professor,at meddele Dem,men siden septem=
ber 1909 har min beslutning om at delta i konkurencen om dette spörs=
maals lösning været fattet.   Mange gange har jeg været paa vei til at
betro det hele til Dem,men altid ventt om ræd,forat De skulle stoppe mig.
Jeg har ofte önsket,at Scott skulle hat greie paa denne min beslutning,
saa det ikke fik utseenne av at jeg ville lure mig derned uten hans
vitenne for at komme ham i forkjöpet:men jeg har ikke vovet noensomhelst
offentliggjörelse   ræd for at bli stoppet.Jeg skal imidlertid gjöre
alt for at træffe ham dernede og meddele ham min beslutning,saa faar han
handle derefter.

Siden september ifjor har altsaa denne beslutning været tat,og jeg tror,
jeg tör si,at vi er gott rustet. Men jeg maa samtidig gjöre opmærksom
paa,at var det lykkes mig at opnaa de midler,som fremdeles var nödven=
dige for min oprindelig paatænkte færd - ca.kr.150000 - da hadde jeg
med glæde latt denne extratur ute:men det kunne der ikke være tanke paa.
Fra Madeira sætter vi kursen mot syd for Syd Victoria Lann.Med 9 mann
er det min hensikt at la mig lannsætte der,og saa la "Fram"gaa ut for at
drive havunnersökelser. Jeg haaper den skal bli istann til at ta to snit
fra Buenos Aires og over mot Cap Verde. Naar "Fram" forlater isen gaar den
mot öst til Punta Arenas og derfra til Buenos Aires. Löitnant Nilsen,som
da har kommandoen ombord , vil antagelig sammen med Kutschin være istann
til at utföre et gott arbeide. Hvor vi kommer til at gaa i lann dernede

Halvorsen & Larsen Ld., Kristiania

Fram-Expeditionen

3

kan jeg ennu ikke bestemme, men er det min hensikt ikke at komme op i hæn=
nerne paa engelsmænnerne. De har selvfölgelig försteretten. Vi faar jo
nöie os med, hvad de vraker.   I februar - mars 1912 vil "Fram" atter
komme ned og hente os. Vi gaar da först innom Lyttelton paa New Zealand
for at telegrafere og derfra til San Francisco for saa at fortsætte det
avbrutte arbeide og, som jeg haaper med et utstyr, som er nödvendig for en
færd av den art. Jeg har bett Helland, som i længere tid har hat kjennskap
til denne plan at overbringe Dem dette brev med haap om, at han muligens
vil være istann til at fremstille min sak i et gunstigere lys, enn jeg
selv kan.   Og naar De saa fæller dom over mig, herr professor, vær da ik=
ke for streng. Jeg har den fulgt den eneste vei, som syntes at staa mig
aapen, og saa faar det da gaa, som det kan.
Samtidig hermed senner jeg Kongen meddelelse om det samme, men forövrig
ingen annen. Noen dage efter mottagelsen av dette vil min bror sörge for
offentliggjörelsen av tillægget i expeditionens plan.
Ennu engang ber jeg Dem. Ta ikke for haartt paa mig. Jeg er ingen hum=
bugmaker, nöden tvang mig.
Og saa ber jeg Dem om tigivelse for, hvad jeg har gjort. Maatte mit kommenne
arbeide hjælpe til at sone, hvad jeg har forbrutt.
        Med min ærbödigste hilsen.

Halvorsen & Larsen Ld., Kristiania

The *Fram*, August 22, 1910

Dear Professor Fridtjof Nansen,

It has not been easy to write you these lines, but there is no way to avoid it, and therefore I will just have to tell to you straight.

When the news from the Cook, and later the Peary, expeditions to the North Pole came to my knowledge last autumn, I instantly understood that this was the death sentence for my own plans. I immediately concluded that after this I could not be expected to secure the financial support I required for the expedition. The Norwegian Parliament's decisions of March and April 1910, to decline my request of NOK 25,000 proved me right.

It never crossed my mind to abandon my plans. The question became how I could raise the necessary funds. Something had to be done to increase the public's interest. Only one challenge remains in the Polar Regions that can be guaranteed to awaken the public's interest, and that is to reach the South Pole. I knew that if I could do this, the funds for my planned expedition would be assured.

Professor, it is not easy for me to tell you that my decision to take part in the competition to reach the South Pole was made in September 1909. There have been many times I have almost confided this secret to you, but then turned away, afraid that you would stop me. I have often wished that Scott could have known my decision, so that it did not look like I tried to get ahead of him without his knowledge. But I have been afraid that any public announcement would stop me. I will, however, do everything I can to meet him and announce my decision, and subsequently he can act as he decides.

As this decision was made in September last year, I think I can say that we are well prepared. From Madeira, we will set course southwards for South Victoria Land. My idea is to take nine men ashore with me and then let the Fram continue doing oceanographic research. My hope is that it will be able to do two incisions from Buenos Aires and towards Cape Verde. When the *Fram* leaves the ice, its course will be east for Punta Arenas and from there to Buenos Aires. Lieutenant Nilsen, who by this time will be in command of the ship, should, together with Kutschin, be well capable of doing a splendid job.

It is not yet possible to decide where we will go ashore, but it is my intention not to get in the way of the English. They do of course have the first right to choose. We have to settle for what they do not want. At some point in February or March 1912, the *Fram* will return to pick us up. We will first go by Lyttelton in New Zealand to cable the news, and from there to San Francisco to continue the voyage north. I have asked Helland, who has for a long time known about the plan, to deliver this letter to you in the hope that he will be able to present my case in a way that I cannot do myself. And when you make your verdict Professor, do not be too hard. I have followed the only road which stood open for me, and then it has to end as it will.

I am currently sending the King the same message, but nobody else. A couple of days after you receive this message, my brother will make a public announcement about the new addition to the expedition's plan.

Once more I beg you. Do not judge me too harshly. I am no hypocrite, but rather was forced by distress to make this decision. And so, I ask you to forgive me for what I have done. May my future work make amends for it.

Respectfully yours,

Roald Amundsen

71

Solar Skib _Fram_ .... paa Reise fra ... Finchal. til ....

Timer.	K.	F.	Vind.	St. Kurs.	Afd.	Dev.	Beh. Kurs.	Afd.	Dist.	Lod-skud.	Baro-meter.	Vandhøide i Pumpen.	Til ...... dag Middag den ......
1.													Tirsdag den 6te september 1910.
2.													Om eftermiddagen tog propellen taget af, de skulde have reist sig
3.													ud... i lægne. Stroducin... liev tillagt for fylding af vand
4.													maskabet gik i land. Samme vagt. Ankerlanternen.
5.													Onsdag den 7de september.
6.													Forlatte arbeidet med propellenakten.
7.													Halvparten af mandskabet havde landlov hele dagen.
8.													Fik ombord ferro vand. Samme vagt. Ankerlanternen.
9.													Torsdag den 8de september.
10.													Fortsatte arbeidet med propellenakten.
11.													Den anden styrmant havde landlov.
12.													Samme vagt. Ankerlanternen.
1.													Fredag den 9de september.
2.													Fortsatte arbeidet med propellaksten.
3.													... i stampikamen ...
4.													... A. Lindstrøm ...
5.													
6.													
7.													
8.													
9.													
10.													
11.													
12.													

Gen. Kurs.	Gen. Dist.	Fr. Br.	Afvign.	Pr. Br.	Obs. Br.	Fr. Lgd.	Pk. Lgd.	Obs. Lgd.	Misvisn.
						Christiania			

Logbook

Friday September 9, 1910

Kept on working on the shaft to the propeller. Finished at 5:00pm in the afternoon. Took a reading on the chronometers over the artificial horizon. Sandvik the cook was sent home. He was replaced by A. Lindstrøm.

At 6:00pm in the afternoon, it was announced that the scope of the expedition was to be expanded to include the South Pole area. The entire crew agreed to stay on.

The last day off in Funchal.
Next stop Antarctica.
Photo: FM

ROYAL GEOGRAPHICAL SOCIETY

TELEPHONE:
No. 57 MAYFAIR.

1, Savile Row,
Burlington Gardens,
London, W.

July 4th, 1912.

Capt. Roald Amundsen,
Noreg,
Buenos Aires.
Argentine Republic.

My dear Amundsen,

I have just cabled to you that the words of our President, Lord Curzon, have been grossly misrepresented. I am sending you a copy of the "Geographical Journal" containing Lord Curzon's Address, and you will see on pages 5 and 6 what he said about you. There is nothing there I am sure at which you could possibly take offence. It is very natural that he should allude to your not having said anything about your expedition until you were ready to start. There is no harm in that.

I have just seen a copy of the cable which you sent to your brother. I hope if you have not done so already that you will cable me to say that you intend to carry out the original arrangement and to lecture for the Society on November 15th. There is no feeling in England against you at all, only a feeling of admiration for the work which you have accomplished and the way in which you accomplished it, and I assure you you may be confident of receiving here a most friendly welcome. You need have no hesitation to come to England.

Personally I have great pleasure in congratulating you on what you have done. It was a very brilliant feat. As to other aspects of the matter we can talk about that when we meet and I hope that we shall do so before very long.

With kindest regards, believe me to be,

Yours very truly,

J. S. Keltie

TELEPHONE:
No. 57 MAYFAIR.

ROYAL GEOGRAPHICAL SOCIETY 1830

1, Savile Row,
Burlington Gardens,
London, W.

July 4th, 1912.

Leon Amundsen, Esq.,
Christiania, Norway.

Dear Mr Amundsen,

I am very sorry that a garbled and incorrect
version of the statement which our President, Lord Curzon
made with reference to your brother should have been transmitted to Norway. Mr Christy as I understand sent you a
correct version and you must see from that that there is
nothing but the very greatest good feeling and friendship
and admiration for your brother. Naturally some reference
had to be made to the fact that he took us all by surprise
in suddenly changing his destination from the North to the
South Pole. But there is no harm in that.

I hope that you will cable to your brother at once and
insist that he has taken a mistaken view of the position and
also write to him and send him a copy of the extract from
the Address which you have, and he will see for himself that

he has taken a wrong view of the position. There is no
feeling here at all against your brother. The only one is
one of admiration for what he has been able to accomplish
and he may be perfectly sure that he will meet here with the
most friendly and sympathetic reception.

You refer to the fact that his meeting is to be in the
Queen's Hall. It is the same Hall for which the meetings for
the Duke of the Abruzzi and for Dr Sven Hedin were held. We
took the Hall for Shackleton and for Peary but in the end the
number of applications from our members for seats was so
great that we had to take a larger Hall. There is no intention whatever of depreciating the value of what your brother
has done in any way. We have taken the Hall for the date
arranged for and all our preparations for the meeting have
been arranged. Evidently your brother is labouring under a
delusion and I trust you will do your best to persuade him
that he need have no hesitation whatever in coming to
London as already arranged.

Yours very truly,

1, Savile Row,
Burlington Gardens,
London, W.

TELEPHONE: No. 57 MAYFAIR.

September 11th, 1912.

Capt. Roald Amundsen,
Christinia, Norway.

My dear Amundsen,

Let me congratulate you on your safe return to your native land after so successful and so brilliant an expedition.

We are now making preparations for the meetings of our new session, and as your meeting comes on at an early date, November 15th. I wish to get everything in shape as soon as possible. For one thing, we ought to have an outline or sketch map of the part of the Antarctic where you were, showing your route and indicating your new discoveries that you have made. We always have, as you know, a hand-map for distribution among the audience on the night of the lecture. I should also be glad if you could let me have the manuscript of your lecture as soon as possible. It need not be the actual lecture which you propose to deliver, and which no doubt will deal to a considerable extent with the incidents of the expedition as well as with the geographical results.

What I should like you to send me would be something for publication in the "Geographical Journal" and that should deal mainly with the geographical and other scientific results of the expedition, with a very brief account of your journey. This need not extend to any great length, anything between 5000 and 6000 words might suffice to give a good idea of the main results of your work. As I say, no doubt your lecture will be of a somewhat more popular character dealing at greater length with the incidents of your journey. You will I have no doubt, have plenty of slides to show. I am not sure whether you took any cinematograph films; if so, I should be glad to know so as to make arrangements to have a cinematograph camera ready.

Trusting you may be able to oblige me in these matters, and with kindest regards,

Yours very truly,

FOUNDED 1879.

The Lecture Agency, Ltd.

(GERALD CHRISTY)

The LECTURE AGENCY, LTD. acts as agent for all the principal Lecturers and Entertainers of the day, without proprietary right; and corresponds with all the principal Literary and Scientific Societies, Philosophical Societies, Mechanics' Institutes, Y.M.C.A.'s, Lecture Associations, Colleges, Schools, Entrepreneurs, and Managers throughout the country.

SOLE AGENTS FOR **SIR ERNEST SHACKLETON** AND **COMMANDER PEARY**

Telegraphic Address: "Lecturing, London."
Telephone: "Gerrard 2899."

The Outer Temple,
Strand, London, W.C.

June the Eighth, 1911.

DEAR MR. AMUNDSEN :—

As promised this morning, I write to let you know the conditions and terms upon which we shall be pleased to act as your brother's agents for lectures if he is successful in getting to the Pole.

For the opening lecture in London, and for certain other big towns, where we should run the lecture at our own risk, the arrangement would be that the expenses of the lecture be paid out of the receipts and the net balance divided in the proportions of two-thirds to Captain Amundsen and one-third to ourselves. We take the entire responsibility. The lecturer incurs no liability whatsoever.

In the other large towns it would be better to sell the lecture (instead of running it ourselves) to some society or organisation in each town and let them work it. In these cases we should get from the societies, etc., the best terms possible. In some instances we might be able to get 65% of the gross receipts, or in certain cases it might be advisable to sell the lecture for a definite sum.

Where we do not work the lecture ourselves but place it with a society, etc., we do not share in the profits. Our remuneration takes the form of a commission of 10% on the sum we obtain for Capt. Amundsen from the society, etc.

When we are running the lecture ourselves on a sharing arrange-

ment the expenses to be deducted from the receipts will be the actual out-of-pocket expenses, such as rent of hall, advertising, printing, postage, lantern and operator, etc.

There will be no charge for our time or office expenses.

The terms mentioned above are the same upon which we worked for Scott, Shackleton, Sven Hedin, and Peary.

With regard to the disposal of your brother's time : I think he could make the best use of it by staying eight or ten weeks in Australia and giving lectures, afterwards going to South Africa for two or three weeks, and possibly touching India. This would make it August before he arrived in Europe. August and September are practically dead months for lectures in Europe. October could be utilised by appearing in a few continental cities and getting to London in time to open here at the end of the month. We could then keep him busy until well on towards Xmas. It would then be wise for him to go to America directly after Xmas in order to open there as soon as possible. He could probably lecture there for four or five months.

All this is assuming that your brother has a definite success and that Scott does not. If Scott is equally successful the book by your brother would still have considerable value, but the value of lectures here would be materially lessened.

If Scott is successful he will doubtless lecture here in the autumn, in which case your brother's arrangements should be modified as it would hardly do to have both of them lecturing here at the same time.

The fact of Captain Amundsen having lectured in Australia would not, I think, affect the success of lectures here. Nor would the publication of the book spoil things. In fact, I should be glad if the book is out before the lectures begin here. The papers would be full of reviews and notices and then is the time for the lectures.

If there is any point not sufficiently clear in the above I shall be glad to explain when you call. Don't come on Saturday as I may be away.

YOURS SINCERELY,

THE LECTURE AGENCY, LIMITED
[signature]
MANAGING DIRECTOR

LEON AMUNDSEN, ESQ.,
INNS OF COURT HOTEL,
HOLBORN, W.C.

P.S. I forgot to include in the above that if we can arrange with our correspondents in the British Empire and the U.S. for lecture tours by the Captain our commission is 5% on the net share. In regard to the Continent, we will gladly give all the help and advice we can without charge of any sort.

FOUNDED 1879

The Lecture Agency, Ltd.

(GERALD CHRISTY)

THE LECTURE AGENCY, LTD., acts as agent for all the principal Lecturers and Entertainers of the day, without proprietary right; and corresponds with all the principal Literary and Scientific Societies, Philosophical Societies, Mechanics' Institutes, Y.M.C.A.'s, Lecture Associations, Colleges, Schools, Entrepreneurs, and Managers throughout the country.

LECTURERS.

SOLE AGENTS FOR

SIR ERNEST SHACKLETON

AND

COMMANDER PEARY

ENTERTAINERS, &c.

Telegraphic Address:—
"Lecturing, London."
Telephone: "Gerrard 2899."

The Outer Temple,
Strand, London, W.C.

June the Ninth, 1911.

DEAR MR. AMUNDSEN :—

I am glad that we had the interview at Heinemann's office this afternoon as it has put things into a clearer light. Supposing your brother is successful and Scott unsuccessful it would undoubtedly be better for the book and serial rights if he came back to Europe at once. Lectures in Australasia might damage the value of the book and the serial rights. As far as lectures are concerned, I do not think that lectures in Australia would make much difference to lectures here. People would want to see and to hear the man who had first reached the South Pole, whether he had lectured elsewhere or not. It is the man who attracts.

Supposing both Scott and your brother should be successful, Scott will undoubtedly lecture here directly he returns and go on a tour

tour of Great Britain in the autumn. It would hardly do for Captain Amundsen to be lecturing here at the same time. As a matter of policy it would be unwise for him to do so. In that case, I should think your brother's better plan would be to stay a time in Australia and lecture there and go to America to lecture in the autumn. He could then come here later. He would still get a great reception from the R.G.S. here and we could book up a number of lectures.

I was very glad to see that you realised it would never do for both men to be here at once and competing in the lecture field. Such competition would look rather bad and in any case Scott would stand to win as his is a national expedition.

YOURS VERY SINCERELY,

THE LECTURE AGENCY, LTD.,
MANAGING DIRECTOR

LEON AMUNDSEN, ESQ.

The Lecture Agency, Ltd.

(GERALD CHRISTY)

LECTURERS.

Abbot, Rev. W. H., M.A. (Oxon.)
Abraham, Ashley P.
Allport, D.
Amos, Norman
Bacon, Miss
Bartlett, Captain Robert A.
Ballingham, Edgar
Benson, Capt. W., P., F.R.G.S.
Bottomley, Prof. W. B., M.A.
Bridge, Sir Frederk, C.V.O.
Bullen, Frank T., F.R.G.S.
Burgess, Harry
Churchill, Winston S., M.P.
Coles, S. K.
Compton-Rickett, Dr.
Cook, E. T., M.A.
Cox, Prof. John, M.A.
Creighton, Mrs.
Curran, T. B.
Davies, Dr. Walford
Dewar, Sir Wm.
Dibdey, Arthur
Dolmetsch, Arnold
Dunning, A. H., F.R.G.S.
Enock, Fred., F.R.E.S.
Ferguson, A. Foxton, B.A.
Garstang, Prof. J., F.R.G.S.
Garrood, W. Herbert, F.R.G.S.
Gaze, W. F., F.R.G.S.
Gill, F. Wm, F.R.G.S.
Grenada, Julian, F.R.G.S.
Green, Rev. E. F.
Grenfell, Dr. W. T., C.M.G.

Grundy, Rev. C. H., M.A.
Hall-Edwards, Dr.
Hampson, Dr. W.
Hele-Shaw, Dr., F.R.S.
Herkomer, Sir Hubert, R.A.
Hill, Alex M., M.D., F.R.C.S.
Hopkins, Father
Hughes, Spencer Leigh, M.P.
Jeffery, E. C.
Jones, Edgar R., M.P.
Kearton, R., F.Z.S.
Kerr, Richard, F.G.S., F.R.A.S.
King, F. Ashe, M.A.
Leason, Emily
Lewis, Prof. Vivian B.
Lynton, The Earl of
McCulloch, Francis
Mackinder, H.J., M.P.
MacVeagh, Jeremiah, M.P.
Malden, Arthur
Marshall, Dr.
Masterman-Cannon, J.H.B., M.A.
McClintock, Walter
Mills, J. Travis, M.A.
Milne, Prof., F.R.S.
Money, L. G. Chiozza, M.P.
Montanaro, E. T., M.A.
Moscheles, Felix
Mountmorres, Viscount
Nansen, Dr. Fridtjof
Needham, Mrs., T., F.R.G.S.
Nogales, Rev. J. L.
O'Connor, Miss Madeleine
Owen, Will
Peary, Commander Robert E.
Perrin, Prof. of Flinders, F.R.S.

Phillips, Maberly, F.S.A.
Pitt, Geo. E., B.Sc.
Preece, H. C.
Pulleine, Rev. John R.
Raven-Hill, L. (of Punch)
Rawling, Capt. C. G.
Rolleston, T. W. G. (of Gaol)
Ridge, W. Pett
Rose, Dr. J. Holland
Salesby, C. W., M.D., F.R.S.E.
Saunders, Charles
Scott, Capt. R.F., R.N., F.R.G.S.
Seton, Ernest Thompson
Shackleton, Sir Ernest, C.V.O.
Smith, S. C. Kaines, M.A.
Spielmann, M. H., F.S.A.
Stanton, V. G., M.A., F.R.A.S.
Sterling, Frank
Stevens, Frank
Storr-Best, F.A.
Synan, V. C. G.
Teagarthen, J. C.
Villiers, Frederic
Wallis, Whitworth, F.S.A.
Watts-Dunton, Ada
Webber, Dr. George, C.I.E., etc.
Webber, Stafford, R.A., Bishop
Whitfield, Richard
Wilson, Dr. Andrew, F.R.S.E.
Wilson, Miss Mary, A.R.A.M.
Winn, Capt. R. C. A., F.R.S.
Wing, Tom
Withers, Dr., F.S.S.
Wood, Dr. George, F.E.S.
Woollatt, Dr. G. H.
Worthington, Prof. A.M., F.R.S.
Yeats, W. B.
Yoxall, Sir James, M.P.

ENTERTAINERS.

Artistes of all kinds
Bands, etc., various
Bowich, Miss Ellen
Brand, Olliery
Byrd-Page, Dr.
Capper, Alfred
Cinematograph, The
Cramer, Miss, The Largest
Crocker, Miss Grace Jean
Denny, Ernest
Drew, Mr. and Mrs. Dennis
Bantock Glee Singers
Fisk Jubilee Trio
Frân-Song Quartette, The
Fisk Jubilee Quartette
French, Percy
Garcia, Emile
Hastings, Everet
Hercul
Hill, Harrison
Jackson, Nelson
Kendal, Mrs.
Leoni Ladies' Quintette
Marr, Miss Helen
Millar, Gertie
Moore, Madame Bertha
Tremblat
Shaw, Miss Gwendolin
Smithson, Miss Laura
Tree, Lady Beerbohm
Upson, Arthur
Walom Quartette
Wesser, Arthur
Webber, Stafford
Wessely String Quartette
Westminster Singers

DUM LOQUOR HORA FUGIT

The LECTURE AGENCY, Ltd. (Founded 1879), acts as agent, without proprietary right, for all the leading Lecturers and Entertainers of the day, and corresponds with all the principal Societies, Scientific and Philosophical Societies, Mechanics' Institutes, Y.M.C.A.'s, Lecture Associations, Colleges, Schools, Entrepreneurs, and Managers throughout the country.

Telephone: GERRARD 2899

Telegrams: "LECTURING, LONDON"

The Outer Temple, Strand, London, W.C.

MARCH EIGHTH, 1912

DEAR MR. AMUNDSEN :-

First of all let me offer you my warmest congratulations on the success of your brother, Captain Roald Amundsen.

Of course, until we also definitely hear the result of Captain R.F.Scott's expedition it will probably be difficult for you to make final plans.

I have heard from our friend Carlyle Smythe of Australia that he has arranged with you for Captain Amundsen to lecture there before he returns to Europe. I imagine that Captain Amundsen will lecture in Australia irrespective of whether Captain Scott is successful, especially as it is highly improbable that Scott will lecture in Australia, or, at any rate, give more than one official lecture. Captain Scott would have to give one lecture, because of the support given him by the Commonwealth Government. Otherwise, I am sure that Scott will reserve himself for Great Britain.

When you were here you agreed that it would be unwise for Captain Amundsen to come for lectures here until Scott had lectured provided Scott does get to the South Pole. I think that this attitude is wise and is likely

to

-- 2 --

to secure the sympathy of the British public ; but if Captain Scott has failed to get to the South Pole, there will then be no reason why your brother should delay his visit to Great Britain and he should come here as soon as convenient after his return to Europe.

I think that Captain Amundsen should certainly visit England before going to any other European country --- excepting, of course, your own land.

Captain Scott is unlikely to be lecturing here later than the end of November or the beginning of December. He is a naval officer and will not be able to devote as much time to lectures as a mean would who was not in the Royal Navy.

I am sure you will keep me fully posted as to Captain Amundsen's movements. People are already writing to me for particulars as to what Captain Amundsen intends to do.

I will write again as soon as there is news of any kind of Scott and his expedition. It will then be much easier to lay plans and will prevent any feeling that there might be that we were trying to get Captain Amundsen in without giving a fair show to Scott. We must have the public with us to ensure a big success, as you will fully understand.

With kind regards,
YOURS SINCERELY,
[signature]

LEON AMUNDSEN, ESQ.,
CHRISTIANIA,
NORWAY.

All fees quoted include travelling and other personal expenses, unless otherwise stated. The Lantern, Kinematograph, and Operator or Piano and Accompanist (where such may be required) must be provided by the Society engaging, unless special arrangements be made. In case an engagement be unavoidably cancelled by reason of sickness, accident, or other unavoidable cause, it is understood that there be no claim for damages, but a new date will be given the same season when possible.

LEON AMUNDSEN.

-2-

P.S.   I think I can say definitely that September would

be a very bad time to lecture here. That is the holiday

month even more than August. Everybody who is anybody is

out of London and Parliament will be closed.

The Lecture Agency, Ltd.

(GERALD CHRISTY)

LECTURERS.

Abbot, Rev. W. H., M.A.(Oxon.)
Abrahams, Ashley P.
Allport, J. W.
Angell, Norman
Bacon, Miss
Baildon, Captain Robert A.
Bellairs, Commander, R.N.
Bellingham, Edgar
Mignahni, Fabio
Hughes, Spencer Leigh, M.P.
Jeffery, E. G.
Jones, Edgar R., M.P.
Kearton, R., F.Z.S.
Kearton, Cherry
Kerr, Richard, F.G.S., F.R.A.S.
King, Hall, Baldwin, M.A.
Lowes, Emily
Lowes, Prof. Vivian B.
Lytton, The Earl of
Churchill, Winston S., M.P.
Cody, S. F.
Coller, Percy
Compton-Rickett, Dr.
Cook, E. T., M.A., SL, F.R.A.S.
Corbin, Prof. John, M.A.
Cox, Prof. John, M.A.
McCabe, Joseph
Maiden, Arthur
Marriott-Watson, H.B.
Martin-Duncan, F.
Macfarren, Walter
Mills, Ernest H., M.A.
Milne, Prof. John, F.R.S.
Crosland, Wilf, M.P.
Curran, T. H.
Davies, Dr. Walford
Dibley, Arthur, F.R.G.S.
Dittmarsdt, Arnold, F.R.G.S.
Donnina, A. H., F.R.G.S.
Enock, Fred., F.R.E.S.
Fergusson, A. Foster, B.A.
Fergus John Foster, F.R.G.S.
Money, L. G. Chiozza, M.P.
Moore, Madame Bertha
Moore, Viscount
Mountmorres, Viscount
Nansen, Dr. Fridtjof
Neddon, Mrs.
Norgate, Rev. T. T., F.R.G.S.
O'Conor, Miss Madeleine
Garrison, W. Herbert, F.R.G.S.
Gay, W. E., F.R.G.S.
Gill, T. P., F.R.G.S.
Gleeson, Rev. John, F.R.G.S.
Grande, Julian, F.R.G.S.
Greer, W. P., F.R.G.S.
Grenfell, Dr. W. T., C.M.G.
Peary, Commander Robert E.
Petrie, Prof. Flinders, F.R.S.

Phillips, Maberly, F.S.A.
Pitt, Geo. E., B.Sc.
Preston, H. G.
Raphael, John A. (of Punch)
Rawling, Capt. C. G.
Read, W. Prof Powell
Robertson, J. M., M.P.
Russ, D. J. Ireland
Salesby, C. W., M.D., F.R.S.E.
Saunders, Charles
Schooling, J. Holt
Schomberg, Capt. F., R.N., F.R.G.S.
Selons, F. C.
Scharp, Capt. Jas. Thompson
Sharp, Cecil J., B.A.
Smith, Dr. Gurlain, M.A.
Spielmann, M. H., F.S.A.
Spitta, Dr. R. J., F.R.A.S.
Stirling, Dr. Dr., B.A.
Sumatharent, F. C. de
Turneareana, G.
Villiers, Frederic
Wallis, Whitworth, F.S.A.
Ward, Miss Ada C.I.E., etc.
Watson, J. Steinfort
Webber, Stafford, B.A.
Wild, The Very Rev. Bishop
Whiteman, Richard
Wild, Frank
Wilson, The Andrew, F.R.S.E.
Wilson, Miss Mary, A.R.A.M.
Windle, Prof. B. C. A., F.R.S.
Withers, Dr. Percy
Wood, Rev. Theodore, F.E.S.
Worsfold, W. Basil
Worsfold, Dr. T. Cato
Worthington, Prof.A.M., F.R.S.
Yoxall, Sir James, M.P.

ENTERTAINERS.

Artistes of all kinds
Bands and Orchestras, various
Bowick, Miss Ellen
Brough, Gilbury
Bryceson, Dr.
Capper, Alfred
Churcher, Walter
Cinematograph, The
Cooper, Miss Margaret
Crocker, Miss Grace Joan
Dale, Frederic
Drew, Mr. and Mrs. Dennis
English Glee Singers
Folk-Song Quartette, The
French Minuet Quartette
French, Percy
Gandy, Sidney
Hercaut
Hill, Harrison
Jaxon, Frank G.
Kendall, Mrs.
Lamberti, Professor
Lauder Quintette
Mdr. Miss Helen
Moore, Madame Bertha
Sewell, Ernest
Shaw, Miss Gwendolyn
Smithson, Miss Laura
Tomalin, Miss Gertrude
Tree, Herbert Beerbohm
Ujile-Smith, A.
Upton, Mrs. Frederic
Watson, Quartette
Watson, Alexander
Webber, Stafford
Welldoferd, Ernest
Westminster String Quartette
Westminster Singers

Telegrams:
"LECTURING, LONDON"

The LECTURE AGENCY, Ld. (Founded 1879), acts as agent, without proprietary right, for all the leading Lecturers and Entertainers of the day, and corresponds with all the principal Literary, Scientific, and Philosophical Societies, Mechanics' Institutes, Y.M.C.A.'s, Lecture Associations, Colleges, Schools, Entrepreneurs, and Managers throughout the country.

Telephone:
GERRARD
2899

The Outer Temple, Strand, London, W.C.

March 26th, 1912.

Dear Mr. Amundsen:-

Many thanks for your letters of the 19th instant and

the 21st instant. I shall hope to be able to write you fully

to-morrow but I have not yet had a chance to see Sir Ernest

Shackleton as he is away until to-morrow and I should also like

to try and find out what the Geographical Society are thinking

of doing.

When Captain Scott went he was quite prepared to stay

a second year if necessary and he had stores sufficient for a

second year. People are now beginning to say that it is quite

likely he is staying. However, it is quite impossible to come

to any conclusions of the sort for some while yet.

YOURS SINCERELY,

LEON AMUNDSEN, ESQ.,
CHRISTIANIA.

All fees quoted include travelling and other personal expenses, unless otherwise stated. The Lantern, Kinematograph, and Operator or Piano and Accompanist (where such may be required) must be provided by the Society engaging, unless special arrangements be made. In case an engagement be unfulfilled by reason of sickness, accident, or other unavoidable cause, it is understood that there be no claim for damages, but a new date will be given the same season when possible.

The Lecture Agency, Ltd.

(GERALD CHRISTY)

LECTURERS.

Abbot, Rev. C. H., M.A. (Oxon.)
Abraham, Ashley P.
Allbutt, V.
Angell, Norman
Bacon, Miss
Bartlett, Captain Robert A.
Bellars, J., Commander, R.N.
Bellingham, Edgar
Benson, Capt. W. J. P., F.R.G.S.
Bingley, E. C.
Bottomley, Prof. W. B., M.A.
Bowring, Rev. Peter, Rev. C.B.,M.A.
Bridge, Sir Frederick, C.V.O.
Bullen, Frank T., F.R.G.S.
Burge, Rev. J.
Churchill, Winston S., M.P.
Cody, S. F.
Collins, A. M., M.A.
Compton-Rickett, D.
Cook, E. T., M.A., S.J., F.R.A.S.
Cox, Prof. John, M.A.
Creighton, Mrs.
Curran, T. B.
Davies, Dr. Walford
Davies-Duncan, W.
Dibley, Arthur, F.R.G.S.
Dolmetsch, Arnold
Dunning, A. H., F.R.G.S.
Enock, Fred., F.E.S.
Ferguson, A. Foxton, B.A.
French, Field, Franc, F.R.G.S.
Garrison, W. Herbert, F.R.G.S.
Gass, W. E., F.R.G.S.
Grande, Julian, F.R.G.S.
Gleeson, Rev. John, F.R.G.S.
O'Connor, Miss Madeleine
Owen, Will
Penrose, Commander Robert E.
Petrie, Prof. Flinders, F.R.S.

Grundy, Rev. C. H., M.A.
Hall-Edwards, Dr.
Hampson, Dr. W.
Hedin, Dr. Sven
Hole-Shaw, Dr., F.R.S.A.
Hill, Alex., M.A., M.B., F.R.C.S.
Hopkins, Father
Hughes, Spencer Leigh, M.P.
Jeffery, E. C.
Jones, Edgar R., F.Z.S.
Kearton, R., F.Z.S.
Kernahan, Coulson
Kerr, Richard, F.G.S., F.R.A.S.
King, A. Ashe, M.A.
Lessar, Emile
Lister, Prof. Dylan B.
Lytton, The Earl of
McCullagh, Francis
Mackinder, H. J., M.P.
MacVeagh, Jeremiah, M.P.
Mahaffy, Joseph
Malden, Arthur
Marshall, Dr. Eric
Masterman-Canon J.H.B., M.A.
Milne, Prof. John
Mills, J. Travis, M.A.
Money, L. G. Chiozza, M.P.
Monteith, E. H., M.A.
Moscheles, Felix
Mountmorres, Viscount
Nansen, Dr. Fridtjof
Norgate, Rev. T. T., F.R.G.S.

ENTERTAINERS.

Artistes of all kinds
Bands and Orchestras, various
Bowie, Miss Ellen
Brindley, Oliver
Byrd-Page, Dr.
Chester, Frederick
Churcher, Walter
Cooper, Miss Margaret
Crocker, Miss Grace Jean
Dale, Frederick
Denny, Ernest
English Opera Singers
Fisk Jubilee Trio
Folk-Song Quartette, The
"Frau Musica" Quartette
French, Percy
Gunter, Silvester
Hastings, Ernest
Hervat
Hill, Harrison
Jackson, Nelson
Jacoby, Leopold
Lambert, Leslie
Leoni Ladies' Quintette
Meister Glee Singers
Moore, Madame Bertha
Seale, Frederick
Shaw, Miss Gwendolyn
Svendsen, Miss Laura
Tree, Lady Beerbohm
Upton, Mr. and Mrs. Frederick
Walton Quartette
Weaver, Antley
Webber, Stafford
Westminster Glee Party
Wessely String Quartette
Westminster Singers

Phillips, Maberly, F.S.A.
Pitt, Geo. E., B.Sc.
Preston, H. G.
Raphael, John R.
Ravens-Hill, L. (of Punch)
Reed, E. T. (of Punch)
Ridler, W. Pett
Rose, Dr., Holland
Sidebury, C. W., M.D., F.R.S.E.
Scott-Cope, F.R.A., R.N., F.R.G.S.
Seton, Ernest Thompson
Shackleton, Sir Ernest, C.V.O.
Smith, S. C., Kaines, M.A.
Spittin, Dr. E. J., F.R.A.S.
Stevens, Frank
Stuart, Dr. Wm.
Sunniehurst, F. C. de
Tregarthen, J. C.
Villiers, Frederic
Ward, Miss Ada L.
Watts, Sir Geo., C.I.E., etc.
Weldon, The Rt. Rev. Bishop
Whiteing, Richard
Wilson, Dr. Andrew, F.R.S.E.
Wilson, Miss Mary A.R.A.M.
Wing, Tom
Wood, Rev. Theodore, F.E.S.
Woollatt, Dr. G. H.
Worthington, Prof. A.M., F.R.S.
Yeats, W. B.
Voxall, Sir James, M.P.

Telegrams: "LECTURING, LONDON."

Telephone: GERRARD 2899

The LECTURE AGENCY, Ltd. (Founded 1879), acts as agent, without proprietary right, for all the leading Lecturers and Entertainers of the day, and corresponds with all the principal Literary, Scientific, and Philosophical Societies, Mechanics' Institutes, Y.M.C.A.'s, Lecture Associations, Colleges, Schools, Entrepreneurs, and Managers throughout the country.

The Outer Temple, Strand, London, W.C.

March 26th, 1912.

DEAR MR. AMUNDSEN :-

Since I wrote you yesterday I have had a long talk with Sir Ernest Shackleton. He naturally says that nothing whatever can be arranged until we hear some news of Captain Scott. It is quite possible to hear from him in at least a fortnight, and it might also be quite three weeks; but if he is not back by then it will certainly look as if something had prevented him from getting back this year at all. When he went out he was quite prepared to stay a second year if necessary, and if we do not hear from him within one month from now it will be fairly certain that he is not coming back this year.

Until this month has elapsed I don't see how anything can be settled definitely for England, as if Scott has had success and is lecturing it would never do for your brother to be here also. If Scott's expedition has been a complete failure, or if he doesn't come home at all this year I don't see why the field should not be clear for your brother.

I think it is quite natural that the interest in the expedition should be greater in the German and Scandinavian countries than in England, as your brother is a Scandinavian, and the British public naturally wanted the Britisher to be successful. By this I don't mean that there is any ill feeling. Quite the reverse. The English public would rather a Norwegian

were

−2−

were successful than any other nationality.

With regard to a guarantee : I may say definitely that I will not give one. I did not give a guarantee in the case of Nansen, Shackleton, Scott or Peary, and what was good enough for them ought to be good enough for Amundsen. It is quite possible there are people in England who would give him a good guarantee, but surely the money side of the question is not everything. Other things have to be considered and I imagine your brother would like to come to England under the best possible auspices and have his tour managed in the best possible way. It might be that more money could be obtained if your brother were to appear in theatres and music halls here end under the management of a music hall manager ; but he would lose caste socially and his prestige would be seriously damaged. I would run him when he does come on the usual sharing arrangement, and there is no plan which will give a greater return to the lecturer than the sharing arrangement.

I have also had a talk with Dr. Keltie and tried to learn from him what the Royal Geographical Society's plans are likely to be. Of course, he could say nothing definite until the uncertainty about Captain Scott is entirely cleared up. The impression I gathered from what Dr. Keltie said was, that he was rather doubtful whether they would be able to arrange for a great public welcome as they did in the cases of Scott and Shackleton. Of course, they would send you an invitation for your brother to come over and give them a lecture. He would have a hearty welcome and an enthusiastic audience. I think it would rather damp their enthusiasm if he did not come over to give them a lecture until after he had been all round the continent. To my mind the best plan would be for him to set aside a particular month, say November, for the visit to England, and then go on again in Germany up till, say, the end of January, and be ready to open in America early in February. Lectures go on a good deal later into the spring in America than they do here.

September would be quite useless here, and October is not a very good month. November and December are our best months. The Royal Geographical Society does not generally commence its autumn session until the last Monday in October or the first Monday in November. I am sure they would like to have your brother for the opening meeting. My suggestion is, to fill October on the continent, November in England, December and January on the continent, and possibly February : and then go to America.

However, as I have said, it is impossible to decide anything definitely until we have news of Scott.

Have

All fees quoted include travelling and other personal expenses, unless otherwise stated. The Lantern, Kinematograph and Operator or Piano and Accompanist (where such may be required) must be provided by the Society engaging, unless special arrangements be made. In case an engagement is unfulfilled by reason of sickness, accident, or other unavoidable cause, it is understood that there be no claim for damages, but a new date will be given the same season when possible.

The Right Hon. A. J. BALFOUR, when presiding at a lecture given by Sir Ernest Shackleton at North Berwick on Sept. 22nd, 1910, said, in proposing a vote of thanks—"'I confess my own expectations have been greatly surpassed. A more moving story of heroic effort, of physical endurance, of boundless courage, I do not think has ever been put before an audience.''

PUBLIC HALL, SUTTON.

UNDER THE PATRONAGE OF—

The Hon. Mrs. FRANCIS COLBORNE.
Sir WILLIAM VINCENT, Bart., J.P.,
Sir EDWARD COATES, Bart., M.P.
Rev. H. W. TURNER, M.A.
A. SPENCER JACKSON, Esq.

E. J. HOLLAND, Esq., J.P., C.C.
R. W. WOOTTEN, Esq.
A. HYSLOP, Esq., J.P.
Mrs. COLMAN.
S. BARROW, Esq., Jun., J.P.
E. H. HENSLEY, Esq., M.A.
And many others.

Messrs. WILLIAM PILE, Ltd. have the honour to announce that they have arranged with THE LECTURE AGENCY, Ltd., of London for

Sir ERNEST SHACKLETON, C.V.O, F.R.G.S.

TO GIVE HIS

POPULAR LECTURE

ENTITLED

"The South Pole"

ON

Tuesday, May 7th, 1912,

AT 8.30 P.M.

In addition to giving a popular account of his own South Polar Expedition, SIR ERNEST will describe and explain the Expeditions under Captain SCOTT and Captain AMUNDSEN.

The Lecture will be fully illustrated from photographs and some very **striking kinematograph films** taken during the Expedition.

The Chair will be taken by

HENRY KESWICK, Esq., M.P.

RESERVED SEATS, 5/- & 3/-; UNRESERVED, 2/- & 1/-.

Carriages at 10. Commence at 8.30.

Plan of Hall and Tickets are NOW READY at Messrs. WILLIAM PILE, LTD.'s, 26 High Street, Sutton.

TELEPHONE SUTTON 4.

Photo by Thomson, New Bond Street.

—3—

        Have you fixed for the book in England yet? It would be well to get that settled as soon as possible. I hope it will be possible for you to let Heinemann have it. He is about the most influential publisher here, and far away the most energetic.

                        With kind regards,

                                YOURS SINCERELY,

                                [signature]

LEON AMUNDSEN, ESQ.,
CHRISTIANIA,
Norway.

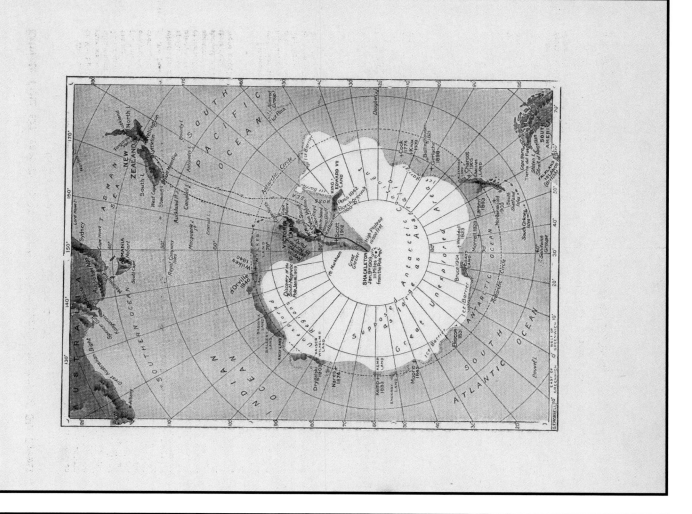

O F all the deeds that men have endeavoured to accomplish none has so aroused the enthusiasm and held the imagination of mankind as the many gallant efforts to penetrate the mysterious regions about the Northern and Southern Poles. Heroes of various nationalities have ventured their lives upon the search, and tragedy has hallowed the long record of Polar Exploration. British explorers occupy a prominent position in the roll of these redoubtable navigators, and our people are always eager to acclaim the man, no matter what his race, who has succeeded in reducing the weary leagues that divide us from a knowledge of either Pole.

To Sir Ernest Shackleton, of the *Nimrod*, belongs the high distinction of having come within a degree or so of the South Pole. Up to the reaching of the South Pole by Captain Roald Amundsen, the record for Antarctic discovery was held by the Shackleton Expedition. Needless to say, such a notable achievement entailed much suffering and privation. Lieutenant Shackleton and his dauntless companions on the famous sledge-journey were men inured to hardship, and they knew that such an attempt as theirs must be a perpetual conflict with death itself. Day after day, for over four months, they forced their way over the illimitable ice, covering a distance of 1,708 miles, encountering blizzards that blew at a rate of seventy miles per hour, and all the while the thermometer registered from seventy to seventy-two degrees of frost. Eight ponies were taken on board the *Nimrod*, but unfortunately four of these died before the great sledge-journey began. Otherwise the British flag might have been hoisted at the South Pole. Only men of the highest intrepidity could have made their way over the enormous glacier giving access to the Antarctic tableland. Numerous crevasses and ice-falls presented considerable danger. On January 9th of this year the southernmost point was reached, and, finding their provisions were almost exhausted, the party reluctantly started for the *Nimrod*. Nothing could be seen to the southward save a vast expanse of snow, and the Southern Pole still preserved its mystery despite their heroic effort.

The observations of the Expedition will enrich our knowledge of the world in which we live and the conditions which gave it birth. Coal measures were discovered, proving that at some remote time this frost-bound desert supported a rich vegetation. There were glacial indications which showed that in another age the cold was even greater than at present.

Sir Ernest Shackleton and his comrades have covered themselves with undying honour, and have written their names among the greatest of Polar explorers. They have won for their country the glory of an exploit which stands unparalleled. They have nobly discharged their promise to the King and Queen to carry the British flag a long stage nearer to the goal of all efforts—to the heart of the land which lies round the Southern Pole.

Sir Ernest Henry Shackleton, Commander of the Royal Victorian Order and gold and silver medallist of the Royal Geographical Society, is the eldest son of Henry Shackleton, M.D., of Kilkea, County Kildare, and Sydenham, London. He was born in 1874, and received his education at Dulwich College. At the age of sixteen he went to sea in the merchant service, and was an officer on a troop-ship during the South African War. In 1901 he joined the National Antarctic Expedition, and in 1902 accompanied Captain Scott on the famous sledging journey that resulted in the attainment of the then "farthest south" record, latitude 82° 17' S., being reached. At the end of 1902 he was invalided. He assisted to fit out the Argentine Relief Expedition which went to the aid of the Swedes; and he also fitted out, under an Admiralty Committee, the *Discovery* Relief Expeditions. For a time he was assistant secretary and treasurer, but he resigned this appointment to contest Scottish Geographical Society appointed him secretary and treasurer. He married in 1904. The Royal Dundee at the Election of 1906. He then became personal assistant to Mr. William Beardmore, of the Glasgow firm of armour-plate manufacturers and battleship builders, and in 1907 he organized and fitted out the British Antarctic Expedition, afterwards leading it with that conspicuous success now known to all the world. The honour of Knighthood was conferred upon him in November, 1909.

ALL THE KINEMATOGRAPH FILMS USED IN THIS LECTURE ARE NON-INFLAMMABLE.

The Lecture Agency, Ltd.

(GERALD CHRISTY)

LECTURERS.

Abbot, Rev. W. H., M.A. (Oxon.)
Abrahams, Arthur P.
Albert, A.
Angell, Norman
Bacon, Miss
Bartlett, Captain Robert A.
Bellairs, C. Commander, R.N.
Bellingham, Edgar
Bennett, Sir T., R., M.A.
Borwell, Montague
Boyd-Carpenter, Rev.A.B.,M.A.
Bridge, Sir Frederick, C.V.O.
Bullen, Frank T., F.R.G.S.
Burgess, Harry
Churchill, Winston S., M.P.
Cody, S. F.
Cooper, Rev. A. N., M.A.
Compton-Rickett, Dr.
Cook, E. T., M.A.
Cortie, Rev. A.L., S.J.,F.R.A.S.
Cox, Prof. John, M.A.
Creighton, Mrs.
Crooke, Will, M.P.
Curran, Pett
Danby, Dr. Wakford
De Windt, Harry
Diósy, Arthur, F.S.G.S.
Dighenesco, A. Rudolph, F.R.G.S.
Dunmore, G. A., F.R.F.C.S.
Enock, Fred., F.E.S.
Ferguson, A. Foxton, B.A.
Fraser, John Foster, F.R.G.S.
Garrison, W. Herbert, F.R.G.S.
Gibbon, Perceval, F.R.G.S.
Gill, T. W., F.R.G.S.
Glazier, Rev. John, F.R.G.S.
Grande, Julian, F.R.G.S.
Green, Thos. W., F.R.G.S.
Grenfell, Dr. W. T., C.M.G.

Grundy, Rev. C. H., M.A.
Hall-Edwards, Dr.
Hannah, Ian, M.A.
Hedin, Dr. Sven
Heerfordt, T. Edw., F.R.S.
Herkomer, Sir H. von, R.A.
Hill, Alex. M.A., M.D., F.R.C.S.
Hopkins, Father
Hughes, Spencer Leigh, M.P.
Jefferys, E. C.
Jones, Edgar R., M.P.
Kernahan, Coulson
Kerr, Richard, F.G.S., F.R.A.S.
Julian, J. R., F.R.G.S.
Lessate, Emile
Lewes, Prof. Vivian B.
Lynch, Arthur, M.P.
McCullagh, Francis
Macdonald, Rev. F. W.
Mackintosh, Rev. J. S., M.A.
MacVeagh, Jeremiah, M.P.
McCabe, Joseph
McClure, Nathan
Marshall, Dr. Eric
Martin-Duncan, F.
Mercer, Wm. J., J.H.B., M.A.
McClintock, Walter
Mills, J. Travis, M.A.
Milne, Prof. John, F.R.S.
Mitchell, P. Chalmers, M.P.
Montanban, E. H., M.A.
Moore, Madame Bertha
Nansen, Dr. Fridtjof
Needham, Mrs.
Noailles, Rev., T., F.R.G.S.
O'Connor, Miss Madeleine
Owen, Will
Peary, Commander Robert E.
Petrie, Prof. Flinders, F.R.S.

ENTERTAINERS.

Artistes of all kinds.
Bands and Orchestras, various
Bowle, Miss Ellen
Brough, Mary
Byrd-Page, Dr.
Caprer, Alfred
Churcher, Walter
Cunnninngham, The
Crocker, Miss Grace Jean
Denny, Ernest
Drew, Mr. and Mrs. Dennis
Elliott-Page Singers
Féa Jubilee Trio
Falace Male Quartette, The
Falace Opera Singers Quartette
French, Percy
Hastings, Ernest
Hercat
Hill Harrison
Jackson, Nelson
Landini, Leslie
Leoni Ladies' Quintette
Meister Glee Singers
Moore, Madame Bertha
Shaw, Miss Gwendolyn
Sewell, Miss Fanny
Tomalin, Miss Gertrude
Tree, Lady Beerbohm
Upton, Mr. and Mrs. Frederic
Walenn Quartette
Weaver, Astley
Wethered, Ernest
Westminster Singers
Weesely String Quartette

Phillips, Mabwrby, F.S.A.
Pitt, Geo. H., B.Sc.
Preece, H. C.
Raven-Hill, L. (of Punch)
Rawling, Capt., C. G.
Richmond, G. (of Punch)
Ridge, W. Pett
Robertson, J., M.P.
Saleeby, C. W., M.D., F.A.S.E.
Saunders, Charles
Scott, Capt., R.F., R.N., F.R.G.S.
Selous, Ernest Thompson
Shackleton, Sir Ernest, C.V.O.
Smith, S. C. Kaines, M.A.
Spielmann, M. H., F.S.A.
Stevens, Frank
Stirling, J. C.
Teagarten, J. C.
Villiers, Frederic
Wallis, Whitworth, F.S.A.
Watt, Sir Geo., C.I.E., etc.
Wellby, Mrs. of Mrs. Bishop
Whitelaw, Richard
Wild, Frank
Wilson, Dr. Andrew., F.R.S.E.
Wilson, Miss M., A.R.C.M.
Wing, Tom
Wood, Rev. Theodore, F.E.S.
Woollcott, Dr. G. H.
Worthington, Prof. A.M., F.R.S.
Yoxall, Sir James, M.P.

Telegrams:
"LECTURING,
LONDON."

Telephone:
GERRARD
2899

The Outer Temple, Strand, London, W.C.

April 17th, 1912.

Dear Mr. Amundsen :—

Since I wrote you last I have spoken to Dr. Keltie, and I find that the Royal Geographical Society would have a very strong objection to your brother appearing at the public luncheon suggested by the Royal Societies' Club on any date prior to their lecture. Absolutely the first public appearance in England must be *your lecture* for them. I think it is very important that you study them in every way. I am therefore telling the Royal Societies' Club that the luncheon they propose to give cannot be before the meeting on November 18th.

May I tell the Royal Societies' Club that Captain Amundsen will be very pleased to accept the invitation for a luncheon on November 19th, or some convenient date after that ?

Yours sincerely,

LEON AMUNDSEN, ESQ.

Extracts from the reports in the London daily papers concerning Sir Ernest Shackleton's Lecture in the Albert Hall.

The Times.

The Royal Geographical Society gave a reception in Mr. Shackleton's honour in the Albert Hall, when he gave an account of the results of his expedition, illustrated with lantern slides ; and afterwards the Prince of Wales, as Vice-Patron of the Society, presented medals to Mr. Shackleton and his comrades. The Princess of Wales was also present. The scene in the hall was brilliant in the extreme, every division of the building being crowded with ladies in evening dress and gentlemen who wore distinguished orders.

Mr. Shackleton was received with great cheering when he stepped forward to give his lecture. He spoke easily and clearly, and he was heard distinctly all over the hall. His humorous descriptions of the habits of the rotifer, which can endure the extremes of heat and cold apparently without discomfort, and of the penguins, which showed an almost human curiosity in the explorers and their dog, were heard with great appreciation. The Lantern slides were excellent.

The Standard.

Lieutenant Shackleton's first formal account of his expedition to the South Pole was given last night by the explorer at a special meeting of the Geographical Society, held, and held necessarily, in the Royal Albert Hall. The Prince and Princess of Wales honoured the occasion by their presence, and the great hall was packed from floor to ceiling.

From the moment that Lieutenant Shackleton commenced his address until its close he held his whole audience spellbound. It was a wonderful gathering, and capable of appreciating to the full a wonderful narrative modestly told—a narrative of intrepid heroism, in which every member of the party had his honoured place, and the story of a feat worthy to rank high among the greatest geographical exploits, and of an enterprise that has advanced the credit of the race and brought distinction on the British flag.

The Daily News.

The most remarkable of the scenes of enthusiasm through which Lieutenant Shackleton and his brave men have passed since their return to England from the historic dash to the South Pole was witnessed last night beneath the vast dome of the Albert Hall. In his breezy Irish way and in the simplest language the intrepid explorer told the story of his adventures and achievements and the vast audience, which packed the huge hall from floor to ceiling, listened spellbound.

The Morning Post.

Mr. Shackleton, whose magnificent voyage to the South Polar regions has called forth the admiration of the whole civilized world, received the welcome of his countrymen last evening in the Albert Hall. The occasion was a special meeting of the Royal Geographical Society to hear the explorer, surrounded by the majority of his comrades, tell the thrilling story of his journey. A distinguished company assembled to do honour to Mr. Shackleton and the members of his expedition. Their Royal Highnesses the Prince and Princess of Wales were present, the Prince occupying a seat on the platform, the Princess of Wales, with her suite, being seated in the front row of the arena. There was no part of the vast hall unoccupied, even the rows from which no view of the screen could be obtained being crowded. As long as three hours before the meeting began ticket holders were awaiting admittance. Mr. Shackleton spoke for more than an hour in an easy-going narrative style without notes, and he held the interest of the vast audience without a moment's pause. After the extraordinary endurance of the explorers, described in the simplest of language by their leader, the feature of the address was the dry humour in which Mr. Shackleton told many incidents which occurred during the long period of exile. Nor were all the pictures serious, and the animated photographs which were shown at the close of the address to illustrate life in the Antarctic regions were the first of their kind to be presented. The last part of the proceedings was devoted to the handing of the Society's special gold medal to Mr. Shackleton by the Prince of Wales, who made a speech of commendation and expressed his pride "as a brother sailor" in what had been achieved.

The Daily Mail.

In the simplest, most matter-of-fact language, with no attempt at rhetoric, no flourishes, but with all the eloquence that comes from sincerity and intimate knowledge of the subject, Lieutenant Shackleton, the famous explorer, last evening delivered one of the most fascinating lectures ever heard in London.

It was a wonderful scene in the Albert Hall, where the lecture—the first by Mr. Shackleton since his return after his memorable journey in the Antarctic—was given under the auspices of the Royal Geographical Society. A splendid audience gathered to listen to the young explorer. The Prince of Wales, wearing the ribbon of the Garter, was on the platform, and the Princess of Wales sat in a front stall.

When the lantern slides were displayed, it became evident that the photographic record of the Shackleton expedition is not the least remarkable of the successes achieved. One realized the Antarctic in these extraordinary pictures—one felt its vast desolation, its mystery, its beauty, and its terror. Again and again the spectators cheered as Mr. Shackleton showed some picture of weird snow or ice formation, of strange clouds and stranger light effects, or some picture indicating the hardships the expedition suffered, and the cheerfulness with which they were encountered.

Telegrams: "Lecturing, London."

Telephone: Gerrard 2899.

Sole Agents for Sir ERNEST SHACKLETON: THE LECTURE AGENCY, LTD., The Outer Temple, London, W.C.

All fees quoted include travelling and other personal expenses, unless otherwise stated. The Lantern, Kinematograph, and Operator or Piano and Accompanist (where such may be required) must be provided by the Society engaging, unless special arrangements be made. In case an engagement be cancelled by reason of sickness, accident, or other unavoidable cause, it is understood that there be no claim for damages, but a new date will be given the same season so soon as possible.

Letter 1

The Lecture Agency, Ltd.

(GERALD CHRISTY)

LECTURERS. ... ENTERTAINERS. ...

Telegrams: "LECTURING, LONDON"

Telephone: GERRARD 2899

The Outer Temple, Strand, London, W.C.

June 3rd, 1912.

DEAR MR. AMUNDSEN :-

I am obliged by your favour of the 31st ultimo, and note what you say in reference to Lord Curzon's speech at the Dinner of the Royal Geographical Society on the 21st ultimo. I read that speech myself, and thought that it might give quite a wrong impression of the feeling of Englishmen in regard to your brother's exploit. I think you can very easily pay too much attention to what Lord Curzon said ; and, if you will remember, he himself wound up his speech in quite a nice way practically removing the impression to which I have referred. I do not find the least feeling anywhere likely to interfere with the success of your brother's lectures, and now that I have announced his visit and have already made some engagements it would look very strange if your brother did not come

Letter 2

The Lecture Agency, Ltd.

(GERALD CHRISTY)

Telegrams: "LECTURING, LONDON"

Telephone: GERRARD 2899

The Outer Temple, Strand, London, W.C.

May 14th, 1912.

DEAR MR. AMUNDSEN :-

Thanks for your letter of the 9th instant which arrived here on Monday morning. I can't imagine why Dr. Nansen should tell you that there is any feeling in this country against your brother. He must have been misinformed. I have shown your letter to Dr. Keltie, and he says he knows of no antipathy to your brother. Doubtless there may be one or two individuals who are jealous of the fact that your brother got to the South Pole before Scott, and possibly one such individual may have written to Dr. Nansen. However, any such opinion is purely personal, and there is no earthly reason why your brother should not come over here and lecture. I think he will have a very successful trip. We have already arranged some dates, so that it would be impossible to run back now. If there were any such feeling it could only make a very slight difference and not enough to take any notice of whatever.

With kind regards,
Yours sincerely,

LEON AMUNDSEN, ESQ.,
CHRISTIANIA,
Norway.

The Lecture Agency, Ltd.

(GERALD CHRISTY)

The Outer Temple, Strand, London, W.C.

Telegrams:
"LECTURING, LONDON."

Telephone:
GERRARD 2899

LECTURERS.

Abbot, Rev. W. H., M.A. (Oxon.)
Adams, Ashley P.
Albert, D. W.
Amundsen, Capt.
Angell, Norman
Bacon, Miss
Bellairs, G., Commander, R.N.
Benson, Capt. W. J. P., F.R.G.S.
Beerbohm, Max
Borwell, Monsieur
Bottomley, Prof. W. B., M.A.
Bottomore, Horace A. B., M.A.
Branden, Dr. Georg
Bridge, Sir Frederic, C.V.O.
Bullen, Frank T., F.R.G.S.
Churchill, Winston S., M.P.
Compton-Rickett, Dr.
Cooper, Sir A. C.
Corbett-Smith, Capt., F.R.G.S.
Cortie, Rev. A., S.J., F.R.A.S.
Crabtree, Mrs.
Cronin, T. B.
Davies, Dr. Walford
Dearmer, Mrs.
Déjar, Arthur, F.R.G.S.
Delmetsch, Arnold
Doughty, Sir H. M., M.A.
Dunning, A. H., F.R.G.S.
Ferguson, A., B.A.
Forbes, Robert B.
...
Nansen, Dr. Fridtjof
...

ENTERTAINERS.

Artistes of all kinds
Bands and other theatres, various
Bard, Cyril
Brough, Oldbury
Byrd-Page, Dr.
Scott, Capt. R.F. R.N., F.R.G.S.
Shackleton, Sir Ernest, C.V.O.
Smith, S. C. Kaines, M.A.
...

June 20th, 1912.

DEAR MR. AMUNDSEN :-

Many thanks for your letter of the 10th instant.

I haven't yet been able to see Lord Curzon, as he has been out of London. I have, however, seen Dr. Keltie, and he has asked me to tell you definitely that there is no feeling in the Royal Geographical Society nor in the country generally against your brother, and that there is no earthly reason for you to think for another moment about the question.

I enclose herewith a copy of Lord Curzon's speech in which you will see that he has paid a very generous tribute to the work your brother has done. Probably this was not included in the newspaper report that you read. If you will read the speech you will see that there is nothing unkindly in what he says about your brother going on his southern expedition without letting Scott know. The subject had to be referred to, and I think Lord Curzon did it very nicely. A less tactful man might have made people think that the Society was jealous. Apart from all this, the general public does not bother who started first or whether due notice was given. They know that your brother made a fine journey and reached the Pole, and they want to see and hear him. The English public is never jealous of the success of a foreigner in things of this sort -- although naturally they would like their own nationals to be first. That is a feeling common to all nations.

Dr. Keltie has told me that he will write a note to Lord Curzon telling him what you say ; and he says that Lord Curzon

---

-2-

come here. I think you have a mistaken idea in regard to the position in this country -- it is difficult to judge from a distance, I know -- but I can assure you that I have not come across anything that would lead me to advise your brother to drop the proposed visit. I was reading only the other day a report of a conversation with Captain Scott, in which Scott stated that if your brother could succeed in getting to the South Pole in the way that he intended to try, then he would thoroughly deserve his success. If Scott himself feels in this manner towards your brother I don't know what other Englishman is going to make a fuss. I think you will do well to put the notion of cancelling your brother's visit altogether out of your mind. Of course, I attach a great deal of importance to Dr. Nansen's opinion, as he knows England well and I have known Dr. Nansen for so many years ; but I venture to suggest, as I have stated above, that too much importance can be attached to one or two of the remarks that Lord Curzon made.

The British people want to hear Captain Amundsen's story, and you must bear in mind that they will feel a little aggrieved if he goes to every other country in the world before coming here. The interest in polar exploration in this country has always been exceptionally keen, and no man who has worked so intrepidly as your brother -- no matter what his nationality -- has ever visited this country without an enthusiastic reception.

With kind regards,

Yours sincerely,

Gerald Christy

LEON AMUNDSEN, ESQ.,
CHRISTIANIA,
Norway.

The Lecture Agency, Ltd.

(GERALD CHRISTY)

CARL AMUNDSEN. SOLE ... FOR ...

The Outer Temple, Strand, London, W.C.

Telephone: GERRARD 2899

Telegrams: "LECTURING, LONDON."

LECTURERS.

Abbot, Rev. W. H., M.A. (O'xon.)
Abraham, Ashley P.
Allbut, D. W.
Amundsen, Capt.
Angell, Norman
Bellairs, Lt. Commander, R.N.
Bellingham, Edgar
Bickerton, Prof.
Boswell, Montague
Boswell, Gurdon
Boyd-Carpenter, Rev. A. B., M.A.
Brabourne, Lord
Bride, Sir F. Gale, C.V.O.
Bruce, Rev. Dr. Rosslyn
Bullen, Frank T., F.R.G.S.
Burgess, Harry
Churchill, Winston S., M.P.
Cooper, Rev. A. N., M.A.
Cortbett-Smith, Capt., F.R.A.S.
Cox, Prof. John, M.A.
Crooks, Will, M.P.
Curran, R.
De Windt, Harry
Dumore, A. Radcliffe, F.R.G.S.
Grenfell, Dr. W. T., C.M.G.

ENTERTAINERS.

Artistes of all kinds
Bands and Orchestras, various
Bowick, Miss Ellen
Casper, Alfred
Churcher, Frederick
Cinematograph, The
Crocker, Miss Grace Jean
Drew, Mr. and Mrs. Dennis
French, Percy
Jackson, Nelson
Kenney, Reginald
Westminster Singers

JULY 2nd, 1912.

DEAR MR. AMUNDSEN :—

I am in receipt of your letter of the 29th ultimo and your two telegrams.

I was afraid your letter would upset your brother. I am very sorry all this trouble has arisen, because there is no necessity for it whatever. I have just had a long talk with Dr. Keltie, and he has asked me to say again that there is absolutely no ill-feeling in this country against your brother, and that he can't imagine why you should make so much of this. Lord Curzon's letter to Dr. Nansen was to assure him that he was quite mistaken in thinking there was any feeling here against Captain Amundsen, and asking him to do his best to remove from the minds of Captain Amundsen and yourself the idea that there was any hostility on the part of the English public.

If you will look at the report of Lord Curzon's speech you will see that there is not a single word in it that is said in an unkindly way.

Directly I got your telegram I wired you that it was impossible to cancel. We have booked halls in certain places, and the Geographical Societies and others to which we are booking the lecture have booked halls ; and it would land them in endless muddle and expense. If from now on you banish from your mind any idea that Captain Amundsen will

not

—2—

Curzon will probably write you a letter explaining more fully what he meant.

Anyhow, please don't think any more about it. I am speaking for the general public and Dr. Keltie for the Royal Geographical Society when we say that there is no feeling of the sort against your brother in this country. I hope you haven't written to your brother a letter that will unsettle him and make him think that there is any feeling here against him. It would be a pity if he got that into his head.

The hall that the Royal Geographical Society has taken for its meeting is the large Queen's Hall.

I am filling up all the dates from November 18th to December 13th. If you find that it will be possible for your brother to stay in England over into the next week, please let me know, as I think I can book all the dates you can give me.

I return herewith the Royal Scottish Geographical Society's letter. It is very good of them to give the medal. I think you had better reply to the letter yourself saying that you are sending it on to your brother, and that you are sure he will be very sensible of the honour they are conferring upon him, and that he himself will write to them in due course. I expect the Royal Geographical Society will be giving something of the sort ; but, of course, if anything is done by them it won't be announced until much nearer the time.

With kind regards,

Yours sincerely,

Gerald Christy

LEON AMUNDSEN, ESQ.,
CHRISTIANIA,
Norway.

The Lecture Agency, Ltd.

(GERALD CHRISTY)

The Outer Temple, Strand, London, W.C.

LECTURERS.

Abbot, Rev. W. H., M.A. (Oxon)
Abraham, Ashley P.
Albert, D. W.
Amundsen, Capt.
Ashton, Norman
Bacon, Miss
Bellairs, C., Commander, R.N.
Bellingham, Roger A.
Bickerton, Prof.
Bottomley, Prof. W. B., M.A.
Branden, Dr. Georg
Bridge, Sir Frederick, C.V.O.
Buxton, Rev. H. J.
Ballen, Frank T., F.R.G.S.
Burgess, Harry
Churchill, Winston S., M.P.
Compton-Rickett, J.P.
Corbett-Smith, Capt., M.F.R.G.S.
Cortis, Rev. A.J.-S.J.,F.R.A.S.
Creighton, Mrs.
Crooks, Will, M.P.
Davies, Dr. Walford
De Windt, Harry
Ditson, Arthur
Dolmetsch, Arnold
Dunning, A. H., F.R.G.S.
Fletcher, J. F.R.S.
Forbes, H. O.
Freire, John Foster
Gibson, W. Hamilton
GI, F. W., F.R.G.S.
Greenwood, F. R.R.G.S.
Green-Thompson, J.A.
Grenfell, Dr. W. T., C.M.G.

ENTERTAINERS.

Artistes of all kinds
Bands and Orchestras, various
Bard, Cyril
Brough, Oldbury
Byrd-Page, Dr.
Caanter, Alfred
Chester, Frederick
Churcher, Walter
Cooper, Miss Margaret
Crocker, Miss Grace Jean
Denny, Ernest
Dew, Mr. and Mrs. Dennis
English Opera Singers
Paul Jubilee Trio
"Frau Musika" Quartette
French, Percy
Gorton, Arthur
Hastings, Ernest
Hill, Harrison
Jackson, Nelson
Kenney, Reginald
Lambert, Leslie
Mar, Miss Helen
Sewell, Ernest
Van Biene, Auguste
Waldron, Rev. A.J.
Weatherhead, Ernest
Westminster Singers

The LECTURE AGENCY, Ltd.
Founded 1879.
Telephone: GERRARD 2899

Telegrams: "LECTURING, LONDON"

JULY THIRD 1912

MY DEAR MR. AMUNDSEN :-

I am writing again to give every additional emphasis possible to what I said in my letter of yesterday. I cannot conceive of anything more disastrous to your famous brother, so far as the people of these islands are concerned, than a blunt refusal to come here and tell his story, especially after all arrangements have been completed. We have spread it far and wide that Roald Amundsen will give an account of his journey, and halls have been booked in various parts of the country and announcements made. To go back on it now would put your brother in an exceedingly invidious position.

Captain Roald Amundsen must come to England ; he is definitely committed to that, and it is in his highest and best interests that he should come. Believe me, he will never regret it. Englishmen are not so churlish as to slight a brave man, and I must beg of you, in justice to my countrymen, to put any such utter misconception wholly out of your mind. There is nothing I regret so much as I do the fact that your brother has somehow got the idea that there is a feeling against him in Great Britain. It is most unjust to our people, and I cannot think of anything that they would resent more keenly than this notion that they could be guilty of what they would call un-sportsmanlike conduct. Your brother got there fairly, and you cannot tell me of any representative Briton who has ever said

-2-

not receive a truly hearty welcome, everything will go right and I don't suppose you will ever hear of the matter again. Over the remains of any feeling there might have been at one time. But if, instead of this, you rake it all up again, and Captain Amundsen abandons his English visit -- then indeed the English public will begin to wonder, and would then probably get the idea that Captain Amundsen himself must feel that he had done something that was not quite sporting, and, in consequence, did not like to come to England.

Do please get the idea out of your head and let things go on as though nothing had happened. Dr.Keltie says he will get Lord Curzon to write direct to your brother, and I hope you will also write him saying that everything is settled.

The invitation to address the Royal Geographical Society has been announced, and it would be excessively impolitic to cancel things now.

You are wrong in what you say about the hall. Nansen was in the Albert Hall, it is true ; but Nansen's expedition had about it certain dramatic elements that made it stand out far more prominently than any other expedition of any sort ever has or ever will do again. His lectures here attracted far more attention than Scott's or Shackleton's. Jackson did not go to the Albert Hall : the Duke of the Abruzzi did not go to the Albert Hall, but to the Queen's Hall. Scott, Shackleton, and Peary were first of all booked for the Queen's Hall, and the Society afterwards transferred to the Albert Hall when they got sufficient applications to warrant this. They will very likely do so in your brother's case if they get sufficient applications for tickets to justify this. The Queen's Hall is a magnificent hall, and far better from many points of view than the Albert Hall.

You must surely see that your brother in South America is not in a position to realise how things stand here. Surely the assurances of Lord Curzon, Dr.Keltie, and myself as to how matters stand should be enough for you. I shall hope to hear from you that all is now in order and that you have written to your brother that everything is arranged satisfactorily.

With kind regards,

Yours sincerely,

LEON AMUNDSEN, ESQ.,
CHRISTIANIA,
Norway.

The Lecture Agency, Ltd.

(GERALD CHRISTY)

DUM LOQUOR, HORA FUGIT

SOLE AGENTS FOR CAPT. AMUNDSEN.

LECTURERS.

Abbot, Rev. W. H., M.A. (Oxon.)
Abraham, Ashley P.
Allen, Grant
Amundsen, Capt.
Ansell, Norman
Bacon, Miss
Bellairs, C., Commander, R.N.
Bellingham, Edgar P., F.R.G.S.
Bensusan, S. L.
Bickerton, Prof.
Boswell, A. Mitchell
Bottomley, Prof. W. B., M.A.
Boyd-Carpenter, Rev. A. B., M.A.
Brandes, Dr. Georg
Bridge, Sir Fredk., C.V.O.
Bruce, Rev. Dr. Rosslyn
Bullen, Frank T., F.R.G.S.
Burgess, Harry
Churchill, Winston S., M.P.
Compton-Rickett, Dr.
Cooper, Rev. A. N., M.A.
Corbett-Smith, Capt., F.R.G.S.
Cortis, Rev. A., S.J., F.R.A.S.
Cox, Prof. John, M.A.
Crockett, S. R.
Crooks, Will, M.P.
Curzon, F. N.
Davies, Dr. Walford
De Windt, Harry, F.R.G.S.
Delmar-Morgan, E. H., M.A.
Dittmar, Arnold
Drummond, A. H., F.R.G.S.
Slatin Pasha, F.R.G.S.
Forbes, John
Foster, Wm. Frost, M.A.
Freer, John Bacon, M.A.
Gardiner, Gordon
Gibbs, Philip
Green, Prof. F. W., F.R.G.S.
Green, Thos. F., F.R.G.S.
Greenwood, Major, M.R.C.S.
Grenfell, Dr. W. T., C.M.G.

Grundy, Rev. C. H., M.A.
Hall-Edwards, Dr.
Hampden, Dr. Wm.
Handa, Alfred
Hedin, Dr. Sven
Hebe-Shaw, Dr., F.R.S.
Hill, Alex., M.A., M.D., F.R.C.S.
Hughes, Spencer Leigh, M.P.
Jeffery, J. J.
Jones, Edgar R., M.P.
Kearton, Cherry
Keane, A. H., M.A.
Kernahan, Coulson
Kerr, Richard, F.G.S., F.R.A.S.
King, Joseph, M.P.
Landor, A. H. Savage
Lessage, Emile
Lytton, The Earl of
Macdonald, J. Ramsay, M.P.
Macluagh, Jeremiah, M.P.
Malden, Arthur
Marshall, Dr. Eric
Martin-Duncan, Prof., J.H.B., M.A.
McCabe, Joseph
Milne, Prof. John, F.R.S.
Mills, Ernest H.
Montanaro, E. H., M.A.
Monsell, J. C. Bayly
Nansen, Dr. Fridtjof
Oliver, D. G., M.A.
Orr, John, M.A.
Peary, Commander R. E.
Perry, Mat. Robert E.
Pigott, Prof. Edgar, F.R.S.
Pike, Prof. E. L.
Parker, Gilbert
Pollen, H. C.
Raphael, John R.

ENTERTAINERS.

Artistes of all kinds
Bands and Orchestras, various
Bard, Cornil
Bowde, Miss Ellen
Bund, Oldbury
Byrod-Page, Dr.
Cather, Alfred
Chew, Frederick
Churcher, Walter
Cooper, Miss Margaret
Crocker, Miss Grace Jean
Dale, Frederic
Denny, Ernest
Dale Quartette
Folk Jubilee Trio
French, Percy
George, Arthur
Hastings, Ernest
Hill, Harrison
Jackson, Nelson
Kendal, Marie
Kenney, Reginald
Lambert, Leslie
Lauchesne Quintette
Mar, Miss Helen
Moore, Madame Bertha
Sewell, Ernest
Stanilland, Miss Gwendolyn
Terriss, Miss Ellaline
Tree, Miss Viola
Van Biene, Auguste
Waldron, Rev. A. J.
Wallis, Whitworth, F.S.A.
Warde, Willie
Warwick, The Countess of
Weston, Dr. Geo., C.B., etc.
Wilson, The Rt. Rev. Bishop
Westminster Singers

Telephone:
GERRARD
2899

Telegrams:
"LECTURING,
LONDON."

The Outer Temple, Strand, London, W.C.

July 3rd, 1912.

Dear Mr. Amundsen:—

Since writing the accompanying letter I have had
another letter from Dr. Keltie. He says that Lord Curzon tells
him that he does not think it would be any good his writing any
further, and that he cannot understand why you should have got
into your head the idea that there was any ill-feeling against
your brother in this country. Dr. Keltie goes on:—

"You should telegraph to Leon Amundsen
and to Captain Amundsen that they are
mistaken about the Queen's Hall. It was
engaged for the Duke of Abruzzi, Dr. Sven
Hedin, Sir Ernest Shackleton, and Commander
Peary, and the last two were only changed
to the Albert Hall because of the exceptional
demand for tickets. To Captain Amundsen you
should also telegraph that he has been misinformed both about the feeling in England and
about Lord Curzon's speech, the text of which,
is in possession of his brother. The Royal
Geographical

— 2 —

a word to the contrary.

If Captain Roald Amundsen lectures everywhere else
and pointedly declines to visit Britain, what is more likely
to give rise to such a feeling as he now believes — and quite
wrongly — exists at present?

Moreover, your brother by taking such a course will
put a slight upon the Royal Geographical Society, the most
notable organisation of the kind in the world. My letter of
last night fully explained the circumstances to which you
referred. It is not quite fair to put Dr. Fridtjof Nansen
in the same category as other men. Nansen has always been
a popular hero here. In the whole of my experience I cannot
think of another man who has aroused so much intense enthusiasm. Nansen occupies a peculiar position in relation to
England. You must remember that he had given many lectures
in this country before he started on his great expedition;
he had made thousands of friends and acquaintances here, and
his wonderful personality took a big hold on everybody.

It is for you to put the matter straight. If I
only out for business and do not care about any other
point of view. It is not so; but the only way to make
sure about things is for you to cable him that he must
come to England and that he will receive a reception which
will effectually disabuse his mind of any doubts as to the
genuine regard and admiration of the British people.

I have lectures booked that represent pretty well
2000 guineas. Halls have been definitely booked, and these
cannot be given up without a severe monetary loss. As a
matter of fact, I cannot lay too much stress upon the disagreeable situation that will arise if your brother does not now
come to this country. I rely upon you to do all that is
necessary in the matter.

About this I am certain: your brother will have
no reason to complain of the treatment he will get from
Englishmen, Scotsmen, Welshmen and Irishmen. I have booked
him for lectures in the four countries, so you can see that
the interest in his exploit is general.

With kind regards,

YOURS SINCERELY,

Gerald Christy

LEON AMUNDSEN, ESQ.

All fees quoted include travelling and other personal expenses, unless otherwise stated. The Lantern, Kinematograph and Operator, or Piano and Accompanist (where such may be required) must be provided by the Society engaging, unless special arrangements be made. In case an engagement be unfulfilled by reason of sickness, accident, or other unavoidable cause, it is understood that there be no claim for damages, but a new date will be given the same season when possible.

The Lecture Agency, Ltd.

(GERALD CHRISTY)

Telephone: GERRARD 2899

Telegram: "LECTURING, LONDON."

LECTURERS.

Abbot, Rev. W. H., M.A.(Oxon.)
Abraham, Ashley P.
Adair, H.
Amundsen, Capt.
Angell, Norman
Bacon, Miss
Bellairs, C., Commander, R.N.
Benson, Capt. W. J. P., F.R.G.S.
Billingham, Edgar
Richardson, Prof.
Botterell, Mrs.
Bottomley, Prof. W. B., M.A.
Brandes, Dr. George
Bridge, Sir Frederick, C.V.O.
Burgess, Harry
Compton-Rickett, Dr.
Corbett-Smith, Capt., F.R.G.S.
Cortie, Rev. A., S.J., F.R.A.S.
Creighton, Mrs.
Crooke, Will, M.P.
Davies, Dr. Walford
Dibdy, Arthur, F.R.G.S.
Dunning, A. E., F.R.G.S.
...

ENTERTAINERS.

Bands and orchestras, various
Bard, Cecil
Brough, Oddbury
Byrd-Page, Dr.
Chester, Frederick
Churchill, Walter
Cinematograph, The
Cooper, Miss Margaret
Dale, Frederic
Folk-Song Quartette, The
"Frau Müska" Quartette
George, Arthur
Hastings, Ernest
Hill, Harrison
Keeney, Reginald
Marr, Miss Helen
Moore, Madame Bertha
Shaw, Miss Gwendolyn
Westminster Singers
...

SOLE AGENTS FOR CAPTAIN AMUNDSEN

The Outer Temple, Strand, London, W.C.

Enclosure.

SEPTEMBER 24th, 1912.

DEAR MR. AMUNDSEN :-

Thanks for yours of the 20th instant. I am glad to hear that there are kinematograph films in addition to slides for illustrating your brother's lecture. Will you please let me know by return whether the lecture can be given without the films, if necessary ? I ask because in some towns there may be difficulties in the way of providing the necessary apparatus. There is no trouble with slides.

I don't think you need have any fear about the Royal Geographical Society providing a good operator for their meeting. Anyhow, we shall have a firstrate man for the public Queen's Hall lecture on the 19th of November.

I enclose herewith a list of the bookings up to date. With regard to the address in each case : I certainly think it would be better for you always to write or telegraph to Captain Amundsen here whilst he is in England, as the post is very quick here and a letter sent on would catch him within a few hours, wherever he might be.

I will send you a fuller list later on, as at present I don't know the names of all the halls in which the lectures are to be given.

Be sure and let me know in plenty of time when Captain Amundsen will arrive in England. I hope it will be not later than November 14th, so that interviews, etc., with him

All fees quoted include travelling and other personal expenses, unless otherwise stated. The Lantern, Kinematograph and Operator or Piano and Accompanist (where such may be required) must be provided by the Society engaging, unless special arrangements be made. In case an engagement be unfulfilled by reason of sickness, accident, or other unavoidable cause, it is understood that there be no claim for damages, but a new date will be given the same season when possible.

- 2 -

Geographical Society has never wavered in its intention to render him due honour, and he may rely upon a very cordial welcome. I hope that by doing so the matter will be put right.

It is exceedingly difficult to put all of this into a cable, except at a very great expense. Besides, if he does get a cable from me it won't carry nearly as much weight as a cable would from you. Will you please cable him that matters have been put right, and follow it up by a letter explaining the circumstances?

YOURS SINCERELY,

[signature: Gerald Christy]

LEON AMUNDSEN, Esq.,
CHRISTIANIA,
Norway.

The Lecture Agency, Ltd.

(GERALD CHRISTY)

LECTURERS.
Abbot, Rev. W. H., M.A. (Oxon.)
Abraham, Ashley P.
Allford, Mr. W.
Amundsen, Capt.
Angell, Norman
Bacon, Miss
Barnes, Rt. Rev. Bishop
Bohun, C., Commander, R.N.
Bellingham, Robert
Benson, Capt. W. J. P., F.R.G.S.
Beketon, Rev.
Borwell, Montague
Bottomley, Prof. W. B., M.A.
Boyd-Carpenter, Rev. A. B., M.A.
Brandes, Dr. Georg
Bridge, Sir Frede., C.V.O.
Brun, Rev. Dr. Nygaard
Bullen, Frank T., F.R.G.S.
Burgess, Harry
Burrell, Arthur M., M.A.
Caullie, Dr. Jas. M.A., F.R.C.S.
Cavells, Rev.
Coteridge, Hon. Stephen
Compston-Rickett, Dr.
Corbett-Smith, Capt., F.R.G.S.
Coreton, Rev. A. A.
Cox, Prof. John, M.A.
Creighton, Mrs.
Curran, T. B.
Davies, Dr. Watford
Delay, Arthur, F.R.G.S.
Dolmetsch, Arnold
Dumville, Rev. F.R.G.S.
Edgerton, A. Fenton, A.
Fiske, John Foster
Gaskin, Mr.
Gill, T. W., F.R.G.S.
Grenfell, Julian, F.R.G.S.

Green, Thos. E., F.R.G.S.
Greenwood, A. M.D., B.Sc.
Grundy, Rev. C. H., M.A.
Hall-Edwards, Dr. W.
Hands, Alfred
Helie-Shaw, Dr., F.R.S.
Hill, Alex., M.A., M.D., F.R.G.S.
Hughes, Spencer Leigh, M.P.
Jeffery, K. C.
Johnston, Sir Harry, M.P.
Keartons, Cherry
Kearton, R. F.G.S.
Kennalin, Coulson
Kerr, Richard, F.G.S., F.R.A.S.
Landor, A. H. Savage
Leange, Emilie
Lawes, William B.
Lytton, The Earl of
Macdonald, Rev. F. W.
MacVeagh, Jeremiah, M.P.
Marshall, Dr. Eric
Martin-Duncan, F.
McCabe, Joseph
McClintock, Walter, M.A.
Mills, Ernest H.
Mumm, Fred. G. Ghorm, M.P.
Nansen, Dr., F.R.G.S.
Norgate, W. T. H., F.R.G.S.
Owen, Will
Peary, Commander Robert E.
Pettie, Geo. Mrs. F.R.S.
Pitt, Geo. E., B.-ès-L.

ENTERTAINERS.
Artistes of all kinds
Bands and Orchestras, various
Bard, Corali
Bostic, Mrs. Ellen
Brough, Oldbury
Byrd-Page, Dr.
Chester, Frederick
Cicennaie, Walter
Cinematograph, The
Cooper, Miss Margaret
Dale, Frederic
Denny, Ernest
Dent, Mr. and Mrs. Dennis
English Opera Singers
Folk-Song Quartette, The
"Frau Musika" Quartette
French, Percy
Genese, Arthur
Hastings, Ernest
Hill, Harrison
Jackson, Nelson
Kendall, Marie
Kenney, Reginald
Meister Glee Singers
Morris, Madame Bertha
Sewell, Ernest
Shaw, Miss Gwendolyn
Tomalin, Miss Gertrude
Vooman, Dr. F. R.
Watson, Alexander
Wellington Prof.
Yosall W. F., M.P.
Westminster Singers

SOLD AMUNDSEN FOR ALL

The Outer Temple, Strand, London, W.C.

Telegrams:
"LECTURING ESTRAND LONDON"
(Two words)

Telephone:
GERRARD 2899

OCTOBER 9th, 1912.

DEAR MR. AMUNDSEN :-

Would you kindly let me know if the films are printed on what is called "Non-flam" material? If they are on ordinary inflammable film there may be a difficulty about getting them shown in some of the halls, but this difficulty is obviated if they are on "Non-flam" material.

Please let me know.

Yours sincerely,

LEON AMUNDSEN, ESQ.

All fees quoted include travelling and other personal expenses, unless otherwise stated. The Lantern, Kinematograph and Operator, or Piano and Accompanist (where such may be required) must be provided by the Society engaging, unless special arrangement be made. In case an engagement be unfulfilled by reason of illness, accident, or other unavoidable cause, it is understood that there be no claim for damages, but a new date will be given, the same season when possible.

-2-

him can appear in the papers on the morning of the 15th.

I am glad to hear that John Murray is publishing the book. You need have no fear about him and rest assured that he will do everything in the best possible style.

With kind regards,

YOURS SINCERELY,

LEON AMUNDSEN, ESQ.,
CHRISTIANIA,
Norway.

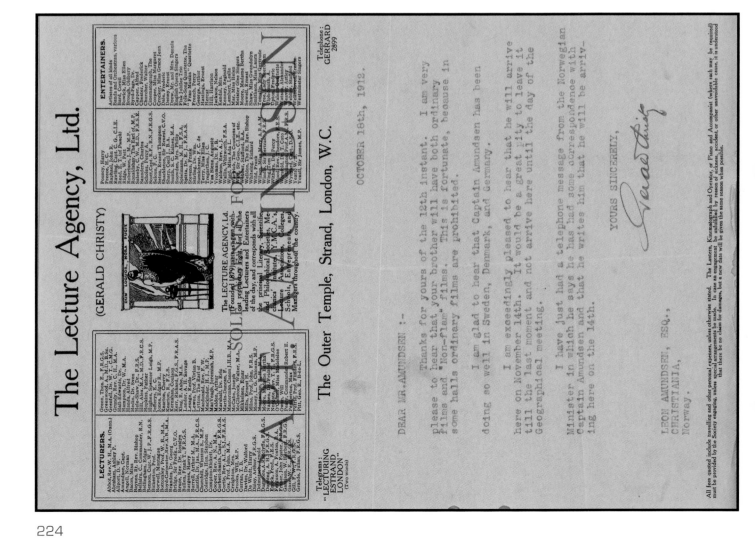

The Lecture Agency, Ltd.

(GERALD CHRISTY)

LECTURERS.

Abbott, Rev. W. H., M.A. (Oxon.)
Abraham, Ashley F.
Allbutt, D. W.
Amundsen, Capt.
Angell, Norman
Bacon, Miss
Bellairs, C., Commander, R.N.
Benson, Capt. W. J. F., F.R.G.S.
Bickerton, Prof.
Botton, Rev. Father
Boyd-Carpenter, Rev. A.B., M.A.
Bridge, Sir Frederick, C.V.O.
Bullen, Frank T., F.R.G.S.
Burgess, Harry
Butler, Arthur H., M.A.
Cantlie, Dr. Jas., M.A., F.R.C.S.
Churchill, Winston S., M.P.
Colville, Mrs. Stephen
Compton-Rickett, Dr.
Cooper-Smith, A. N., M.A.
Corelli, Rev. A. S. J., F.R.A.S.
Creighton, Mrs.
Crooke, Will, M.P.
Davies, Dr. Watford
De Windt, Harry, F.R.G.S.
Doheny
Dunn, Capt. A. D., F.R.G.S.
Foa, Edouard
Forster, John Foster
Fraser, John Foster
Gill, F.R.A.S.
Grande, Julian, F.R.G.S.

Green, Thos. E., F.R.G.S.
Greenwood, A., M.D., B.Sc.
Grenfell, Dr. W. T., C.M.G.
Hall-Edwards, Dr.
Hampson, Dr. W., M.A.
Hedin, Dr. Sven
Hill, Alex., M.A., M.D., F.R.C.S.
Hopkins, Father
Hughes, Spencer Leigh, M.P.
Jeffery, E. C.
Jones, Edgar R., M.P.
Kearton, R., F.Z.S.
Kerr, Richard, F.G.S., F.R.A.S.
King, R. Askie, M.A.
Lewis, Prof. Vivian B.
Macdonald, Rev. F. W.
MacVeagh, Jeremiah, M.P.
Malden, Arthur
Martin-Duncan, F.
Masterman, Canon J.H.B., M.A.
McClintock, Walter, M.A.
Mills, Ernest H.
Milne, Prof. John, F.R.S.
Oliver, Capt., R.N., M.P.
Pitt, Command. Robert E.
Pitt, Geo. E., B.às-L.

ENTERTAINERS.

Artistes of all kinds
Band, Corali
Bowden, Miss Ellen
Brough, Lionel
Byrd-Page, Dr.
Chester, Frederick
Churcher, Walter
Cooper, Miss Margaret
Crocker, Miss Grace Jean
Denny, Ernest
English Opera Singers
"Fran Musica" Quartette
French, Percy
George, Arthur
Hastings, Ernest
Hill, Harrison
Jackson, Nelson
Kennerley, Reginald
Marmion, Leslie
Meister Glee Singers
Sewell, Ernest
Shaw, Miss Gwendolyn
Westminster Singers

Telegrams:
"LECTURING
ESTRAND,
LONDON"
(Two words)

Telephone:
GERRARD
2899

The Outer Temple, Strand, London, W.C.

OCTOBER 18th, 1912.

DEAR MR. AMUNDSEN :-

Please to hear that your brother will have both ordinary films and "Non-Flam" films. This is fortunate, because in some halls ordinary films are prohibited.

I am glad to hear that Captain Amundsen has been doing so well in Sweden, Denmark, and Germany.

I am exceedingly pleased to hear that he will arrive here on November 14th. It would be a great pity to leave it till the last moment and not arrive here until the day of the Geographical meeting.

I have just had a telephone message from the Norwegian Minister in which he says he has had some correspondence with Captain Amundsen and that he writes him that he will be arriving here on the 14th.

YOURS SINCERELY,

Gerald Christy

LEON AMUNDSEN, ESQ.,
CHRISTIANIA,
Norway.

All fees quoted include travelling and other personal expenses, unless otherwise stated. The Lantern, Kinematograph and Operator, or Piano and Accompanist (where such may be required) must be provided by the Society engaging, unless special arrangements are made. In case an engagement be unfulfilled by reason of sickness, accident, or other unavoidable cause, it is understood that there be no claim for damages, but a new date will be given the same season when possible.

Office of Lee Keedick, Manager, Distinguished Lecturers, Readers, Musicians

150 NASSAU STREET, NEW YORK
Telephone 4074 Beekman

CABLE ADDRESS
"KEEDICK, NEW YORK"

Mr. Amundsen -- #2 -- September 26.

Vancouver, $1840 for one lecture. These figures will give you some idea of the results of Sir Ernest Shackleton's tour.

Your suggestion that the first lecture be in Vancouver meets with my approval and it would be my plan to book the lectures following in Tacoma, Seattle, San Francisco, Los Angeles, Sacramento, and then proceed East through the central or Southern part of the United States, and after the lectures in Boston and New York, proceed back to Vancouver or San Francisco by the Northern route. I would follow this itinerary only in the case that Captain Amundsen finds it necessary to close his tour by the first of June. In this country we have Summer Assemblies called Chautauquas, and if Captain Amundsen can remain over during the Summer I feel sure I can secure enough engagements at these Assemblies to make it worth his while. I could book him with the Chautauquas for either a flat rate of $200 per lecture or on a 50 % basis with a guarantee of $200. These Assemblies are held in the rural districts and would not conflict with the city engagements for the Fall. Owing to the great number of cities in the United States and Canada I could book a Fall tour, also.

As you will see, this contract is based upon the condition that your brother discovers the South Pole. I do not believe that it would pay him to tour the United States unless he discovers the Pole or makes a better record than Sir Ernest Shackleton or Captain Scott.

If this contract meets with your approval will you please cable me at my expense as soon as you have signed the same as I am getting out some advertising material of a general nature and wish to make mention as soon as possible of the coming tour of Captain Amundsen.

May I also trouble you to send me some photographs of Captain Amundsen in his former expeditions and also I should be grateful if you would supply me with facts and information concerning your brother's career as an explorer.

Very sincerely yours,

LK/S
Enc.

Office of Lee Keedick, Manager, Distinguished Lecturers, Readers, Musicians

150 NASSAU STREET, NEW YORK
Telephone 4074 Beekman

CABLE ADDRESS
"KEEDICK, NEW YORK"

September 25, 1911.

Mr. Leon Amundsen,
Christiania, Norway.

My dear Sir:-

I acknowledge with thanks, your valued favor dated September 11, which I have read carefully. In accordance with your request I am enclosing contracts for your signature. In drawing these contracts I have been governed by your suggestion that all of Captain Amundsen's expenses be included. I have a similar contract with Alfred Tennyson Dickens, the eldest surviving son of the late Charles Dickens, who tours America under my management beginning the first of October, and in drawing up this contract with you I have inserted the exact clause from his contract bearing on the expense account, and I think that you will find it satisfactory as he is already immensely well pleased with the bookings we have to date and the way we have managed the tour so far.

It is my purpose to keep the expenses as low as possible and I shall not keep an advance man on the road any more then is absolutely necessary, but at the same time I want to have that privilege as I do not want to be handicapped in any way from making this tour a grand success. I have found from experience that a visit by a personal representative gets much better results than can be secured by correspondence.

It will be much more profitable for all concerned to have a representative travel with Captain Amundsen as it is my intention to book all lecture engagements in large cities on a percentage basis. Therefore, it will be to the advantage of both Captain Amundsen and myself to have one of our men present to check up on the receipts.

In reply to your question as to what a place like Carnegie Hall could give for one entertainment, I wish to state that the management at Carnegie Hall does not book lecturers on their own responsibility. However, there are Societies in New York with whom I feel sure I could book Captain Amundsen in case he discovers the Pole, for $1000. I think Chicago, St. Louis, San Francisco, Vancouver and other large cities would pay an equal amount. However, from a financial standpoint I do not think it advisable to accept a flat rate even at this price in the largest cities. I would advise that these engagements be booked on a percentage basis, say for our share 60 % of the receipts with a minimum guarantee of $500. On this basis I am sure that we would realize much more than on a flat rate. The gross receipts for the Shackleton lecture in New York were $3200; in Chicago, $2550.50; in Winnipeg, $2750 for two lectures; in

Office of Lee Keedick, Manager, Distinguished Lecturers, Readers, Musicians

CABLE ADDRESS
"KEEDICK, NEW YORK"

150 NASSAU STREET, NEW YORK
Telephone 4074 Beekman

Mr. Amundsen -- #2 -- December 20.

I mention these facts so that you may have a thorough understanding of the conditions in this country and not be misled by wild and extravagant statements. It is true that Dr. Cook drew large audiences in this country before he was discredited but that was in a measure due to the fact that there was a keen and heated controversy on between Cook and Peary and that the newspapers contained practically nothing else. It would not be possible to get such publicity again possibly within a century, even though the same condition prevailed again.

two acts of

In the latter part of your letter you state that if I see my way clear to send you contracts in accordance with your suggestions, that you would propose, in accordance with Dr. Nansen to accept one of the two, but leave to your brother the matter of selecting the one he would prefer on his arrival in the States, and that this would give me more time to prepare my business, and that you could then send the photographs I desire. As previously stated in this letter, the contracts which I have submitted are the very best I am prepared to make and according to your own statement, which I have just quoted, I will be seriously handicapped if I am forced to wait for your brother to decide who is to manage his American tour, and if I am selected, of course he cannot expect me to get the same results as I could obtain were I notified immediately whether or not I am to manage this tour. Of course, if your brother cannot come to America by the first of April it would be better for him to postpone his tour until September, but by that time the interest in the man and his subject would be so lessened that this receipts would not be half as much as in the Spring. My advice, therefore, would be that from a financial standpoint it would pay him to come to America direct from New Zealand, and then tour Australia later.

While your brother is well-known to men interested in geographical affairs, yet the general public in America are not familiar with his name and it seems to me that it would be very advantageous to begin a publicity campaign in this country as early as possible so that the general public would be well informed as to what he has accomplished.

I note in your letter that your brother is an Honorary Member, and you has received Gold Medals from different Geographical Societies in the States, and you intimate that he would be willing to speak before these Societies without charge. I would consider such an arrangement inadvisable. Sir Ernest Shackleton received Gold Medals from the American Societies but they also paid him liberally for his lecture and they were perfectly satisfied, so I see no reason why these same arrangements should not be effected for your brother.

I would consider it a great favor if you will arrange another conference with Solicitor Nansen and decide at once whether or not I am to have the management of your brother's lecture tour. I have other plans that I wish to put through during April and May if Captain Amundsen is not to be under my management. If I have

---

Office of Lee Keedick, Manager, Distinguished Lecturers, Readers, Musicians

CABLE ADDRESS
"KEEDICK, NEW YORK"

150 NASSAU STREET, NEW YORK
Telephone 4074 Beekman

December 20, 1911.

Mr. Leon Amundsen,
Christiana, Norway.

Dear Mr. Amundsen:-

My delay in replying to your letter dated November 25 has been occasioned by my absence from the city. I have been on an extended trip through the West in the interests of Lieutenant-General Sir Robert Baden-Powell and Alfred Tennyson Dickens.

I have read your letter carefully. The propositions contained in the contracts already submitted to you are the best that I can make. As you will see by copies of the enclosed letters and by the copy of the letter from Sir Ernest Shackleton which I enclosed in my last letter to you, I have established a reputation in this country for getting the highest prices that the public will pay. If there is a general interest in any speaker I can get the highest possible price for his services but if there is not a general interest I cannot afford to make a contract with anyone which will bind me to pay a high price for the public's lack of interest in a speaker. In other words, I have the facilities for conducting his lecture bureau business so as to get the highest possible efficiency but no Manager can make the public attend a lecture unless they want to, and the people's lack of interest should not compel a Manager to pay to the speaker as much as the public would have paid if they were thoroughly interested in the man and his subject. Within the last month I have sold thirteen engagements for General Baden-Powell in a block for $15,000 but I would not have thought of guaranteeing him in advance a third of this amount.

I note the contents of your Post Script and I am afraid that you have been misinformed concerning the amount of money paid in this country for individual lecturers.

Dr. Cook was never paid $10,000 for any lecture in the United States. He did receive $5000 in one town where a Fall Festival was being held and he was engaged more as an exhibit than as a lecturer but this committee lost heavily on the deal and it would be extremely difficult to book another explorer in this particular city at anywhere near the same rate. There are not any Halls in this country, with the possible exception of two or three, with a seating capacity of more than $2500 where a lecturer can be heard and only popular prices can be charged in such Halls. For Armories and Convention Halls with a seating capacity of several thousand a very low rate of admission has to be charged for the people know in advance that they cannot expect to hear the speaker. They only go to see him.

CABLE ADDRESS "KEEDICK NEW YORK"

TELEPHONE BEEKMAN 4074

LEE KEEDICK
MANAGER OF THE WORLD'S MOST CELEBRATED LECTURERS
150 NASSAU STREET
NEW YORK CITY

May 27, 1912.

[signature]

Mr. Leon Amundsen,

Christiana, Norway.

Dear Mr. Amundsen:-

CAPT. ROALD AMUNDSEN
Discoverer of the South Pole and Winner in the International Race for the Southern Extremity of the Earth.

SOME OTHER FAMOUS LECTURERS NOW OR PREVIOUSLY UNDER MY MANAGEMENT

LIEUT.-GENERAL SIR ROBERT BADEN-POWELL.
SIR ERNEST H. SHACKLETON
COUNTESS OF WARWICK
COUNTESS LYDIA ROSTOPCHINE
ALFRED TENNYSON DICKENS
JOHN MITCHELL, THE GREAT LABOR LEADER
HON. LESLIE M. SHAW, EX-SECRETARY U. S. TREASURY
HON. HENRY CLEWS, WALL STREET BANKER
COL. S. S. McCLURE, EDITOR OF McCLURE'S MAGAZINE
A. RADCLYFFE DUGMORE, F. R. G. S.
DR. JOHN WESLEY HILL
DR. G. STANLEY HALL
I. M. TARBELL
HAMILTON WRIGHT MABIE
PROFESSOR BRANDER MATTHEWS
WILLIAM R. GEORGE
DR. WILLIAM B. GUTHRIE
COL. JOHN TEMPLE GRAVES
SENATOR ALBERT B. CUMMINS

It was fortunate that you wrote me concerning Dr. Cook's visiting your brother in Christiana upon his return. I would consider such a meeting a fatal mistake for your brother. The very fact that Captain Amundsen received Dr. Cook would be great advertising for the latter and very detrimental advertising for the former. While all Americans deeply regret the attitude that Commander Peary assumed in the controversy with Cook, they believe Cook to be an impostor and it would do your brother only harm to have his name linked with Cook in any manner whatsoever. Since Cook has been discredited he has gone about the country lecturing in out-of-the-way places at exceedingly low prices, and I have noticed in some of his advertisements that he has quoted references to himself from your brother's books. I have regretted to note this attempt on the part of Cook to boost himself at your brother's expense but it would be a thousand times worse for your brother to receive Cook. Captain Amundsen's great achievements are unquestioned by anyone in this country and I would be loath to have him do anything that would make it appear to some people that he had any faith or confidence in Cook; so I hope that you will see to it that such a meeting as Cook suggests is made impossible.

I have just returned from a trip through the middle West where I secured many satisfactory lecture engagements for Captain Amundsen. The latter part of this week I start on a special trip to the Pacific Coast in his interests. I am giving the tour a great deal of personal time and attention as well as putting representatives on the road to secure bookings.

I wish to thank you for giving me the right to make arrangements with the phonograph and with the motion picture men. I wish that you would let me know by

CAPTAIN AMUNDSEN'S AMERICAN LECTURE TOUR WILL BE UNDER MY EXCLUSIVE MANAGEMENT. WRITE FOR TERMS AND OPEN DATES—TOUR BEGINS IN JANUARY 1913.

Office of Lee Keedick, Manager, Distinguished Lecturers, Readers, Musicians

150 NASSAU STREET, NEW YORK
Telephone 4074 Beekman

CABLE ADDRESS "KEEDICK, NEW YORK"

Mr. Amundsen -- #3 -- December 20.

the management of the tour I want to make a big success of it, and I would rather not attempt it at all under such a serious handicap as being compelled to wait until your brother reaches New Zealand and then perhaps be delayed considerably thereafter if he should decide to tour Australia first.

I infer from your letter that you have not the power to act in this matter and as already stated, I would rather have an answer in the negative at this time than to have all my other plans held up by the uncertainty of not knowing whether I am to manage the tour or not.

Thanking you for the consideration you have shown me, and asking for an immediate reply, I remain

Very sincerely yours,

Lee Keedick

P. S. Concerning a Business Manager I wish to state that if the man proposed by me is not entirely satisfactory to your brother I would agree to any change he might desire. It would be much better to have a Business Manager who was well acquainted with affairs in this country in this particular line of business so that he would understand checking up on the Box Office receipts and looking after other details connected with the business. It may be possible that I could arrange to accompany Captain Amundsen myself.

Mr. Leon Amundsen - #3 - May 27, 1912.

graph was carried to the Pole and motion pictures secured there of the planting of the Norwegian Flag, etc. Will you kindly let me know the name of the firm in the United States that will publish Captain Amundsen's book on his South Polar Trip.

Under separate cover I am sending some post cards we have had printed and which we are sending broadcast throughout the country.

I shall be glad to have you answer the questions asked in this letter at your very earliest convenience.

Thanking you in advance for this favor, and with kind regards, I remain

Very sincerely yours,

LK/S

Mr. Leon Amundsen - #2 - May 27, 1912.

return mail if I may not have the right to sell to some American Syndicate the motion picture films which Captain Amundsen secured on this South Pole trip. I believe that this matter should be left in my hands so that I may make all arrangements as to the time these films are to be shown in the motion picture houses, for if these pictures should appear in America prior to the termination of the lecture tour it would interfere with the success of the tour and mean a financial loss to both Captain Amundsen and myself. I feel confident that you will protect me in this matter, and if you can place in my hands the authority for making arrangements to have these films presented in the big motion picture houses at the proper time, I shall deem it a great favor on your part. I feel confident that I can get as high a price for those rights as anyone.

I am sparing no expense to make this lecture tour a great success but I feel that I cannot help thinking that from a business standpoint I am not sufficiently protected in case your brother should, by reason of illness or death, be prevented from fulfilling the engagements I booked. Life and Accident Insurance would give me ample protection.

Immediately upon receipt of this letter I wish that you would get into communication with your brother and have him submit to a physical examination and take out $10,000 worth of Life and Accident Insurance, made payable to me and send me a bill for the expense of the same, and I will remit to you at once. I want to be fair about this matter and I am willing to pay the cost of the Insurance, and as it is to the interest of Captain Amundsen that I be handicapped in no way in putting forth my best efforts to make this tour a success, I hope that he will readily agree to my proposition and take out the Insurance without delay. The loss I sustained by the sudden death of Alfred Tennyson Dickens, who was on a lecture tour of America under my management, has made me more cautious and I feel loath to spend as much money under the circumstances as I would if I were fully protected by Insurance.

Can your brother make arrangements to bring with him to America the personal equipment he used in making the dash to the Pole, that is, his fur clothing, his skies, and one sledge. If he could arrange to bring a couple of dogs with him I believe that they could be made the means of helping our advertising campaign. Part of this paraphernalia could be placed on exhibition on the platform after the lecture and I believe that these things would add materially to the people's interest. When Commander Peary lectured in New York he had his North Pole equipment on the stage and after the lecture the people were permitted to examine the same. Notice of this added feature was published in the papers and served to arouse much interest.

How many reels of motion picture films will your brother show during his lecture, and about how many stereopticon pictures does he propose to use? The lecture should be made about an hour and a quarter in length.

I would like to have you advise me also if the cinemato-

Mr. Leon Amundsen - #2 - October 10.

Society and I am pledged by contract to them that Captain Amundsen shall not accept any social engagement without their written consent. In this country a great many Societies and individuals are only too anxious to entertain a distinguished visitor at a luncheon or banquet but they are reluctant to assume the management of a lecture. It is only fair to the local organizations that assume financial risk that they shall be consulted about all social engagements. The matter of social engagements is so important that you will see that I insert a clause covering the same in all contracts. Experience has taught us that the only Societies that are entitled to give these receptions and banquets to noted speakers are the ones whose members have shown sufficient interest to have purchased tickets for the lecture in advance. In other words, if the members of a Society are not sufficiently interested in Captain Amundsen's lecture to purchase tickets for the same, Captain Amundsen should not be sufficiently interested in their Society to give them a free talk, which is always expected at a banquet or dinner. We have found by experience that the best plan is for the speaker to refer all social invitations to us, saying that all such matters are arranged by his Manager. Then we can consult with the local organization having charge of the lecture and if they are willing, we can accept the social engagement. Such a system protects Captain Amundsen and also avoids conflicts and confusion.

I feel sure that the National Geographic Society will want to have full charge of Captain Amundsen's time while in Washington, and as they are the best organization in the country, I feel that they should have this privilege. In New York, the lecture is to be under the auspices of the National Norwegian League, and any engagements that Mr. Glade may make that this organization approves of will be satisfactory to me. I understand that your brother is to be the guest of Mr. Glade and I think the National Norwegian League understands this.

Please do not misunderstand me in this matter. I am not attempting to be dictatorial in any way, but I am working in the interests of Captain Amundsen and I know how easy it is for a speaker to lessen the attendance at his lectures by accepting social engagements. I wish, therefore, that he would refrain from accepting any other engagements until he reaches this country and then we can talk the matter over and work out the social schedule.

I thank you sincerely for the photographs and information you have sent me from time to time. It would be a profitable thing if you could engage the services of a press representative and have him cable to the American papers the news concerning Captain Amundsen's lectures abroad.

I enclose a Draft for Kr. 547.20 in payment of the amount due on the insurance policy which you so kindly sent me. I thank you sincerely for this favor.

Upon receipt of this letter will you please cable me at my expense, telling me the number of lectures that Captain Amundsen feels he can deliver each week. I do not want to over-work him and yet I do not want him to have too much idle time. It seems to me that he could deliver four or five lectures per week.

TELEPHONE
BEEKMAN 4074

CABLE ADDRESS
"KEEDICK NEW YORK"

LEE KEEDICK
MANAGER OF THE WORLD'S MOST CELEBRATED LECTURERS
150 NASSAU STREET
NEW YORK CITY

October 10, 1912.

Mr. Leon Amundsen,
Christiana, Norway.

Dear Mr. Amundsen:—

CAPT. ROALD AMUNDSEN
Discoverer of the South Pole and Winner in the International Race for the Southern Extremity of the Earth.

SOME OTHER FAMOUS LECTURERS NOW OR PREVIOUSLY UNDER MY MANAGEMENT

LIEUT.-GENERAL SIR ROBERT BADEN-POWELL
SIR ERNEST H. SHACKLETON
COUNTESS OF WARWICK
COUNTESS LYDIA ROSTOPCHINE
ALFRED TENNYSON DICKENS
JOHN MITCHELL, THE GREAT LABOR LEADER
HON. LESLIE M. SHAW, EX-SECRETARY U. S. TREASURY
HON. HENRY CLEWS, WALL STREET BANKER
COL. S. S. McCLURE, EDITOR OF McCLURE'S MAGAZINE
RADCLYFFE DUGMORE, F. R. G. S.
DR. JOHN WESLEY HILL
DR. G. STANLEY HALL
M. TARBELL
HAMILTON WRIGHT MABIE
PROFESSOR BRANDER MATTHEWS
WILLIAM R. GEORGE
DR. WILLIAM B. GUTHRIE
COL. JOHN TEMPLE GRAVES
SENATOR ALBERT B. CUMMINS

I hope you will pardon my delay in writing you. Your communications have been held at the office awaiting my return from the West. I am so anxious to make this lecture tour by Captain Amundsen the greatest success possible that I personally made a three months' trip to the Pacific Coast, looking over conditions and booking engagements. We now have practically 100 lecture bookings. All of these are with the very best auspices in each city. The terms which we have secured are 60 % of the gross receipts with a minimum guarantee that the 60 % will amount to not less than $500. Of course, in most of the places we expect our share to amount to several hundred dollars.

The method of booking in the United States differs greatly from that in Europe. Here owing to the tremendous distances we do not assign the definite dates as fast as we book the cities but arrange the itinerary in a later period. Captain Amundsen's American tour will begin on January 10 when he speaks in Washington under the auspices of the National Geographic Society. His New York lecture will be on January 14. I am working on the complete itinerary now and shall assign the Chicago date within a few days. It is my present plan to have your brother deliver several lectures in the East, then work Westward to Chicago, and South to California, up along the Pacific Coast, and back through the Dakotas, Minnesota, etc. By pursuing this course he could escape the severe weather in the Northwest avoiding railway delays of several days which are bound to occur in that section of the country in that season of the year. By pursuing this plan we would undoubtedly secure the attendance of thousands of tourists who are in California for the Winter.

Mr. John A. Glade has written me that he has had a letter from you asking him to arrange social engagements in Chicago, New York, and Washington. In Chicago the lecture is to be under the auspices of the Chicago Geographic

CAPTAIN AMUNDSEN'S AMERICAN LECTURE TOUR WILL BE UNDER MY EXCLUSIVE MANAGEMENT.
WRITE FOR TERMS AND OPEN DATES—TOUR BEGINS IN JANUARY 1913.

CABLE ADDRESS "KEEDICK NEW YORK"

TELEPHONE BEEKMAN 4074

LEE KEEDICK
MANAGER OF THE WORLD'S MOST CELEBRATED LECTURERS
150 NASSAU STREET
NEW YORK CITY
PUBLISHER OF CAPTAIN AMUNDSEN'S WORK IN TWO VOLUMES
"THE SOUTH POLE"

January 25, 1913.

CAPT. ROALD AMUNDSEN
Discoverer of the South Pole and Winner in the International Race for the Southern Extremity of the Earth.

SOME OTHER FAMOUS LECTURERS NOW OR PREVIOUSLY UNDER MY MANAGEMENT

LIEUT.-GENERAL SIR ROBERT BADEN-POWELL.
SIR ERNEST H. SHACKLETON
COUNTESS OF WARWICK
COUNTESS LYDIA ROSTOPCHINK
ALFRED TENNYSON DICKENS
JOHN MITCHELL, THE GREAT LABOR LEADER
HON. LESLIE M. SHAW, EX-SECRETARY U. S. TREASURY
HON. HENRY CLEWS, WALL STREET BANKER
COL. S. S. MCCLURE, EDITOR OF McCLURE'S MAGAZINE
RADCLYFFE DUGMORE, F. R. G. S.
DR. JOHN WESLEY HILL
M. TARBELL
HAMILTON WRIGHT MABIE
PROFESSOR BRANDER MATTHEWS
WILLIAM R. GEORGE
DR. WILLIAM B. GUTHRIE
COL. JOHN TEMPLE GRAVES
SENATOR ALBERT B. CUMMINS

Mr. Leon Amundsen,
Christiania, Norway.
Dear Mr. Amundsen:--

Please pardon my delay in replying to your communication, but I have never been so busy in my life as during the past month. I have been putting in about eighteen hours work per day. However, the report I have to send you is a good one. Your brother has been well received in this country. We planned the publicity campaign with great care, and I have been told by a advertising men that it has been exceedingly well conducted. As you know Polar exploration received a blow over the Peary and Cook controversy. People became so disgusted that neither Cook nor Peary could get audiences large enough to pay expenses shortly after their controversy broke out. Therefore, we had much to overcome; and it required most careful handling in order to get your brother started in the right manner with his lecture work in this country. Captain Amundsen's first lecture in New York drew more dollars in the box office than any lecture ever given by an explorer in this city. In other places he has had excellent houses. Present indications are that the lecture tour will surpass your expectations. I enclose statement for your inspection. In my first payment to Captain Amundsen I deducted the amount due on the five hundred dollars you were to pay on my expenses of copyrighting the South Pole book. I presume that this meets with your approval. Your brother has instructed me to make weekly statements and settlements to his friend, Mr. John Bade, and I shall do so and send to you each week a duplicate statement. I also enclose the lecture itinerary.

I am negotiating for several dates in June, right up to the first of July. The indications are

CAPTAIN AMUNDSEN'S AMERICAN LECTURE TOUR WILL BE UNDER MY EXCLUSIVE MANAGEMENT. WRITE FOR TERMS AND OPEN DATES-TOUR BEGINS IN JANUARY 1913.

Mr. Leon Amundsen - #3 - October 10'

Your brother wrote me that he would give me his time from January 10 to July first. In one of your letters you state something about extending this time two months. Am I to understand that he wishes to remain in this country until the first of September? Please let me know concerning this matter at your very earliest convenience.

A great many smaller towns and villages have written that while they can not guarantee the $500 they are willing to pay $250 or $300. Would your brother be willing to accept a number of these engagements to be run in on the schedule during the latter part of his visit? Of course, such requests come from small towns where the halls are so small that they really cannot afford to pay a larger sum.

The Committee at San Diego could not have "The Fram" visit that port a day or two previous to his lecture there. I told them that I thought it was highly improbable but I would write you concerning the matter. Kindly let me know about this in your next letter.

Practically all of the committees have requested that Captain Amundsen speak without notes as the use of a manuscript spoils the effect of the lecture. I have told them that I was confident that he would commit his lecture and refrain from using notes in any way. We have advertised that the lecture will be illustrated with motion as well as stereopticon pictures.

It will be necessary for me to use some photographs on the 4-page circular which I am issuing to be given to the local committees for advertising purposes. In your cable please state if I may use the photographs that appeared in Collier's Weekly.

Mr. Glade informs me that Captain Amundsen will sail from Southampton on "The Olympic" on January 1. This is highly satisfactory.

With all good wishes believe me,

Very sincerely yours,
Lee Keedick

Dic. LK/S
Enc. 1 draft.

P.S. I understand that Mr. Gade is an intimate friend of your brother and of course will arrange only such period of lecture engagements in New York as will help the lecture -

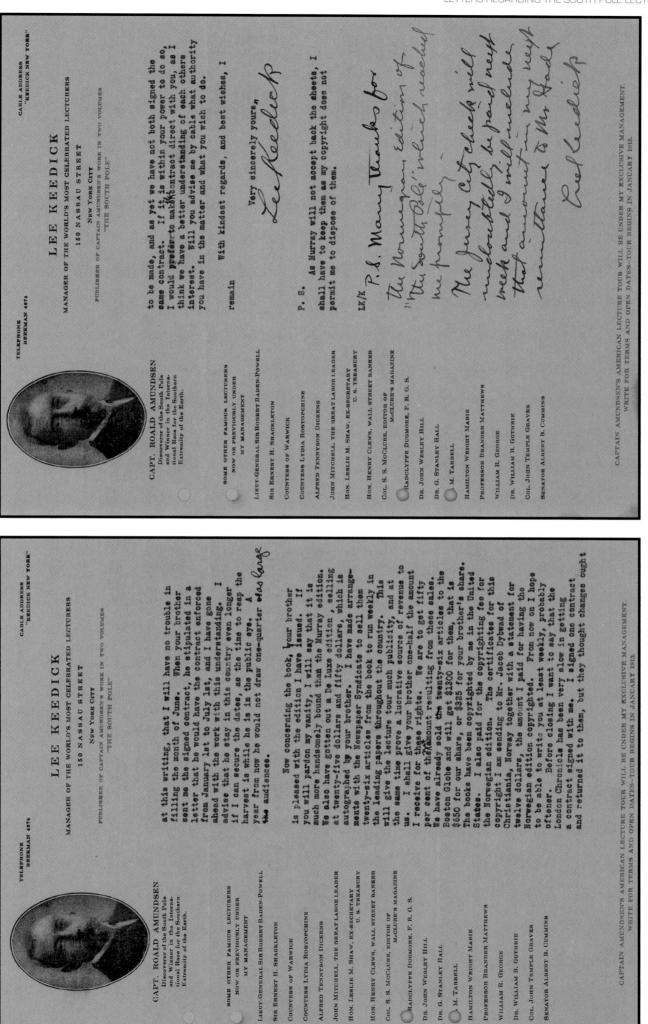

First letter (top):

LEE KEEDICK
MANAGER OF THE WORLD'S MOST CELEBRATED LECTURERS
150 NASSAU STREET
NEW YORK CITY
PUBLISHER OF CAPTAIN AMUNDSEN'S WORK IN TWO VOLUMES
"THE SOUTH POLE"

CAPT. ROALD AMUNDSEN
Discoverer of the South Pole and Winner in the International Race for the Southern Extremity of the Earth.

SOME OTHER FAMOUS LECTURERS NOW OR PREVIOUSLY UNDER MY MANAGEMENT

LIEUT-GENERAL SIR ROBERT BADEN-POWELL
SIR ERNEST H. SHACKLETON
COUNTESS OF WARWICK
COUNTESS LYDIA ROSTOPCHINE
ALFRED TENNYSON DICKENS
JOHN MITCHELL, THE GREAT LABOR LEADER
HON. LESLIE M. SHAW, EX-SECRETARY U. S. TREASURY
HON. HENRY CLEWS, WALL STREET BANKER
COL. S. S. McCLURE, EDITOR OF McCLURE'S MAGAZINE
RADCLYFFE DUGMORE, F. R. G. S.
DR. JOHN WESLEY HILL
DR. G. STANLEY HALL
M. TARBELL
HAMILTON WRIGHT MABIE
PROFESSOR BRANDER MATTHEWS
WILLIAM R. GEORGE
DR. WILLIAM H. GUTHRIE
COL. JOHN TEMPLE GRAVES
SENATOR ALBERT B. CUMMINS

to be made, and as yet we have not both signed the same contract. If it is within your power to do so, I would prefer to make a contract direct with you, as I think we have a better understanding of each others interest. Will you advise me by cable what authority you have in the matter and what you wish to do.

With kindest regards, and best wishes, I remain

Very sincerely yours,
Lee Keedick

P. S. As Murray will not accept back the sheets, I shall have to keep them as my copyright does not permit me to dispose of them.

LK/K

P.S. Many thanks for the Norwegian edition of "The South Pole" which reached me promptly.

The Jersey City check will undoubtedly be paid next week and I will include that amount in my next remittance to Mr. ____
Lee Keedick

Second letter (bottom):

TELEPHONE BEEKMAN 4074   CABLE ADDRESS "KEEDICK NEW YORK"

LEE KEEDICK
MANAGER OF THE WORLD'S MOST CELEBRATED LECTURERS
150 NASSAU STREET
NEW YORK CITY
PUBLISHER OF CAPTAIN AMUNDSEN'S WORK IN TWO VOLUMES
"THE SOUTH POLE"

CAPT. ROALD AMUNDSEN
Discoverer of the South Pole and Winner in the International Race for the Southern Extremity of the Earth.

SOME OTHER FAMOUS LECTURERS NOW OR PREVIOUSLY UNDER MY MANAGEMENT

LIEUT-GENERAL SIR ROBERT BADEN-POWELL
SIR ERNEST H. SHACKLETON
COUNTESS OF WARWICK
COUNTESS LYDIA ROSTOPCHINE
ALFRED TENNYSON DICKENS
JOHN MITCHELL, THE GREAT LABOR LEADER
HON. LESLIE M. SHAW, EX-SECRETARY U. S. TREASURY
HON. HENRY CLEWS, WALL STREET BANKER
COL. S. S. McCLURE, EDITOR OF McCLURE'S MAGAZINE
RADCLYFFE DUGMORE, F. R. G. S.
DR. JOHN WESLEY HILL
DR. G. STANLEY HALL
M. TARBELL
HAMILTON WRIGHT MABIE
PROFESSOR BRANDER MATTHEWS
WILLIAM R. GEORGE
DR. WILLIAM H. GUTHRIE
COL. JOHN TEMPLE GRAVES
SENATOR ALBERT B. CUMMINS

at this writing, that I will have no trouble in filling the month of June. When your brother sent me the signed contract, he stipulated in a letter that he would have the contract enforced from January 1st to July 1st, and I have gone ahead with the work with this understanding. I advise that he stay in this country even longer if I can secure the dates, as the time to reap the harvest is while he is in the public eye. A year from now he would not draw one-quarter of so large the audiences.

Now concerning the book, your brother is pleased with the edition I have issued. If you will pardon my vanity, I will say that it is much more handsomely bound than the Murray edition. We also have gotten out a De Luxe edition, which is selling at twenty-five dollars and fifty dollars, autographed by your brother. I have made arrangements with the Newspaper Syndicate to sell them twenty-six articles from the book to run weekly in the leading papers throughout the country. This will give the lecture tour much publicity, and at the same time prove a lucrative source of revenue to us. I shall give your brother one-half the amount I receive for these rights. We are to get fifty per cent of the amount resulting from these sales. We have already sold the twenty-six articles to the Boston Globe and will get $1300 for them, that is $650 for our share, or $325 for your brother's share. The books have been copyrighted by me in the United States. I also paid for the copyrighting fee for the Norwegian edition. The certificates for this copyright I am sending to Mr. Jacob Dybwad of Christiania, Norway together with a statement for twelve dollars, the amount I paid for having the Norwegian edition copyrighted. From now on I hope to be able to write you at least weekly, probably oftener. Before closing I want to say that the London Chronicle has been very slow in getting a contract signed with me. I signed one contract and returned it to them, but they thought changes ought

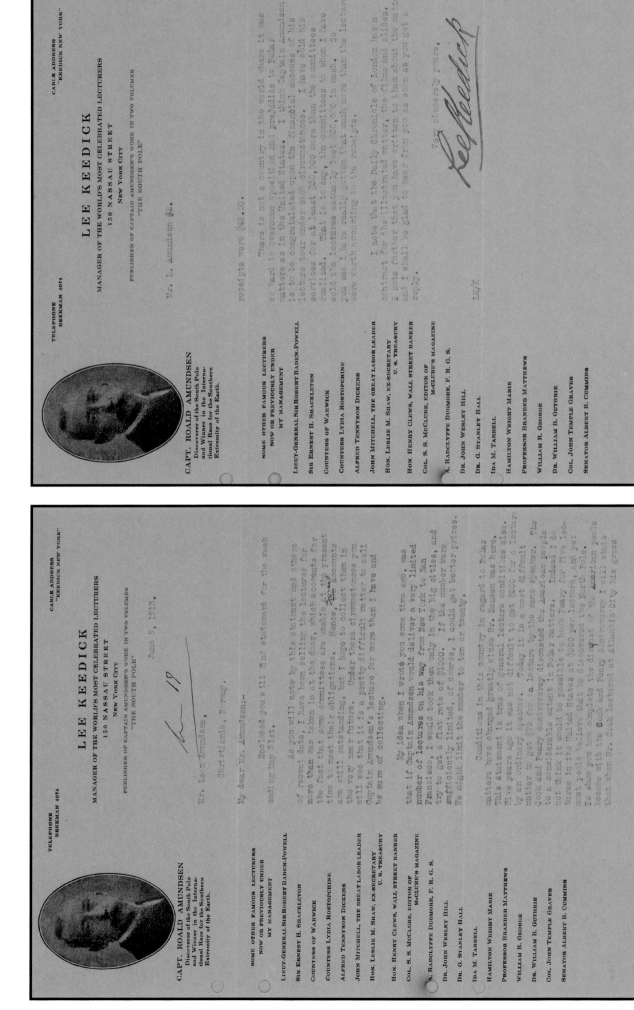

First letter (right):

TELEPHONE
BEEKMAN 4074

CABLE ADDRESS
"KEEDICK NEW YORK"

LEE KEEDICK

MANAGER OF THE WORLD'S MOST CELEBRATED LECTURERS

150 NASSAU STREET
New York City

PUBLISHER OF CAPTAIN AMUNDSEN'S WORK IN TWO VOLUMES
"THE SOUTH POLE"

Mr. L. Amundsen #2.

receipts were $48.00.

There is not a country in the world where it was so hard to overcome opposition and prejudice to Polar matters as in the United States. I think Captain Amundsen is to be congratulated upon the financial success of his lecture tour under such circumstances. I have paid his services for at least $23,000 more than the committees realized. What is to say, the committees to whom I have sold the lectures actually lost $20,000 in cash. So you see I have really gotten that much more than the lectures were worth according to the receipts.

I note that the Daily Chronicle of London has a contract for the illustrated matter, the films and slides. I note further that you have written to them about the matter and I shall be glad to hear from you as soon as you get a reply.

Very sincerely yours,

LK/K

CAPT. ROALD AMUNDSEN
Discoverer of the South Pole
and Winner in the International Race for the Southern
Extremity of the Earth.

SOME OTHER FAMOUS LECTURERS
NOW OR PREVIOUSLY UNDER
MY MANAGEMENT

LIEUT-GENERAL SIR ROBERT BADEN-POWELL
SIR ERNEST H. SHACKLETON
COUNTESS OF WARWICK
COUNTESS LYDIA ROSTOPCHINE
ALFRED TENNYSON DICKENS
JOHN MITCHELL, THE GREAT LABOR LEADER
HON. LESLIE M. SHAW, EX-SECRETARY U. S. TREASURY
HON. HENRY CLEWS, WALL STREET BANKER
COL. S. S. MCCLURE, EDITOR OF MCCLURE'S MAGAZINE
A. RADCLYFFE DUGMORE, F. R. G. S.
DR. JOHN WESLEY HILL
DR. G. STANLEY HALL
IDA M. TARBELL
HAMILTON WRIGHT MABIE
PROFESSOR BRANDER MATTHEWS
WILLIAM R. GEORGE
DR. WILLIAM B. GUTHRIE
COL. JOHN TEMPLE GRAVES
SENATOR ALBERT B. CUMMINS

CAPTAIN AMUNDSEN'S AMERICAN LECTURE TOUR WILL BE UNDER MY EXCLUSIVE MANAGEMENT

Second letter (left):

TELEPHONE
BEEKMAN 4074

CABLE ADDRESS
"KEEDICK NEW YORK"

LEE KEEDICK

MANAGER OF THE WORLD'S MOST CELEBRATED LECTURERS

150 NASSAU STREET
New York City

PUBLISHER OF CAPTAIN AMUNDSEN'S WORK IN TWO VOLUMES
"THE SOUTH POLE"

June 5, 1913.

Mr. Leon Amundsen,
Christiania, Norway.

My dear Mr. Amundsen:-

Enclosed you will find statement for the week ending May 31st.

As you will note by this statement and others of recent date, I have been selling the lectures for more than was taken in at the door, which accounts for the fact that some committees are unable at the present time to meet their obligations. Hence, some accounts are still outstanding, but I hope to collect them in the very near future. Under these circumstances you will see that it is a pretty difficult matter to sell Captain Amundsen's lecture for more than I have and be sure of collecting.

My idea when I wrote you some time ago, was that if Captain Amundsen would deliver a very limited number of lectures on his way from New York to San Francisco, I would book them only in the big cities, and try to get a flat rate of $1000. If the number were sufficiently limited, of course, I could get better prices. We might limit the number to ten or twenty.

Conditions in this country in regard to Polar matters have changed greatly since Dr. Nansen was here. This statement is true of general lecture conditions also. Five years ago it was not difficult to get $200 for a lecture by an ordinary speaker. Today it is a most difficult matter to get $75 for a lecture by the same speaker. The Cook and Peary controversy disgusted the American people to a considerable extent in Polar matters. Indeed I do not think it would be possible to book Peary for five lectures in the United States at $500 per lecture, and yet most people believe that he discovered the North Pole. To show you how complete the disgust of the American people became with the Cook and Peary controversy I will state that when Dr. Cook lectured at Atlantic City his gross

CAPTAIN AMUNDSEN'S AMERICAN LECTURE TOUR WILL BE UNDER MY EXCLUSIVE MANAGEMENT
WRITE FOR TERMS AND OPEN DATES-TOUR BEGINS IN JANUARY 1913.

CAPT. ROALD AMUNDSEN
Discoverer of the South Pole
and Winner in the International Race for the Southern
Extremity of the Earth.

SOME OTHER FAMOUS LECTURERS
NOW OR PREVIOUSLY UNDER
MY MANAGEMENT

LIEUT-GENERAL SIR ROBERT BADEN-POWELL
SIR ERNEST H. SHACKLETON
COUNTESS OF WARWICK
COUNTESS LYDIA ROSTOPCHINE
ALFRED TENNYSON DICKENS
JOHN MITCHELL, THE GREAT LABOR LEADER
HON. LESLIE M. SHAW, EX-SECRETARY U. S. TREASURY
HON. HENRY CLEWS, WALL STREET BANKER
COL. S. S. MCCLURE, EDITOR OF MCCLURE'S MAGAZINE
A. RADCLYFFE DUGMORE, F. R. G. S.
DR. JOHN WESLEY HILL
DR. G. STANLEY HALL
IDA M. TARBELL
HAMILTON WRIGHT MABIE
PROFESSOR BRANDER MATTHEWS
WILLIAM R. GEORGE
DR. WILLIAM B. GUTHRIE
COL. JOHN TEMPLE GRAVES
SENATOR ALBERT B. CUMMINS

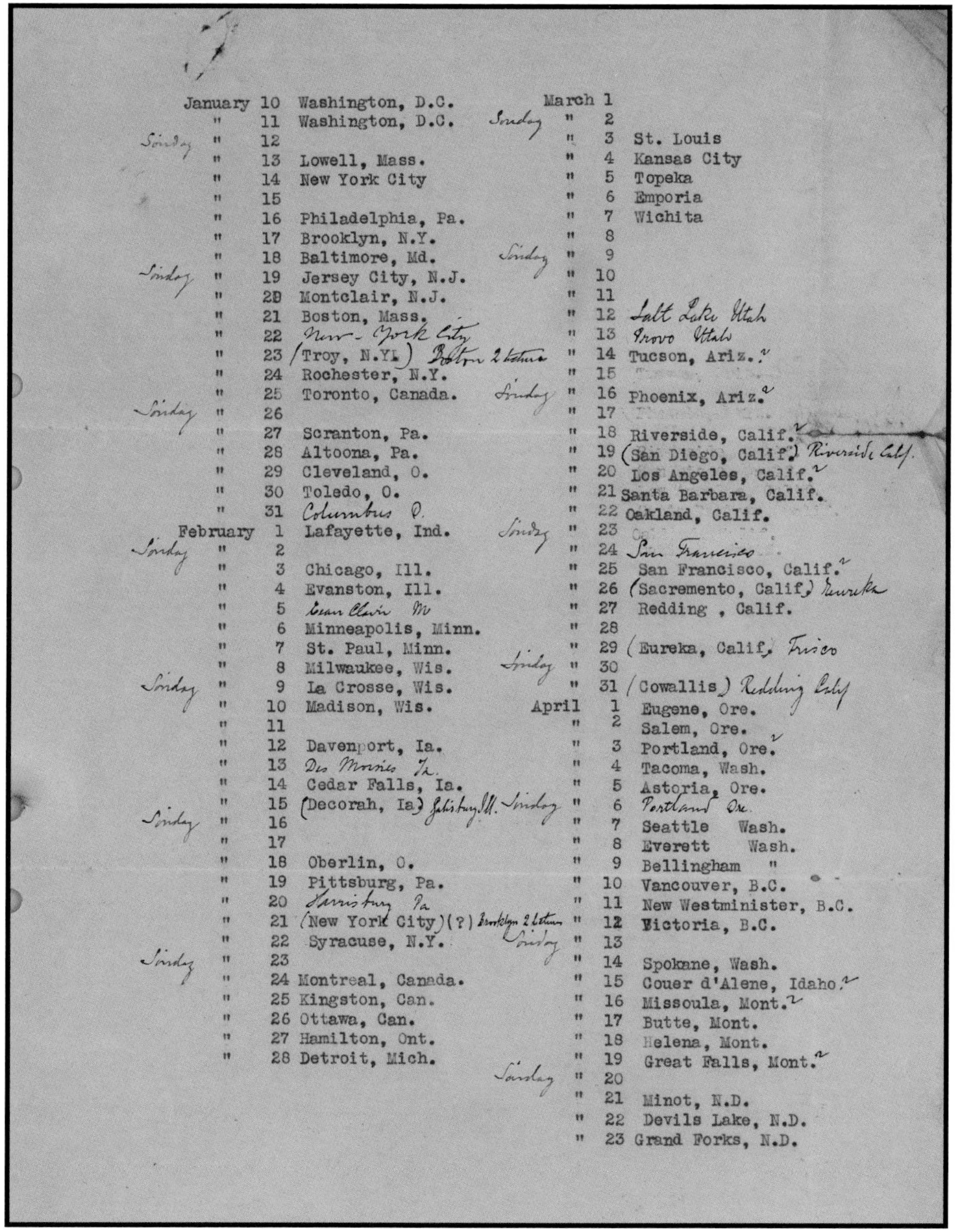

January	10	Washington, D.C.	March	1	
"	11	Washington, D.C. (Sunday)	"	2	
(Sunday) "	12		"	3	St. Louis
"	13	Lowell, Mass.	"	4	Kansas City
"	14	New York City	"	5	Topeka
"	15		"	6	Emporia
"	16	Philadelphia, Pa.	"	7	Wichita
"	17	Brooklyn, N.Y.	"	8	
"	18	Baltimore, Md. (Sunday)	"	9	
(Sunday) "	19	Jersey City, N.J.	"	10	
"	20	Montclair, N.J.	"	11	
"	21	Boston, Mass.	"	12	Salt Lake Utah
"	22	New-York City	"	13	Provo Utah
"	23	(Troy, N.Y.) Boston 2 lectures	"	14	Tucson, Ariz.
"	24	Rochester, N.Y.	"	15	
"	25	Toronto, Canada. (Sunday)	"	16	Phoenix, Ariz.
(Sunday) "	26		"	17	
"	27	Scranton, Pa.	"	18	Riverside, Calif.
"	28	Altoona, Pa.	"	19	(San Diego, Calif.) Riverside Calif.
"	29	Cleveland, O.	"	20	Los Angeles, Calif.
"	30	Toledo, O.	"	21	Santa Barbara, Calif.
"	31	Columbus O.	"	22	Oakland, Calif.
February	1	Lafayette, Ind. (Sunday)	"	23	
(Sunday) "	2		"	24	San Francisco
"	3	Chicago, Ill.	"	25	San Francisco, Calif.
"	4	Evanston, Ill.	"	26	(Sacremento, Calif) Eureka
"	5	Eau Claire W	"	27	Redding , Calif.
"	6	Minneapolis, Minn.	"	28	
"	7	St. Paul, Minn.	"	29	(Eureka, Calif, Frisco
"	8	Milwaukee, Wis. (Sunday)	"	30	
(Sunday) "	9	La Crosse, Wis.	"	31	(Cowallis) Redding Calif
"	10	Madison, Wis.	April	1	Eugene, Ore.
"	11		"	2	Salem, Ore.
"	12	Davenport, Ia.	"	3	Portland, Ore.
"	13	Des Moines Ia	"	4	Tacoma, Wash.
"	14	Cedar Falls, Ia.	"	5	Astoria, Ore.
"	15	(Decorah, Ia) Galesburg Ill. (Sunday)	"	6	Portland Ore
(Sunday) "	16		"	7	Seattle Wash.
"	17		"	8	Everett Wash.
"	18	Oberlin, O.	"	9	Bellingham "
"	19	Pittsburg, Pa.	"	10	Vancouver, B.C.
"	20	Harrisburg Pa	"	11	New Westminister, B.C.
"	21	(New York City)(?) Brooklyn 2 lectures	"	12	Victoria, B.C.
"	22	Syracuse, N.Y. (Sunday)	"	13	
(Sunday) "	23		"	14	Spokane, Wash.
"	24	Montreal, Canada.	"	15	Couer d'Alene, Idaho.
"	25	Kingston, Can.	"	16	Missoula, Mont.
"	26	Ottawa, Can.	"	17	Butte, Mont.
"	27	Hamilton, Ont.	"	18	Helena, Mont.
"	28	Detroit, Mich.	"	19	Great Falls, Mont.
		(Sunday)	"	20	
			"	21	Minot, N.D.
			"	22	Devils Lake, N.D.
			"	23	Grand Forks, N.D.

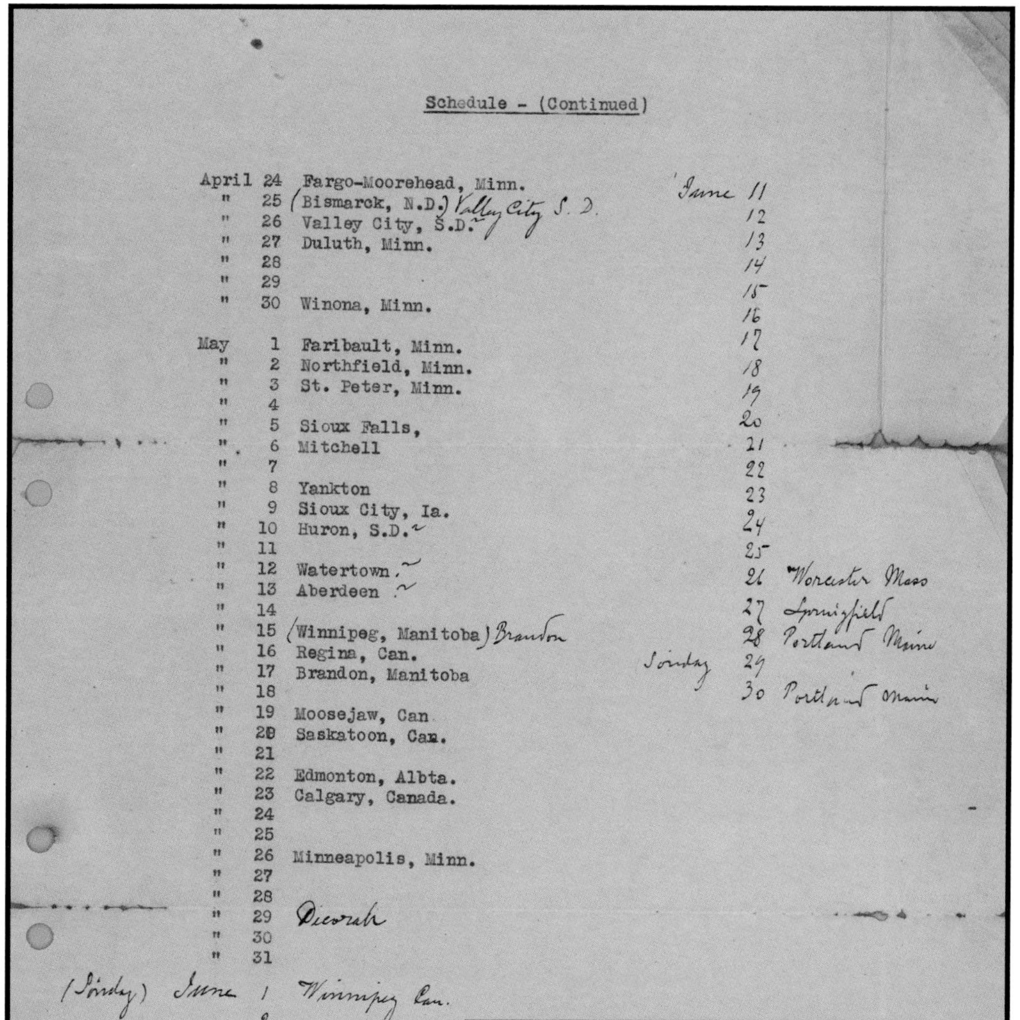

Schedule - (Continued)

April	24	Fargo-Moorehead, Minn.	June 11	
"	25	(Bismarck, N.D.) Valley City S. D.	12	
"	26	Valley City, S.D.	13	
"	27	Duluth, Minn.	14	
"	28		15	
"	29		16	
"	30	Winona, Minn.	17	
May	1	Faribault, Minn.	18	
"	2	Northfield, Minn.	19	
"	3	St. Peter, Minn.	20	
"	4		21	
"	5	Sioux Falls,	22	
"	6	Mitchell	23	
"	7		24	
"	8	Yankton	25	
"	9	Sioux City, Ia.	26	Worcester Mass
"	10	Huron, S.D.	27	Springfield
"	11		28	Portland Maine
"	12	Watertown	(Sunday) 29	
"	13	Aberdeen	30	Portland Maine
"	14			
"	15	(Winnipeg, Manitoba) Brandon		
"	16	Regina, Can.		
"	17	Brandon, Manitoba		
"	18			
"	19	Moosejaw, Can		
"	20	Saskatoon, Can.		
"	21			
"	22	Edmonton, Albta.		
"	23	Calgary, Canada.		
"	24			
"	25			
"	26	Minneapolis, Minn.		
"	27			
"	28			
"	29	Decorah		
"	30			
"	31			
(Sunday) June	1	Winnipeg Can.		
	2			
	3			
	4			
	5			
	6			
	7			
	8			
	9			
	10			

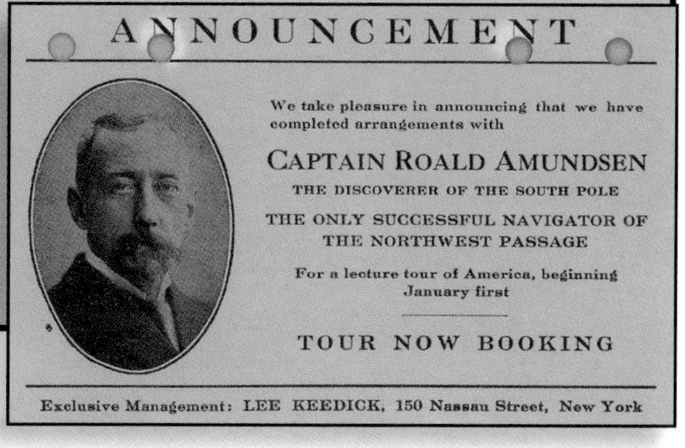
ANNOUNCEMENT
We take pleasure in announcing that we have completed arrangements with
CAPTAIN ROALD AMUNDSEN
THE DISCOVERER OF THE SOUTH POLE
THE ONLY SUCCESSFUL NAVIGATOR OF THE NORTHWEST PASSAGE
For a lecture tour of America, beginning January first
TOUR NOW BOOKING
Exclusive Management: LEE KEEDICK, 150 Nassau Street, New York

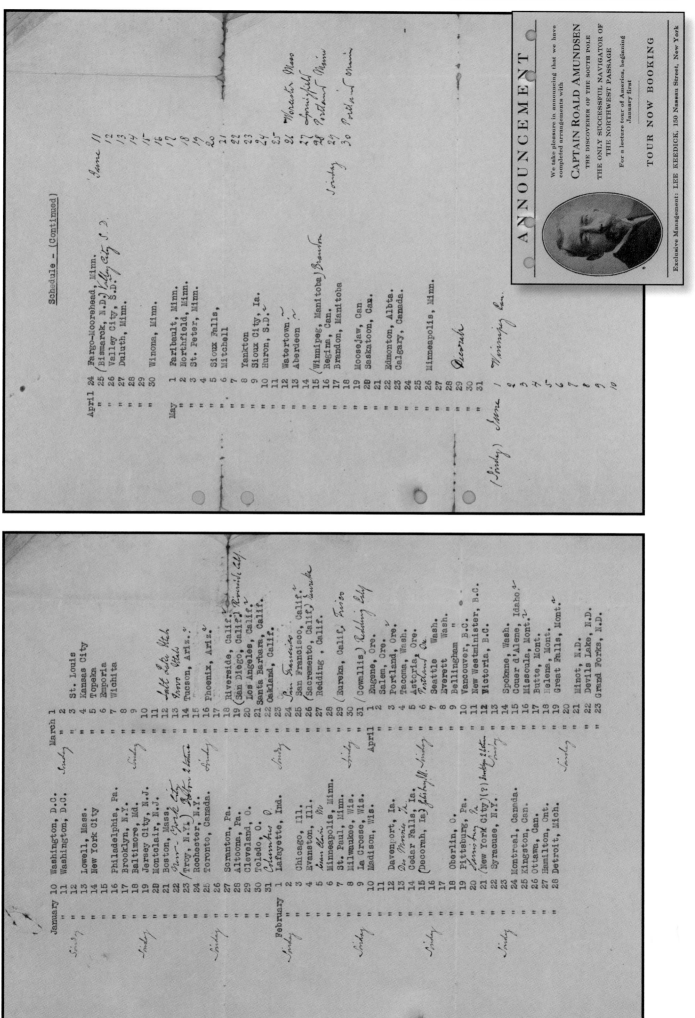

SOUVENIR BOOK OF CAPT ⋅ ROALD AMUNDSEN'S LECTURE

CAPT. ROALD AMUNDSEN

CITY HALL, JUNE 25, 1913, 8 P. M.
PORTLAND, MAINE
SUBJECT:
HOW I DISCOVERED THE SOUTH POLE
Illustrated with Motion Pictures

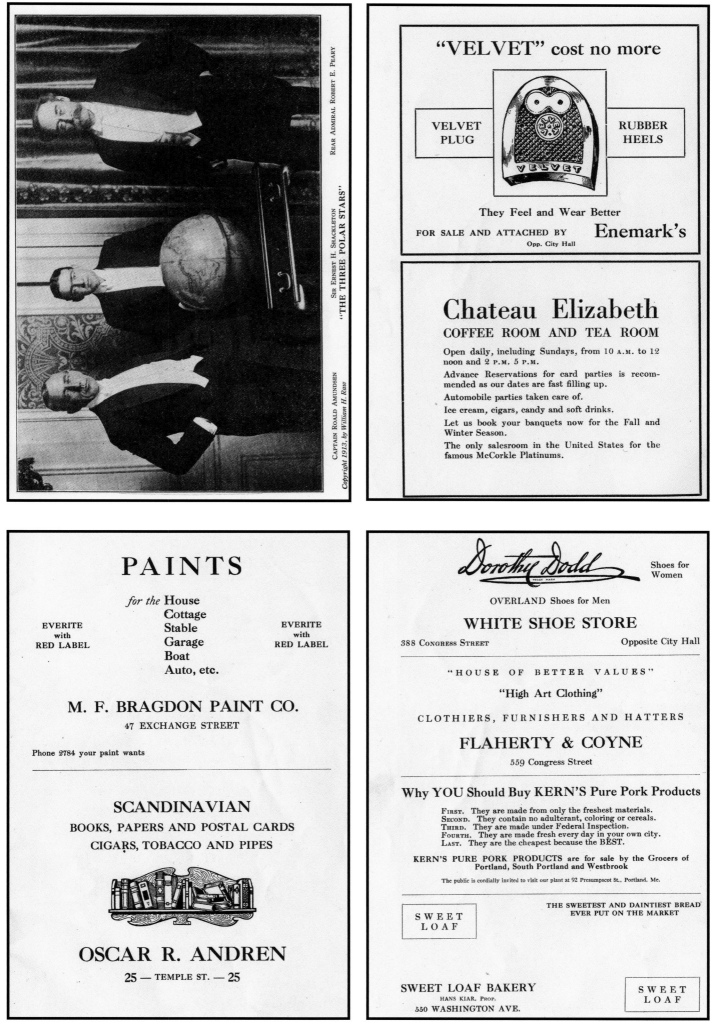

CAPTAIN ROALD AMUNDSEN
Copyright 1913, by William H. Rau

SIR ERNEST H. SHACKLETON
"THE THREE POLAR STARS"

REAR ADMIRAL ROBERT E. PEARY

"VELVET" cost no more

| VELVET PLUG | | RUBBER HEELS |

They Feel and Wear Better

FOR SALE AND ATTACHED BY   Enemark's
Opp. City Hall

Chateau Elizabeth
COFFEE ROOM AND TEA ROOM

Open daily, including Sundays, from 10 A.M. to 12 noon and 2 P.M. 5 P.M.

Advance Reservations for card parties is recommended as our dates are fast filling up.

Automobile parties taken care of.

Ice cream, cigars, candy and soft drinks.

Let us book your banquets now for the Fall and Winter Season.

The only salesroom in the United States for the famous McCorkle Platinums.

PAINTS

for the House
Cottage
Stable
Garage
Boat
Auto, etc.

EVERITE
with
RED LABEL

EVERITE
with
RED LABEL

M. F. BRAGDON PAINT CO.
47 EXCHANGE STREET

Phone 2784 your paint wants

SCANDINAVIAN
BOOKS, PAPERS AND POSTAL CARDS
CIGARS, TOBACCO AND PIPES

OSCAR R. ANDREN
25 — TEMPLE ST. — 25

Dorothy Dodd   Shoes for Women
TRADE MARK

OVERLAND Shoes for Men

WHITE SHOE STORE

388 CONGRESS STREET   Opposite City Hall

"HOUSE OF BETTER VALUES"

"High Art Clothing"

CLOTHIERS, FURNISHERS AND HATTERS

FLAHERTY & COYNE
559 Congress Street

Why YOU Should Buy KERN'S Pure Pork Products

FIRST.   They are made from only the freshest materials.
SECOND. They contain no adulterant, coloring or cereals.
THIRD.   They are made under Federal Inspection.
FOURTH. They are made fresh every day in your own city.
LAST.   They are the cheapest because the BEST.

KERN'S PURE PORK PRODUCTS are for sale by the Grocers of Portland, South Portland and Westbrook

The public is cordially invited to visit our plant at 92 Presumpscot St., Portland, Me.

SWEET LOAF

THE SWEETEST AND DAINTIEST BREAD EVER PUT ON THE MARKET

SWEET LOAF BAKERY
HANS KIAR, PROP.
550 WASHINGTON AVE.

SWEET LOAF

Davis Greenhouses

HANS J. NIELSEN, PROP.

Plants, Cut Flowers, Floral Designs for all Occasions

Telephone 3339-W

67 Brentwood St., Woodfords, Me.

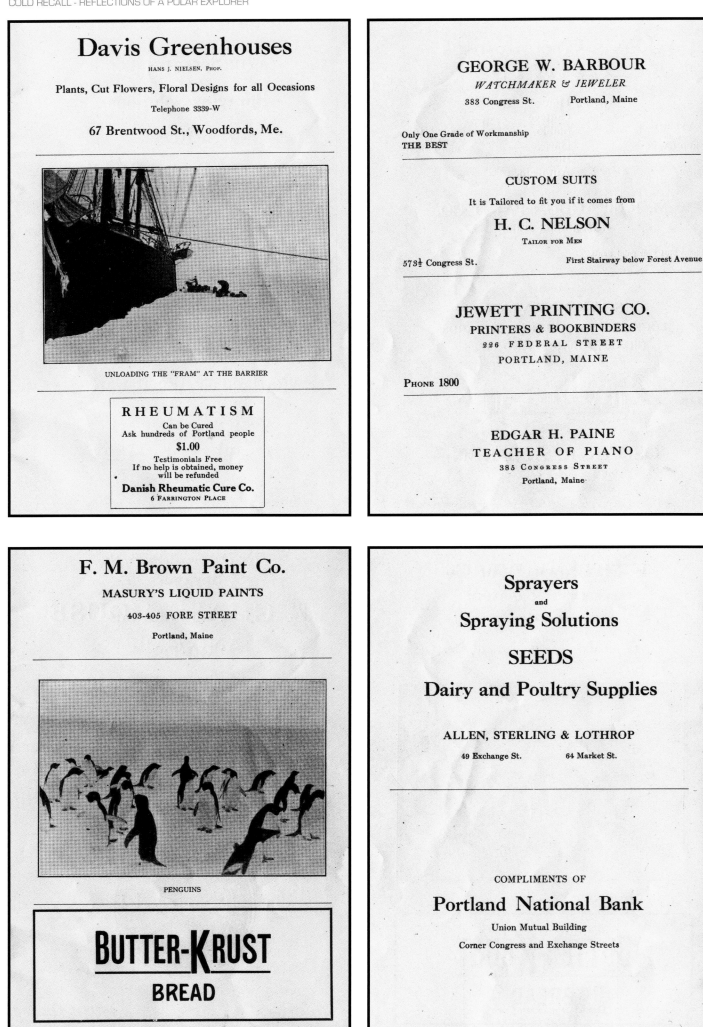

UNLOADING THE "FRAM" AT THE BARRIER

RHEUMATISM
Can be Cured
Ask hundreds of Portland people
$1.00
Testimonials Free
If no help is obtained, money
will be refunded
Danish Rheumatic Cure Co.
6 FARRINGTON PLACE

GEORGE W. BARBOUR
WATCHMAKER & JEWELER

383 Congress St.   Portland, Maine

Only One Grade of Workmanship
THE BEST

CUSTOM SUITS
It is Tailored to fit you if it comes from

H. C. NELSON
TAILOR FOR MEN

573½ Congress St.   First Stairway below Forest Avenue

JEWETT PRINTING CO.
PRINTERS & BOOKBINDERS
226 FEDERAL STREET
PORTLAND, MAINE

PHONE 1800

EDGAR H. PAINE
TEACHER OF PIANO
385 CONGRESS STREET
Portland, Maine

F. M. Brown Paint Co.
MASURY'S LIQUID PAINTS
403-405 FORE STREET
Portland, Maine

PENGUINS

BUTTER-KRUST
BREAD

Sprayers
and
Spraying Solutions
SEEDS
Dairy and Poultry Supplies

ALLEN, STERLING & LOTHROP
49 Exchange St.   64 Market St.

COMPLIMENTS OF
Portland National Bank
Union Mutual Building
Corner Congress and Exchange Streets

CHARLES M. HAY PAINT CO.
8-12 FREE STREET
PORTLAND, ME.

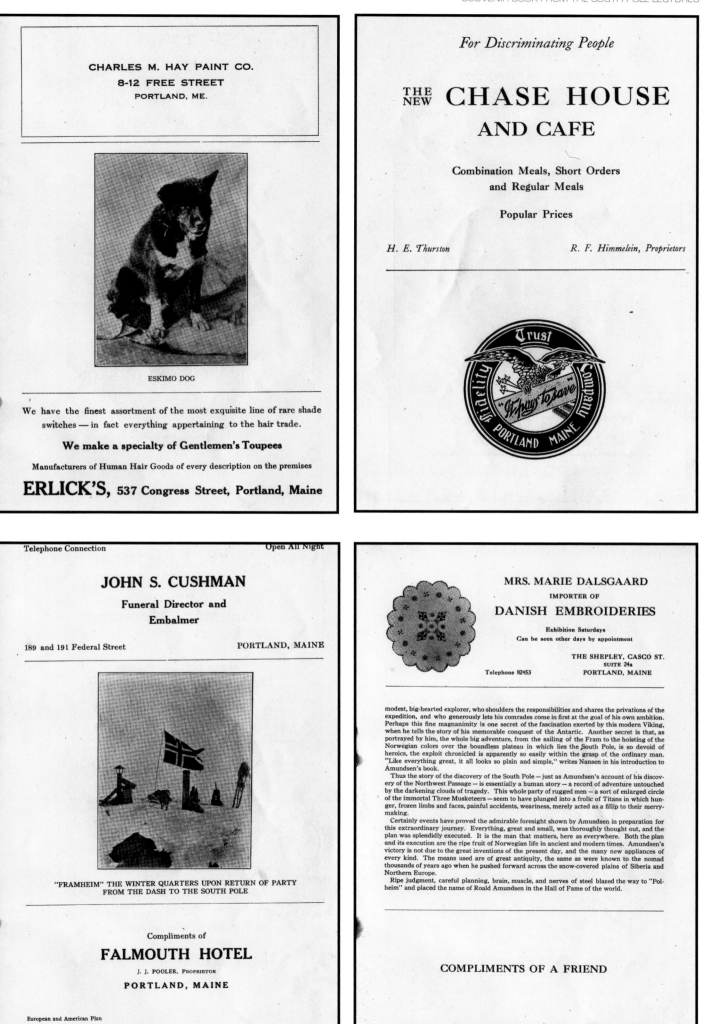

ESKIMO DOG

We have the finest assortment of the most exquisite line of rare shade switches — in fact everything appertaining to the hair trade.

We make a specialty of Gentlemen's Toupees

Manufacturers of Human Hair Goods of every description on the premises

ERLICK'S, 537 Congress Street, Portland, Maine

For Discriminating People

THE
NEW CHASE HOUSE
AND CAFE

Combination Meals, Short Orders
and Regular Meals

Popular Prices

H. E. Thurston   *R. F. Himmelein, Proprietors*

Telephone Connection   Open All Night

JOHN S. CUSHMAN

Funeral Director and
Embalmer

189 and 191 Federal Street   PORTLAND, MAINE

"FRAMHEIM" THE WINTER QUARTERS UPON RETURN OF PARTY
FROM THE DASH TO THE SOUTH POLE

Compliments of

FALMOUTH HOTEL

J. J. POOLER, PROPRIETOR

PORTLAND, MAINE

European and American Plan

MRS. MARIE DALSGAARD
IMPORTER OF

DANISH EMBROIDERIES

Exhibition Saturdays
Can be seen other days by appointment

THE SHEPLEY, CASCO ST.
SUITE 24a
Telephone 82453   PORTLAND, MAINE

modest, big-hearted explorer, who shoulders the responsibilities and shares the privations of the expedition, and who generously lets his comrades come in first at the goal of his own ambition. Perhaps this fine magnanimity is one secret of the fascination exerted by this modern Viking, when he tells the story of his memorable conquest of the Antartic. Another secret is that, as portrayed by him, the whole big adventure, from the sailing of the Fram to the hoisting of the Norwegian colors over the boundless plateau in which lies the South Pole, is so devoid of heroics, the exploit chronicled is apparently so easily within the grasp of the ordinary man. "Like everything great, it all looks so plain and simple," writes Nansen in his introduction to Amundsen's book.

Thus the story of the discovery of the South Pole — just as Amundsen's account of his discovery of the Northwest Passage — is essentially a human story — a record of adventure untouched by the darkening clouds of tragedy. This whole party of rugged men — a sort of enlarged circle of the immortal Three Musketeers — seem to have plunged into a frolic of Titans in which hunger, frozen limbs and faces, painful accidents, weariness, merely acted as a fillip to their merry-making.

Certainly events have proved the admirable foresight shown by Amundsen in preparation for this extraordinary journey. Everything, great and small, was thoroughly thought out, and the plan was splendidly executed. It is the man that matters, here as everywhere. Both the plan and its execution are the ripe fruit of Norwegian life in ancient and modern times. Amundsen's victory is not due to the great inventions of the present day, and the many new appliances of every kind. The means used are of great antiquity, the same as were known to the nomad thousands of years ago when he pushed forward across the snow-covered plains of Siberia and Northern Europe.

Ripe judgment, careful planning, brain, muscle, and nerves of steel blazed the way to "Polheim" and placed the name of Roald Amundsen in the Hall of Fame of the world.

COMPLIMENTS OF A FRIEND

H. H. HAY SONS

TWO DRUG STORES MIDDLE ST. CONGRESS ST.

PURE DRUGS—GOOD SODA—FINE CIGARS

CITY HALL, PORTLAND, MAINE

Tuesday Eve., June 25th, 1913, at 8

CAPTAIN ROALD AMUNDSEN

LECTURE SUBJECT

How I Discovered the South Pole

ILLUSTRATED WITH MOTION PICTURES

Under the auspices of the Scandinavians of Portland, Me.

WHEN a man has done a great thing all the world turns to look at him, and question whether he "can meet with Triumph or Disaster and treat those two impostors just the same." No one who has followed the career of Roald Amundsen can doubt for one moment that here is a man big enough to stand success—a man who is greater than the thing he has done. The closest scrutiny of this simple-hearted hero will fail to reveal the slightest self-vaunting or self-laudation. Honored as few men have ever been—decorated by the most distinguished societies of Europe, received by kings and nobles, praised by scholars and sages, he still remains the same

---

HIGH GRADE PIANOS   PIANO PLAYERS

John Andrew Peterson

18 PREBLE STREET

PORTLAND, ME.

"Going to HOLMES to Shoe the Family"

A GLIMPSE OF CAPTAIN ROALD AMUNDSEN

CAPTAIN ROALD AMUNDSEN, the world's greatest living explorer, in fact one of the five greatest in the world's history, was born and bred amid the rigors of the north of Christiania, Norway. His explorations and discoveries extend over the greatest part of his life.

The discovery of the South Pole is by no means the first achievement and experience of Capt. Amundsen. Among the most valuable scientific and educational knowledge which Capt. Amundsen has given to the world is the discovery of the Magnetic North Pole, the Northwest Passage and finally the recent discovery of the South Pole.

Captain Amundsen has been interested in navigation and exploration since childhood. His spirit was kindled with a desire for adventures in the far-off Polar Regions while he was still in his teens.

He was naturally accustomed to snow and ice and like many other Norwegians he soon became an expert on skis. His first exploration on a ski trip with his brother nearly cost him his life. Had it not been by a fortunate chance of the brother of Amundsen, who during the night while they were asleep in their bags awoke and found young Amundsen buried under a drift of

---

CHESTER L. JORDAN & CO.

All kinds of

INSURANCE and SURETY BONDS

13 Exchange St.   Portland, Me.

Shoes that Satisfy

Lane's
381 CONGRESS ST.
491 CONGRESS ST.
EXCLUSIVE Emerson Dept.
AT UPPER STORE

Compliments of

C. M. Rice Paper Co.

FOUNTAIN PENS

Non-leakable and Always Reliable

FOR SALE

Fessenden News Co.

497 CONGRESS ST.

H. E. DAVIS COMPANY

PRACTICAL PLUMBERS

Steam and Water Heating
General Jobbing

33 FOREST AVENUE

Southworth Printing Company

THIS is a large Booklet and Catalog Printing Plant, whose work is distinguished by a strong, distinctive style in typography and by a mechanical excellence in all details of composition and presswork.

Our customers include many of the large manufacturing and mercantile houses of Portland and out of town.

We invite your correspondence regarding prospective work. We are always glad to send samples of our work to business houses.

105 MIDDLE STREET, PORTLAND, MAINE

HAY & PEABODY

756 Congress St.

York & Boothby Co.

Electric

Wiring and Fixtures

---

a raging snowstorm, this first expedition would have been his last. They had lost their way in the snow storm and were three days and nights on the trip and ninety-four hours without food.

Capt. Amundsen also had a narrow escape from losing his life when he was two years old. He tried to make a voyage across the waters of a big fountain in his father's yard. When he fell in, the servants heard his scream and found him half drowned in the fountain. They had to work on him an hour before he regained consciousness.

Capt. Amundsen attended the Anderson Academy and the University in Christiania. He was considered a bright pupil at the University and it was the intention of his parents to have made a doctor of Amundsen, but he longed for the life of the explorers and outdoor winter sports.

Soon after the death of his mother he left the University and plunged with great delight into the life of his boyhood dreams. The adventures of Capt. Amundsen since then have been repeated to the world over and over again. His lectures have been listened to and his books have been read by many thousand people with great interest. His character, his personality and his achievements have been studied and they have been weighed and found in tune with the foremost heroes that the world has produced.

Portland, Maine, will be near the end of his journey in this country. In a short time he will be on his seven year trip to the North Pole Regions to study the water and air currents and to seek general information in the interest of science and education.

H. W. STRAW & SON

THE HURRY UP

Plumbers

124 Monument St.   Telephone 3932-3

James A. Martin & Son

UNDERTAKERS AND CORONERS

No. 19 Myrtle Street
PORTLAND, ME.

Opticians

Makers of Good Glasses for More than 20 years

MURDOCK CO.

Y. M. C. A. Building

STRAWBERRY SHORTCAKE

The Real Old Fashioned New England Home Style

Any

MERRILL CAFE

TEMPLE ST.   OAK ST.   ST. JOHN ST.

Telephone 3437-4

DR. W. H. ROBERTS

DENTIST

Residence
76 FESSENDEN ST.   542 1-2 CONGRESS ST.
OAKDALE   PORTLAND, ME.

Designs   Estimates

SHAW-THOMPSON CO.

MANUFACTURERS OF

LEADED ART GLASS FOR CHURCHES
AND DWELLINGS

Colonial Leaded Lights
Memorial Windows
Art Lamp Shades

276 Middle Street,   Portland, Maine

N. E. TELEPHONE

Manufacturers and Repairs of

WAGONS and CARRIAGES

of all Descriptions

Automobile Painting

D. E. McCANN'S SONS

Have your Developing and Printing done
by

H. M. SMITH

Photographer

ORDER BY MAIL   Pictures Framed to Order

DO NOT FORGET we do all kinds of Portrait
Photography, Crayon, Water Color, Etc.

8 Elm Street   PORTLAND, ME.

F. B. W. WELCH, Treas.   Telephone 2726-1

THE WELCH STENCIL CO.

MANUFACTURERS OF

RUBBER STAMPS, STENCILS, SEALS

WOOD ENGRAVING AND PRINTING

401 Fore Street   Portland, Maine

EXECUTIVE COMMITTEE

CONSUL PERCY F. KEATING
REV. WILHELM PETTERSEN
HENNING ANDREN
H. JACOB P. ENEMARK

RECEPTION COMMITTEE

MARTIN JENSEN	HANS E. HANSEN
ALBERT MOLBECK	OSCAR HANSEN
WALTER POULSEN	HENRY HANSEN
FRANK HOGLUND	T. SAM EGLUND
OSCAR JOHNSON	MICHAEL JOHNSON
ANDREW ANDREN	JOHN A. JOHNSON
C. HORNDRUP	LUDWIG WESTWIG
MARTIN T. MADSEN	MR. SEIPEL
B. REINERTSEN	HENRY ANDERSON
CHARLES J. FREDERIKSEN	CHR. A. PETERSEN
IVER SWENDSEN	REV. WILHELM PETTERSEN
CARL FLORBERG	

WHOLESALE AND RETAIL   CALENDARS
FRAMING

H. J. BURROWES CO.

PORTLAND, MAINE

225 MIDDLE STREET   TELEPHONE 4296-W

RANDALL & McALLISTER

WHOLESALE AND RETAIL DEALERS IN

ANTHRACITE **COAL** BITUMINOUS

PORTLAND, MAINE

JULIUS JENSEN

BAKER

181 Brackett Street

Compliments of

IRVING E. VERNON

Attorney and Counselor-at-Law

390 CONGRESS ST.

Shaylor ILLUSTRATORS, DESIGNERS AND ENGRAVING Co.
240 MIDDLE ST. PORTLAND, ME.   PHOTO-ENGRAVERS

Moved to our New Location, next door
to Heseltine & Tuttle's, call and
see us selling Good Shoes
there

Heywood Shoes for Women

Urban Shoes for Men

COX, the Shoeman

S. H. & A. R. DOTEN

LUMBER

HARDWOOD FLOORING, HOUSE FINISH
AND STAIR WORK

MILL AND YARD
490-504 Fore and 279 Commercial Streets

COMPLIMENTS FROM

GAMAGE'S

PHARMACY

Cor. Veranda St. and
Washington Ave.

EAST DEERING DISTRICT

Chas. F. W. Stockton

FIRST CLASS BARBER

3 Veranda St.   East Deering

EDWARD M. RING

DRY AND FANCY GOODS

503 Washington Ave., East Deering, Me.

Compliments of

SHALIT BROS.
& MARKSON

A FRIEND

CONANT'S

Dry Cleaning House

18-20 Forest Ave.

KAUFMAN'S

Ladies' Department Store

565 Congress St.,   Portland, Me.

W. J. LUCAS

Groceries, Meats and Provisions

Cor. Washington Ave. and Veranda St.
EAST DEERING, ME.

Deering Laundry Co.

FRED L. SMALL, Proprietor   PHONE 846

EUREKA FUEL CO.
COAL AND WOOD
Hardwood Charcoal and Coke
79 PARRIS STREET

Reliable Clothes
for men and boys
at
reasonable prices
Haskell & Jones Co.
Monument Square

Maine Artificial Stone Co.
A. W. HIGGINS, Proprietor
23 Boyd St.
Tel. 2794

J. H. DUFFEY
Plumber
And Dealer in Plumbers' Supplies
Jobbing Promptly Attended To
Telephone Connection
35 Free Street   Portland, Maine

THUSS, The Candy Man
Ice Cream
and
Soda
OPPOSITE MASONIC TEMPLE

Telephone 1571

Portland Decorating Co.
Painting, Decorating, Paper Hanging
Painting and Varnishing   Hardwood Finishing
Tinting   Decorating   Wall Paper
412 1-2 Congress Street
PORTLAND, MAINE

ALBERT DIRWANGER
FLORIST
Corner
Montreal and North Sts.
Munjoy Hill
STORE, 52 Temple St., PORTLAND, ME.
Telephone Connection

Tel. 2388-M

CHARLES E. DOWNS
WATCHMAKER
51 Temple Street
PORTLAND, MAINE
SPECIALTIES
Chime, French, Hall and Banjo Clocks

Easy Payments

H. E. BAKER
New and Second Hand
National Cash Registers
$15 up
53 Exchange St.

PLUMMER'S
INSURANCE AGENCY
121 EXCHANGE STREET
PORTLAND, ME.
Strong Companies   Low Rates
Prompt Settlement of Losses

COME OVER
to 431 Congress St. and have a game of
Billiards or Pool
Tables to let by the hour
if you wish

J. E. LIBBY
Groceries, Meats, Provisions
and Bakery
410 CONGRESS STREET
Portland, Me.
Telephone 1819

FLYNN, The Painter
14 Custom House Wharf
Absolutely Without an Equal

BRYSON & WELCH
PRINTERS
48 Temple Street
Phone 3504-M

Automobile Accessories
Electric Horns, Remy Magnetos
Storage Batteries Charged
Ford Specialties

L. W. CLEVELAND CO.

USE
WHITE CRESCENT FLOUR
FOR BREAD AND PASTRY
It has no equal
W. L. WILSON CO.
112 Exchange St.   651 Congress St.

BOOKS   CRANE'S LINEN LAWN   POST CARDS
CRANE'S INITIAL STATIONERY

BARBER'S CIRCULATING LIBRARY
428 CONGRESS STREET
PORTLAND, MAINE
OPPOSITE FIRST PARISH CHURCH

WRITER'S SUPPLIES   SOUVENIRS   SWEET GRASS BASKETS
BIRTHDAY AND SEASON BOOKLETS, LETTERS, ETC.

TUCKER AND COUGHLAN
JOB PRINTERS
Portland, Me.

Wedding Invitations   Visit Cards

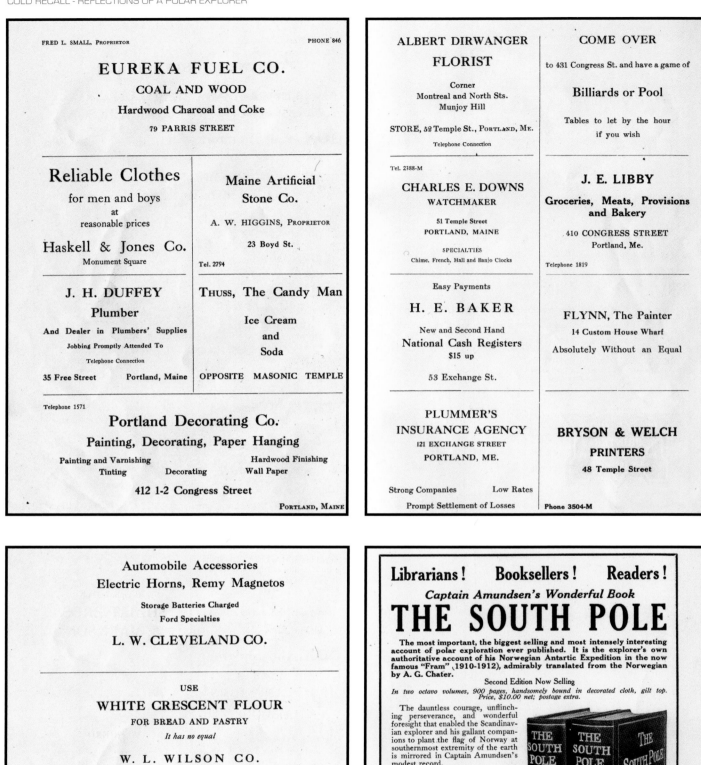

Librarians!   Booksellers!   Readers!
Captain Amundsen's Wonderful Book
THE SOUTH POLE
The most important, the biggest selling and most intensely interesting account of polar exploration ever published. It is the explorer's own authoritative account of his Norwegian Antarctic Expedition in the now famous "Fram" (1910-1912), admirably translated from the Norwegian by A. G. Chater.
Second Edition Now Selling
In two octavo volumes, 900 pages, handsomely bound in decorated cloth, gilt top. Price, $10.00 net; postage extra.

The dauntless courage, unflinching perseverance, and wonderful foresight that enabled the Scandinavian explorer and his gallant companions to plant the flag of Norway at southernmost extremity of the earth is mirrored in Captain Amundsen's modest record.

Dr. Nansen in an introduction pays high tribute to Captain Amundsen and his achievement.

Here is the book that should find its place in every library.

"These two volumes, translated easily and idiomatically, tell of an adventure that must always stand alone in the annals of discovery and tell it so well that one would scarcely suggest a change."—From *The Bookman, Andre Thery.*

"Captain Amundsen writes as well as he discovers."—FROM THE BOSTON TRANSCRIPT.

"Captain Amundsen's story of the discovery of the South Pole is a saga filled with humor and pathos."—NEW YORK TIMES.

LEE KEEDICK
150 Nassau Street
New York
Dear Sir: — Send me Captain Amundsen's book, "THE SOUTH POLE," two volumes, $10.00 net, postage extra.
NAME ....
ADDRESS ....

"Captain Amundsen's own story of his discovery of the South Pole is in every way worthy of his remarkable achievement. The narrative contains scarcely a dull page from first to last," says THE LONDON TIMES.

Send Your Order to LEE KEEDICK, Publisher, 150 Nassau St., New York.

☞ Captain Amundsen is now making a lecture tour under the auspices of his American publisher.

AMUNDSEN COMING TO LECTURE

Accepts the Invitation of the National Geographic Society.

WASHINGTON, March 23.—Roald Amundsen, discoverer of the south pole, will visit the United States in January and give his first North American lecture on the successful antarctic expedition before the National Geographic Society. President Henry Gannett to-day received a cablegram from Capt. Amundsen, accepting the society's invitation.

Other explorers who gave their first American lectures before the society after successful expeditions were Rear Admiral Robert E. Peary, discoverer of the north pole; Sir Ernest Shackleton, who until Capt. Amundsen's expedition had attained the farthest south, and Col. Theodore Roosevelt, who as a faunal naturalist led an expedition into Africa.

SWORE TO FIND THE POLE.

Shirase Persevered in Face of Poor Equipment and Jeers of Critics.

While Amundsen was at his comfortable quarters on McMurdo Sound at the base of Mount Erebus, Capt. Neilson of the Fram found the members of the Japanese expedition, which has just now been reported, living in a tent on the cold heights of the Great Ice Barrier. That they were living in a tent while Amundsen had his portable house, is typical of the two expeditions. The party went into the antarctic with a high enthusiasm, and swearing eternal loyalty to the Emperor, with bonds writ in blood, the accounts say, to find the pole or never return to great Nippon. Devotion had largely taken the place of preparation, and grim determination stood in place of substantial funds.

With many persons in Japan the south-polar expedition of Lieut. Shirase appeared in the light of a foolhardy attempt, and it was considered that withholding of funds was a blessing, for it might stop the party before they put themselves in danger. It was said when they sailed away from Japan in December, 1910, that they would never be heard of again, for they could not succeed, and they would never return to acknowledge defeat. The Emperor withheld his support, and had it not been for Count Okuma, who came forward with money to repair the ship Kanain-Maru after her first disastrous battle with the ice, the expedition would have been a flat failure. Scott's fund was $200,000. Shirasi had all told $21,000.

The equipment of the Japanese expedition was apparently chosen without attention to the lessons of arctic travel that had been taught by Occidentals. The party, which consisted of twenty-seven men, with the crew under Capt. Nomura, were outfitted with heavy fur garments, whereas Shackleton, Amundsen, and Scott had discarded furs for light woolen garments. Shirase trusted to Manchurian ponies for his transportation, and his sledges were built in Tokio after his own plans. Six men were picked for the final dash for the pole, and the rest of the party were to push into the Antarctic Continent along Shackleton's trail and establish depots of supplies to sustain the six men and their ponies on the return trip.

Started in Flimsy Craft.

The Kainan-Maru fulfilled the expectations of engineers when she was crushed by the ice on the first expedition and forced to put back. The ship was of the schooner type and of 199 tons, with an engine of a compound type, which, with boilers and five huge water tanks, occupied most of the available space in the ship. The tanks were of sheet iron and would probably have become useless once the cold regions were reached. The space left was so small that there was scarcely room enough for storage of provisions. The storage of coal for a long cruise was impossible.

The sleeping quarters of the men were along the sides of the boat, the thickness of which was 6 and 8 inches. Reinforcements of sheet iron had been attached by ironwood screws, and the work was badly done. In construction she was quite the opposite of Amundsen's "good old Fram," which had sides two feet thick, and had been built for withstanding the ice pressure.

The only part of the equipment which favorably impressed critical visitors before the sailing was the scientific instruments, which were almost all of foreign make. It was said that the expedition wrote to a merchant of Japan asking him if he had a map of the south pole, and adding that the party had not been able to find one. The merchant replied that his shipping had never extended that far, and that he regretted that he had no map to offer them.

Lieut. Shirase is not an unexperienced man in exploration, but his former expeditions have not been aimed at polar honors. In 1893 he was a member of the party organized and led by Lieut. Gunji, which went into Kurile Island for the purpose of encouraging emigration. The expedition was unfortunate, and the brunt of the work fell on Shirase. He spent two terrible Winters in the Island of Shimshu, the furthest north of the Kuriles. During the second Winter all of his companions, six in number, perished from cold and hunger, Shirase alone escaped and was rescued by the Japanese warship Banjo.

In 1898 he went with a Japanese sealing ship to Bering Sea and Alaska. Disembarking at Point Barrow, he made an inland journey into Alaska and spent a year among the Eskimos. He came out of the experience convinced of his ability to withstand extreme cold.

During the Russo-Japanese war Shirase went into Manchuria and there met Gen. Kodama, an experienced explorer, who was serving on the staff of Field Marshal Oyama. Kodama promised assistance to Shirase and would have been of great assistance in planning the south polar expedition, but death cut him off. Shirase took up the plan single-handed and besought the Government to support an expedition.

In the Summer of 1910, when Capt. Scott set out from London to seek the south pole, the idea of beating the English and placing the flag of the Land of the Rising Sun at the pole instead of allowing the English to set up the Union Jack, made a strong popular appeal, and the expedition became a reality.

Amid all the talk of the project, with patriotism on the one hand warring against prudence on the other, bitter attacks were made by the Japanese press on the character of Shirase as well as his preparations. He found powerful supporters, however, in Count Okuma and Prof. Miyake, who defended his character and gave him money, and he finally sailed in December, 1910, after a public demonstration of great enthusiasm.

ott had only 111 miles of territory left ter he passed beyond the trail of Sir rnest Shackleton.

Filchner is a famous explorer, although experienced in polar lands. He penerated into the forbidden land of Thibet 1903 and explored Turkistan and Per- a in 1905. He left Buenos Aires on his ip, the Deutschland, Oct. 6, 1911, with a lendidly equipped party, sent out under e auspices of the Geographical Society Berlin.

The striking fact about the German expedition is that they planned to drive right ross the south pole. Felchner's plan cluded the establishing of depots of supplies on Shackleton's route. He was then retreat around the great ice barrier the other side of the world at Weddell land, which lies off the tip of South merica. Then he expected to push ross the continent toward the pole and to his supplies on the opposite side. According to this plan he would approach the pole at about 35 degrees west ngitude and retreat from it at about 0 degrees west, which lacks little of beg a march straight across the antctic continent.

The Deutschland is equipped at the cost $375,000, all of which came from prite sources. The ship is wholly of wood, hich has been found best adapted to rest the crushing effects of ice packs. er tonnage is 580. With her auxiliary gine she can make a speed of seven hots. Her propeller is so arranged that can be drawn up when not in use, so to be protected from the ice. The rudr is similarly arranged and can be ised out of way of danger.

As the ship was provisioned for three d a half years, and as it was thought e expedition might take that long, news om Lieut. Filchner is not looked for on.

The New York Times

Published: March 24, 1912

Copyright © The New York Times

SORRY AMUNDSEN KEPT QUIET

Lord Curzon Regrets He Didn't Say He Was Going to the South Pole.

By Marconi Transatlantic Wireless Telegraph to The New York Times.

LONDON, May 20.—Lord Curzon, presiding to-day at the anniversary meeting of the Royal Geographical Society, referred to the race to the antarctic.

He would not, he said, discuss what might be called the "ethical side" of the relations between Capts. Scott and Amundsen. Regret might be felt that Capt. Amundsen did not see his way to take the public into his confidence from the moment when he changed the object of his expedition, which was originally organized to explore the north polar region. Had he openly proclaimed his intention at that time of proceeding to the antarctic instead of to the arctic, he would have avoided all appearance of attempting to forestall Capt. Scott in one at least of the objects which the Englishman had had in view for twelve years.

All geographers, however, said Lord Curzon, united in congratulating Capt. Amundsen on attaining so easily and rapidly the remaining untrodden pole.

Lord Curzon said there could be little doubt that Capt. Scott had reached the south pole long ago, and that he was now on his way back to his base.

Capt. Amundsen has been invited, in the event of his visiting England, to give an account of his expedition at a meeting of the society.

The New York Times

Published: May 21, 1912

Copyright © The New York Times

SCIENTISTS HEAR AMUNDSEN.

Brilliant Audience in London Told of South Pole Journey.

By Marconi Transatlantic Wireless Telegraph to The New York Times.

LONDON, Nov. 15.—Capt. Roald Amundsen delivered at Queens Hall to-night a lecture on his historic journey to the south pole. The big hall was packed with members of the Royal Geographical Society and their friends, who listened with the keenest attention to every word that was uttered by the Norwegian explorer.

Earl Curzon presided, and with him on the platform were Prince and Princess Louis of Battenberg, the Norwegian Minister, Earl Brassy, Gen. Sir R. S. Baden-Powell, Sir Ernest Shackleton, Sir James Crichton Browne, Sir Frank Younghusband, Dr. W. S. Bruce, Dr. J. Scott Keltie, and many other notabilities.

Lord Curzon, in introducing the lecturer, dwelt on the magnificent nature of his performance, at the same time introducing in his speech a reference to Captain Robert F. Scott, in order that the latter should have a share in the honors of the evening.

"In the field of exploration," said Lord Curzon, "we know no jealousy. Even while we are honoring Capt. Amundsend I am convinced that his thoughts, no less than ours, are turned to our own brave countryman, Capt. Scott, who is still shrouded in the glimmering in the half light of the antarctic and whose footsteps reached the same pole doubtless only a few weeks after Amundsen. The names of these two men will perpetually be linked, along with Shackleton's, in the history of antarctic exploration."

Capt. Amundsen delivered his lecture in the great voice of a man accustomed to shout against the winds and swiftly carried his audience of savants into the very atmosphere of the explorer's exploits.

Sir Ernest Shackleton proposed a vote of thanks to Capt. Amundsen and it was seconded by Dr. Bruce and heartily accorded.

AMUNDSEN TO SEEK NORTH POLE IN 1914

South Pole Discoverer, In on the St. Paul, Tells of Projected Five-Year Arctic Trip.

WELCOMERS' PLANS UPSET

Customs Men Wouldn't Let Explorer Quit Liner for Tug—Believed Cook for a Long Time.

Copyright, 1913, Underwood & Underwood.
ROALD AMUNDSEN.

Capt. Roald Amundsen, the Norwegian explorer, who reached the south pole in December, 1911, arrived yesterday on the belated American liner St. Paul from Southampton, and departed immediately for Washington, where he gave his first lecture last night.

In appearance the explorer was younger looking than when he was here in 1906, after passing through the Northwest Passage. This was due no doubt to his having shaved off his mustach and beard. When he landed at the pier Capt. Amundsen had on a blue serge suit and black derby hat, but no overcoat, as he considered it too warm for any extra clothing.

In a talk with the reporters the explorer said that he intended to make a start for the north pole in the Summer of 1914.

"So far as arrangements have been made at present," Capt. Amundsen went on. "I expect to start on my expedition about July 1, and will be away five years. I shall lay my course across the arctic basin, and by constantly drifting I hope to reach the north pole. On the way we will make observations and explore the arctic regions in the interest of science.

"Our start will be made from the Bering Sea and we expect to come out on the Atlantic side.

"The entire voyage will be made if possible in my old ship, the Fram, which is now laid up safe and sound in the harbor of Buenos Aires. If the canal is open by the Spring of next year I shall take the Fram through the new waterway to the Pacific, and if not she will go through the Strait of Magellan."

Concerning the nature of the antarctic regions, the explorer explained that the land was rich in minerals, and that there were some of the largest coal deposits ever discovered, which he hoped would be developed in the future. He added that these coal deposits indicated that the region was a tropical one thousands of years ago. When he was asked whether he believed Admiral Peary discovered the north pole he replied:

"There is not the least doubt that Peary got to the north pole. I have never questioned his claim."

"What about Dr. Cook?" he was asked.

"When I first knew Dr. Cook," said Capt. Amundsen very earnestly, "he was a very fine man. I was with him from 1897 to 1899 in the antarctic regions, and he saved the lives of the men on the expedition. When he came out with the statement that he had reached the north pole I had faith in him, and retained that faith until I went to Copenhagen this last time and saw the proofs they had in the university there. Since then I no longer knew Dr. Cook."

Capt. Amundsen will return to New York on Tuesday to receive a medal from the American Geographical Society, and deliver a lecture at Carnegie Hall that night.

When the St. Paul arrived yesterday morning at Quarantine she was met by the tug Henry Lee, which had been chartered by Christopher Ravn, the Norwegian Consul General in New York, who was accompanied by the reception committee from the Norwegian National League. The tug was gayly decorated and in the cabin there were piles of sardines, smoked salmon, and fried oyster sandwiches with a liberal supply of aqua vita, the fiery spirit of the Viking, and cases of beer.

It was the intention of the Norwegian Leaguers to carry off their distinguished countryman from the St. Paul and land him at the Jersey City pier of the Pennsylvania Railroad, with his baggage, and permission had been obtained from Collector Loeb, who detailed an inspector to go on the tug to clear the baggage. When the Consul General went on board he found that the explorer had a moving picture machine with him, which he wished to use in his lectures at Washington, and the customs officials on board could not pass it without an appraiser fixing the duty to be paid.

Capt. Amundsen, therefore, had to continue on the liner to her pier, and the members of the committee had to remain on the tug and be content with waving their hats to him when he appeared at rail of the St. Paul, but they were very cross. The reporters and photographers were also ordered to remain on the Henry Lee until the ship reached her pier, and one agile young man, who scaled a rope ladder and reached the deck of the St. Paul, was detained by order of the customs inspectors at the gangway in the biting blast until the ship was moored.

The New York Times

Published: January 11, 1913

Copyright © The New York Times

POLE FINDERS MEET ON SAME PLATFORM

Peary Follows with Deep Interest Amundsen's Story of His Dash to the South.

PRAISES HIM TO AUDIENCE

Norwegian's Lantern Slides Include One of His Steam Bath at the Ross Barrier.

Capt. Roald Amundsen, whose full story of his dash to the south pole was published first in THE TIMES, took a large and applauding audience that filled Carnegie Hall over the same expedition last night in an illustrated lecture delivered under the auspices of the American Geographical Society, the American Museum of Natural History, and the Norwegian National League.

Presiding over the exercises that preceded the lecture, Prof. Henry Fairfield Osborn, President of the Museum of Natural History, told the distinguished Norwegian that New York City was proud to have him as a guest. Prof. Osborn enumerated arctic and antarctic expeditions in which New Yorkers had taken part, closing with mention of the Roosevelt, commanded by former Commander, but now Rear Admiral, Robert E. Peary, who, he assured Capt. Amundsen, had intended to lend his presence to the occasion.

Meanwhile Admiral Peary appeared quietly on the stage and took his seat with the other guests, unobserved by the Chairman, who added a few words of excuse for his absence. Hearing the remarks about himself, the discoverer of the North Pole straightway arose from his seat and bowed toward the Chairman in an effort to make known his presence. But Prof. Osborn failed to catch sight of the Admiral and finished his courteous explanation while the polar discoverer stood apparently frozen on the spot.

Capt. Amundsen caught sight of Admiral Peary before Prof. Osborn did, and beckoned him to a neighboring seat. Admiral Peary was then escorted across the stage to the accompaniment of much laughter and applause.

Prof. Osborn read a telegram from Sir Ernest Shackleton expressing his regret that a long-standing engagement prevented him from being present "to offer his most hearty congrtaulations to Capt. Amundsen on his splendid achievement in the discovery of the south pole."

Capt. Amundsen was then welcomed on behalf of the Norwegian National League by Fred Werner, Chairman of the committee representing that organization on the stage.

Admiral Peary, who was introduced next among the welcomers, admitted that on such an occasion he hardly knew what to say. "When I hear a story like that you will hear to-night," he said, "there is no word that can be added to it by any man. There is no man to-day who has achieved the same distinction in polar work, south a d north, that Roald Amundsen has achieved."

The discoverer of the north pole, evidently reminiscent of his own hard struggle to the northernmost point of the hemisphere, pleaded with the audience to look into the eyes of the lecturer as they followd him on his heroic journey to the south pole and see with him the

to the south pole and see with him the hundreds of miles of icefields he had been compelled to push his way across and the thousands of feet of ice-armored plateaux that he had been forced to climb.

Growing more eloquent, Admiral Peary asked his hearers to follow Capt. Amundsen still on to the south and remain with him, "for days while the yellow sun swung across the white horizon until he capped the south pole."

Following Admiral Peary, John Greenough, on behalf of the American Geographical Society, presented to Capt. Amundsen a gold medal in recognition of his discovery.

"By his latest exploit in getting to the south pole he has reached a fitting climax to his discovery of the north magnetic pole and the Northwest Passage," he said, and added that Capt. Amundsen was the third to whom the society's gold medal had been awarded, the other two being Sir Ernest Shackleton and Rear Admiral Robert E. Peary. Engraved on the medal was the following inscription:

Awarded to
Roald Amundsen,
in recognition of the value
of his magnetic observations
in the American Arctic
Achievement of the Northwest Passage
and attainment of the South Pole.
MCMXII.

After expressing his appreciation of the honor conferred on him by the American Geographical Society, and his sense of indebtedness to the Museum of Natural History and Norwegian National League for having arranged the lecture, Capt. Amundsen proceeded with a detailed narration of his expedition to the pole, beginning with the time that the Fram started on her 15,000-mile journey until the party placed the Norwegian flag at the south pole at 3 P. M. on Dec. 14.

The lantern slides illustrating Capt. Amundsen's lecture won enthusiastic applause, but the audience was disposed to doubt the statement of the explorer that the party had a steam bath at its first depot, about two miles from the great Ross Ice Barrier, with its numerous rooms and passageways dug out eight feet under the surface of the barrier. Capt. Amundsen placed the tip of his pointer on one part of the diagram, and said:

"Here was our steam bath."

He produced further evidence of the steam bath later in a picture of it in operation.

The invited guests of the American Museum of Natural History were Admiral Robert E. Peary, Col. David L. Brainard of the Greely expedition, Gen. Thomas H. Hubbard, President of the Peary Arctic Club; Herbert L. Bridgman, Secretary of the Peary Arctic Club; Donald B. MacMillan, leader of the Crocker Land expedition; Emerson McMillin, President of the New York Academy of Sciences; John H. Finley, President of the College of the City of New York; Frederic A. Lucas, Director of the American Museum of Natural History; Sir Ernest Shackleton, and George Bird Grinnell.

The guests of the American Geographical Society were Prof. William M. Davis of Harvard University and Prof. Ellsworth Huntington of Yale University. The following officers of the society: John Greenough, Walter B. James, A. A. Raven, Edwin F. Balch, Banyer Clarkson, L. Holbrook, D. Randall-McKeever, and A. D. Russell.

The guests of the Norwegian National League were Chr. Ravn, Norwegian Consul General; John A. Gade, President American Scandinavian Society; Fred Werner, Chairman of the committee; Peter Benson, President Norwegian National League; G. A. Roberg, Juell Bie, Oskar Pettersen, B. Overland, O. Royon, Jacob Eriksen, President Norwegian Singing Society; A. N. Rygg, editor Nordisk Tidende, and G. T. Leland.

After his lecture Capt. Amundsen was the guest of honor at a supper given by the American Scandinavian Society at Louis Martin's. President John H. Finley of the City College, the toastmaster, paid a high tribute to Amundsen for his achievements as an explorer and his contributions to science. As soon as toasts were proposed to the President of the United States, the three Scandinavian Kings, and Amundsen by John A. Gade, President of the society, a polar bear slowly threaded his way through the excited guests and crowned the discoverer of the south pole with a wreath of white roses.

The New York Times

Published: January 15, 1913
Copyright © The New York Times

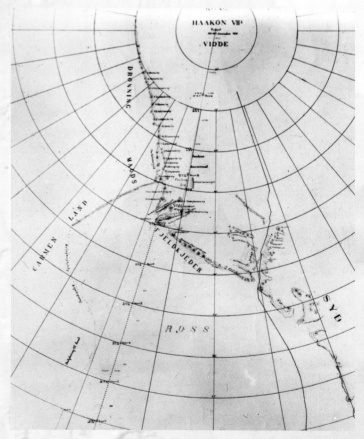

The New York Times

FORBID AMUNDSEN LECTURE

Action of Prussian Authorities Causes Anger in Scandinavia.

By Marconi Transatlantic Wireless Telegraph to The New York Times.

COPENHAGEN, Nov. 4.—The prohibition by the Prussian authorities of a lecture by Capt. Amundsen at Flensburg, Schleswig, has caused general indignation in Denmark and Norway. It is regarded as the more surprising because Capt. Amundsen is on friendly terms with the Kaiser.

It is understood that the explorer will lecture at Flensburg, but that the audience will be specially invited. This the authorities cannot forbid.

Published: November 5, 1913
Copyright © The New York Times

Explorer Plans New Voyage

Captain Amundsen Tells of Arctic Ocean Mysteries.

CAPT. AMUNDSEN is telling his experiences while exploring the Northwest passage, on the lecture platform, and he finds it more arduous than building a snow hut on Northern ice, in a temperature of 79 degrees below. When I last saw him, a year ago, it was after a banquet and dance tendered to him by the Norwegians of Brooklyn, and part of my duty was to pilot him safely back to New York across Brooklyn Bridge. In a speech he delivered there after dinner he was unable to find the Northwest passage on a huge map hung on the wall behind him, but maps are strange and evasive things to your genuine explorer.

"I found the Northwest passage, but I cannot find it on this map," he said, amid roars of laughter.

He was less spruce, erect, and tailor-made then than he is now. His three years spent in sealskins, among the Eskimos, away from sight or sound of civilization, was still evident in the cut of his clothes, in a certain awkwardness of manner, a kind of difficult silence about him.

The past year spent amid the creature comforts of a civilized part of the world, have restored him to the style and trim appearance of a naval officer in active service.

No Discoveries in Lectures.

"You do not fancy this lecturing tour?"

"It is too much traveling," he said petulantly.

"What—for a man who has spent years in exploration?"

"Oh, that is different; there is a motive then, but a lecture is not a discovery."

"You will go back to the unknown region?"

"Yes, surely. In 1910 I shall go North again for five years."

"To discover the North Pole?"

"No, there is nothing in that. The pole is there, and when it is discovered it will mean nothing to science, nothing to the world."

"This search for the North Pole is theatrical?"

"It is simply a little glory to say that you got there first, before the other fellow, which is not a scientific principle, is it?"

"What is more important to do up there?"

"The Arctic Ocean is entirely unexplored, we know nothing about its currents, its actual shore lines. On the map it is a hole, that is all we know. Oh, there is so much to do there, so much to discover," and the Captain regained his poise in the mirage of ice and silence, and cold.

"How will you explore the arctic?"

"Nansen has shown us that the only way is to drift with the ice. In that way the discovery of the arctic region is certain, and, I fear, in no other way. By what has been attempted and failed, we must profit. Of course, the only danger is that a ship will be crushed by the ice, but I consider that is only one chance in a hundred, if the ship is built, to expect that.

"I shall try and take the Fram, Nansen's ship, which is lying in Norway now. It seems to me that she is best equipped for my purpose, being strong and light enough to rise to the top in an ice-squeeze."

"How long do you calculate will it take you to drift over the North Pole?"

"About five years. That is to say, in 1916 I hope to have explored the Arctic Ocean with valuable results to science; that is why I am postponing my starting time for over two years, so as to have time to get ready."

"It will take that long?"

"You cannot pick up a bag and start for the North Pole as you would go to Philadelphia. It will take all of two years to get ready, to provision the ship with five years' rations. You see, the food has to be especially carefully prepared, otherwise the men get scurvy, and it is no use to be an explorer unless you live to come back.

"There is nothing to eat up there, nothing to kill, no life whatever. The bears do not go so far north, nor the seals."

"Can you get Eskimos to stay with you so long?"

"How can they get back before we do?" said the explorer, far too gently. "Besides, they are a patient people, very intelligent, very peaceable," he added.

He seemed to look forward to the five years in the dead line of the earth with exuberance, and when this phase of his intentions was mentioned, he shrugged his shoulders and explained that he would be so busy during those five years that he would not notice the time.

"We expected to stay four years during our last trip, and we were all quite happy and contented to do so. We discovered the magnetic pole, but the full detailed report of our observations is still in the hands of the scientists. It will be five years before we know the complete results. The scientists are carefully studying our figures, and I hope our work will result in some new scientific facts."

"The magnetic pole does not have any bearing upon the origin of earthquakes?"

"No, I am sure it does not. The magnetic pole is influenced by currents above, and earthquakes come from the earth beneath. How much it may reveal for wireless telegraphy is something of a possibility."

"Will you use wireless telegraphy in the North?"

"I think so. I should like to. It would be most useful for communication between the sledges and the ship, but that, too, would be an experiment."

We gradually left Peacock Alley, and New York, and civilization for the uninhabitated North, which to the uninitiated brought up the question of man's endurance, not so much against cold and ice, but his endurance of extreme loneliness from human environment.

"There were seven white men in our little boat that lived three years together, in three small cabins, in almost harmony and contentment," said the explorer, "and, of course, the Eskimos live there, in the ice, always.

"Of course, in any expedition it is important to select men who will be equal to the conditions. I never read the references a man brings to me, when he applies for a position with us in an exploring trip. I can generally tell, after observing him closely and talking to him awhile, if he will be equal to the strain, and I have never been mistaken. It is important to get the right sort of men, for one weak man will disorganize the rest. The main thing is always to keep busy, to keep the men at work all the time, and to keep at work yourself."

"No matter how cold it is?"

"You may be sure it is always cold enough. An average temperature is 50 below zero, more often 60. Of course, we have to dress for it, but there is really no difficulty when you are clothed from head to foot in sealskin.

"The best way is to wear a complete sealskin garment, with the fur worn next to the skin, and over that other furs, and a coat with the fur outside. Your under fur garments must be loose enough to let the air circulate. Great care must be taken to avoid getting wet; that is the principal recreation in the north, the drying of skins and furs."

"How do you get fuel up there?"

"We use oil entirely, seal oil chiefly. There is no cozy fireside for the arctic explorer till he gets back, and no steam heat, thank goodness. Just oil lamps. Most of the time, of course, the temperature in our cabins was zero—but that is very healthy, almost tropical, compared to what we had outside. Our greatest trouble was to avoid losing our noses or our cheeks by frost bite."

A waiter went by with a dish of crushed ice, and Capt. Amundsen kept a weather eye on it till the waiter disappeared through a door into the restaurant.

"I have some pictures of fine ice," he said, feelingly, and one could almost see his eyes kindle with pleasure at the memory of some particularly artistic iceberg.

Your arctic explorer revels in a field of ice, as a farmer delights in a wheat field.

An arctic diversion, Capt. Amundsen describes, was the building of a snow hut, the native domicile of the Eskimos.

"It is a very difficult thing to build," said the Captain, "and the white men must learn it from the Eskimos. A snowhouse is built of large square blocks of snow cut with a big knife, and piled together. Only a certain kind of snow can be used for this purpose. It takes about an hour and a half of hard work to build one of them, and if there is a gale blowing at 60 miles an hour and the temperature is 70 below zero, you don't linger, but make the shelter as quickly as you can.

Plenty of Comfort On Snow Hut.

"And it makes a very perfect shelter, absolutely airtight, and warmer than a ship's cabin. When it is complete, you light your oil lamp, spread some skins to sleep on, and you are almost as comfortable as you would be in the Waldorf. One of the first things to learn in the arctic regions is to make a snow hut, because there is always plenty of snow, and it is the only available shelter when you are away from the ship. Tents would be of no use whatever."

The expense in fitting out an expedition that would last five or six years, Capt. Amundsen calculated would be a difficult feature of his undertaking, and for that reason he was giving the matter two years' thought and time. He had not secured the Fram, but he said that there is no other ship better fitted for the task.

"You don't mind a few years' exile?" I asked him.

"It is not exile, it is work, work that I would rather do than anything else. And, I assure you, it is work."

"You discipline your ship's work just as if you were in a civilized part of the world?"

"Absolutely, but I have never had any trouble with my men. I choose them carefully, and I have been fortunate in making a good choice. I prefer Norwegians, because I understand them, but there are good and bad men in any race. For instance the Scandinavians and Norwegians are one people, but since we have separated our Governments and are separate kingdoms it is better. On the principle that a man prefers to conduct his own business it is better as it is now."

Capt. Amundsen spoke warmly of Fiala, with whom he had had a long conference that morning.

"I like that man," he said with enthusiasm, "he is so eager and so quick."

"It is not necessary that your explorer should be phelgmatic?" I asked.

"No, he must on the contrary be keenly alive, enthusiastic always, but with executive ability. Yes, that he must have, to be ready to meet emergency."

Capt. Amundsen regarded Nansen as the only man who had accomplished really valuable results in the arctic, and to him he gave the chief honors for showing the way through northern ice for the explorer.

The New York Times

Published: November 5, 1913
Copyright © The New York Times

The Amundsen lantern slides. Photo NB

OPEN ONLY IN A RUBY LIGHT.

KEEP COOL AND DRY.

LANTERN PLATE RAPID SERIES.

1 Dozen, 3¼ × 3¼.

These plates which give **black** tones only, are sufficiently rapid for reduction in Camera by artificial light, or may be used for contact printing with very short exposure, as per instructions enclosed.

In case of any difficulty apply direct, giving full particulars and the following

REFERENCE NUMBER } **769 R10**

NOTICE.—The utmost care is taken to render these plates as perfect as possible, and any reasonable complaint made direct to the Works will receive immediate attention. But they are sold WITHOUT LEGAL WARRANTY of any kind expressed or implied.

PAGET PRIZE PLATE COMPANY, LIMITED, WATFORD, ENGLAND.

SOURCES:

ROALD AMUNDSEN: THE NORTHWEST PASSAGE (1907)

ROALD AMUNDSEN: THE SOUTH POLE (1912)

ROALD AMUNDSEN: SYDPOLEN (1912)

J.E. BERNIER: MASTER MARINER AND ARCTIC EXPLORER (1939)

CARSTEN E. BORCHGREVINK: NÆRMEST SYDPOLEN AARET 1900 (1905)

TOR BORCH SANNES: FRAM (1989)

ROLAND HUNTFORD: THE AMUNDSEN PHOTOGRAPHS (1987)

GEIR O. KLØVER (ED.): ROALD AMUNDSEN AND THE EXPLORATION OF
THE NORTHWEST PASSAGE — A FRAM MUSEUM EXHIBITION (2008)

W. GILIES ROSS (ED.): AN ARCTIC WHALING DIARY (1984)

THE PROCEEDINGS OF THE ROYAL GEOGRAPHICAL SOCIETY 1907, 1910, 1911, 1912 & 1913

THE AMUNDSEN ARCHIVES IN THE NATIONAL LIBRARY OF NORWAY

THE FRAM MUSEUM ARCHIVES

THE NEW YORK TIMES WEBSITE

THE WELSH HERITAGE AND CULTURE WEBSITE

EDITOR:

GEIR O. KLØVER

OTHER CONTRIBUTORS:

ANNE RIEF, CHARLOTTE WESTERENG SYVERSEN, JO BARR,
STEPHANIE STEWART & MATTHEW DE VILLIERS

PHOTOS:

THE AMUNDSEN LANTERN SLIDES. COPYRIGHT: THE FRAM MUSEUM/JFO. RESTORED AND DIGITIZED
AT THE NATIONAL LIBRARY OF NORWAY

OTHER PHOTOS: THE NATIONAL LIBRARY OF NORWAY (NB) AND THE FRAM MUSEUM (FM)

THE LETTERS FROM THE ROYAL GEOGRAPHICAL SOCIETY, LECTURE AGENCY LTD, LEE KEDDICK AND
THE LETTER TO NANSEN: THE AMUNDSEN ARCHIVE IN THE NATIONAL LIBRARY OF NORWAY

SOUVENIR BOOK FROM THE SOUTH POLE LECTURES: THE FRAM MUSEUM

THE NORTH MAGNETIC POLE BOOKLET: THE NATIONAL LIBRARY OF NORWAY

THE LOGBOOK OF THE FRAM: THE FRAM MUSEUM

THE CARDIFF SOUTH POLE LECTURE POSTER: CARDIFF CENTRAL LIBRARY

PREVIOUS TITLES IN THE FRAM MUSEUM EXHIBITION SERIES:

ROALD AMUNDSEN AND THE EXPLORATION OF THE NORTHWEST PASSAGE

A Fram Museum Exhibition

Including:
- The Mystery of the North Magnetic Pole
- A 30-page illustrated timeline on the exploration of the Northwest Passage 1497–1906

In 1903-1906 Roald Amundsen established himself as a sailor and explorer of the first order when he successfully navigated the Gjøa through the entire length of the Northwest Passage, a treacherous ice-bound route that winds between the current northern Canadian mainland and Canada's Arctic islands. The expedition was a landmark event in the history of Arctic exploration.

This book tells the story of the Gjøa and her crew. It is fully illustrated with original photos from the expedition and contains several excerpts from Roald Amundsen's diary. The book includes a 30-page fully illustrated timeline of all the main efforts to find the Northwest Passage and a chapter on the mystery of the north magnetic pole.

"The voyage of Amundsen stands forth unrivalled as to scant means, scientific work, and successful navigation. Under his skilful handling the tiny Gjøa is the first ship to make the Northwest Passage, and the redetermination of the location of the north magnetic pole is a most notable contribution to science. It should be borne in mind that these results have been produced by the labor of only seven men, without undue suffering, and with the most modest equipment. The outcome stamps Amundsen as a man endowed with high qualities of administration, judgment, and resourcefulness".

- A.W. Greely, Major General U.S. Army

"Son of the Vikings navigates the Northwest Passage. Capt. Roald Amundsen achieves undying fame – Success crowns his efforts where Sir John Franklin and others have failed".

- The New York Times, December 10, 1905

ISBN 978-82-8235-001-3

AVAILABLE AT THE FRAM MUSEUM
TEL: + 47-23 28 29 50 FAX: +47-23 28 29 51
E-MAIL: ORDER@FRAM.MUSEUM.NO

Fridtjof Nansen

Scientist and Humanitarian
A Fram Museum Exhibition

Including:
- Fridtjof Nansen's "The Food Situation in Norway (1917)" and "Adventure (1926)"

In the summer of 1922, the last of the German and Austria-Hungarian soldiers who had been in Russian captivity after the First World War were shipped home across the Baltic. On the return voyage, the ships carried the last Russian prisoners-of-war from Germany. Altogether, over 400,000 prisoners were exchanged in less than two years. The credit for this was given mainly to the Norwegian Fridtjof Nansen. That autumn he was awarded the Nobel Peace Prize. Nansen did his country great service as a politician and diplomat, but he acquired his international renown primarily as a scientist, polar exploration hero, and the altruistic champion of people in times of distress.

This is the story of Fridtjof Nansen's tireless work on the refugee situation in Europe in the aftermath of the Great War. The book is illustrated with many of Nansen's own photos.

"The life and the efforts of Fridtjof Nansen provide us with the inspiration to strive for human progress, dignity and development – for this generation and those to come."

- Dr. Gro Harlem Brundtland,
Director-General of World Health Organization,
former Prime Minister of Norway

ISBN 978-82-8235-002-0